POLITEXT 184

The ISPS Code - 1
Ship-port interface operativity

EDICIONS UPC

POLITEXT

Ricard Marí Sagarra

The ISPS Code - 1
Ship-port interface operativity

EDICIONS UPC

Publication sponsored by the Ministry of Public Works (2009)

First edition: September 2009
Reprint: November 2009

©   Ricard Marí Sagarra, 2009

©   Edicions UPC, 2009
     Edicions de la Universitat Politècnica de Catalunya, SL
     Jordi Girona Salgado 1-3, 08034 Barcelona
     Tel.: 934 137 540   Fax: 934 137 541
     Edicions Virtuals: www.edicionsupc.es
     E-mail: edicions-upc@upc.edu

Production: LIGHTNING SOURCE

Legal deposit: B-36522-2009
ISBN: 978-84-9880-369-3

This work may only be reproduced, distributed, publicly disclosed or transformed with permission from its copyright holders, with the exception provided by the law. If you need to photocopy or scan a part of this work, please contact CEDRO (Spanish Centre for Reprographic Rights) at www.cedro.org.

Index

Introduction 11

1. The ship as the object of the threat 15
    1.1 Organisational means 15
    1.2 Ship related determinants 16
    1.3 Ships in block "A" 18
    1.4 Ships in block "B" 22
    1.5 Ships in block "C" 25
    1.6 Ships in block "D" 28
    1.7 Ships in block "E" 31
    1.8 Ship related conclusion summary 35

2. The port as a threat to the ship 39
    2.1 Determinants associated with the port 39
    2.2 Access control philosophy and principles 40
    2.3 Access security control (personnel, vehicles and merchandise) 42
        2.3.1 Control zones 42
        2.3.2 Access control to restricted zones 44
        2.3.3 Personnel control 48
        2.3.4 Maritime area 50
        2.3.5 Criteria for establishing the water surface 51
    2.4 Identifying and analysing risks at the port facility 53
        2.4.1 Risk classification 55
        2.4.2 Deriving from social activities 59
    2.5 Vulnerability evaluation 61
    2.6 Execution of an attempt 64
    2.7 Checklists 65

3. Ship's threats and risks 73
    3.1 The ship as a threat receiver 73
    3.2 Security controls for cargo containers 75
        3.2.1 Entry/exit operations 77
        3.2.2 Gate operations analysis 77
        3.2.3 Gate automation 79
        3.2.4 Various constituting processes of gate operations 81

3.3 Technological elements at the gates 86
    3.3.1 EDI 86
    3.3.2 TOS (Terminal Operating System) 87
    3.3.3 Video systems 88
    3.3.4 Optical Character Recognition (OCR) 88
    3.3.5 RFID 89
    3.3.6 Magnetic Identification Cards (MIDC) 89
    3.3.7 Electronic gantry signs 89
    3.3.8 Intercom 91
    3.3.9 Electronic scale technology 91
    3.3.10 Mobile Data Terminal (MDT) 91
    3.3.11 Electronic seals at the gate 92
    3.3.12 Simulation models 92
    3.3.13 Automatic container code reading system 93
3.4 Railway 95
3.5 Result verification 95
3.6 Conclusion 97

4 Merchandise transfer enhancements 99
4.1 Introduction 99
4.2 Registry of companies authorised at the PF 100
    4.2.1 Obtaining an authorisation 101
    4.2.2 Authorised company personnel accreditation 102
    4.2.3 Transportation means accreditation 104
4.3 Merchandise road transport 104
    4.3.1 Merchandise entry from road transport 105
    4.3.2 Merchandise departure by road transport 113
    4.3.3 List of certificates and documents to be examined 117
    4.3.4 List of clear grounds for a more detailed inspection 120
4.4 Ship control procedures 120
    4.4.1 Ships subject to expanded inspection 120
    4.4.2 Expanded procedure for certain ship categories 121
    4.4.3 Ship detention criteria 124
    4.4.4 Deficiency reference list 125
4.5 Deficiencies in the IBC Code scope 127
4.6 Inspection report 131
4.7 Data provided in the context of monitoring implementation 132
4.8 Procedures relating to refusal of access at Community ports 133
4.9 International and European Community minimum requirements related to Voyage Data Recorders 134
4.10 Manoeuvring within port premises 135
4.11 Loading and departure of road transport vehicles 137

5 Identification technology 139
5.1 Fundamentals of biometric authentication 139
5.2 Various biometric technologies 147
    5.2.1 Facial recognition technology 148
    5.2.2 Fingerprint recognition 148

    5.2.3 Hand geometry recognition 150
    5.2.4 Iris recognition 150
    5.2.5 Writing (signature) recognition 157
    5.2.6 Voice recognition 159
    5.2.7 Other biometric recognition systems 161

6 Control of individuals and goods 163
  6.1 Passenger control and baggage search 163
  6.2 Ticket control and baggage search area 164
  6.3 Access control 165
  6.4 Passenger access control structure 166
  6.5 Non admitted or restricted goods at the access 167
  6.6 Suspect identification through body language 171
  6.7 Observable indications 173
  6.8 Light weapons, incendiary and explosive items 174
    6.8.1 Introduction 174
    6.8.2 Light weapons 174
    6.8.3 Types of light weapons 175
    6.8.4 Light weapons, bullets and penetrating traumas 176
    6.8.5 Countermeasures 177
    6.8.6 Explosive and incendiary devices 180
    6.8.7 Injury types 181
    6.8.8 Explosive and incendiary device types 181
    6.8.9 Countermeasures 182
  6.9 Selecting technical equipment and means that may be installed 183
  6.10 Conclusions 187

7 Human response to security related situations 189
  7.1 Human behaviour under pressure 189
  7.2 Individual behaviour 189
  7.3 Shock and panic reactions 191
  7.4 Simulation drills 193
  7.5 Psychological aspects of stress situations 194
  7.6 Option consideration interfering factors 195
  7.7 Communications and messages 196
  7.8 Seamen views prior to the ISPS 199
    7.8.1 Regarding merchant ships 200
    7.8.2 Regarding the commercial ports survey 204

8 Conclusions 207
  8.1 Introduction 207
  8.2 Conclusions 208

Bibliography 215

Introduction

Compliance with Chapter XI-2 of the SOLAS Convention, known as the ISPS Code, adopted on 12th of December, 2002, in force since 1st of July, 2004, as well as the Regulation of the European Parliament and of the Council adopted on the 31st of March, 2004, in force since the 20th of May, 2004 (OJEU of the 29th of April, 2004), in its progressive application to ships,

   a) National maritime transit, 1st of July, 2005 (passengers)
   b) Other ship categories (2007)

has originated a new field of operating relationships between the ship and the port facility, within the framework of the sole intention of preventing criminal situations (level 1) as the priority objective, and of openly opposing resistance, when security level 3 is reached.

Implementation of mandatory regulations within marine environment security represents a difficult challenge for those responsible for safety. The main concern is the security of the ship-port interface, and all procedures should be aimed at creating a tight barrier to all past, present and future threats.

The new terrorist attack methods and the use of new technologies by attackers enormously hinder security tasks, which until now had a minimum impact on port procedures.

All studies done to the present moment by various entities are pessimistic with respect to the capability of preventing in real time an attempt at a port facility. Events to date demonstrate this. The port of Ashdod provides a clear example that in the face of terrorist resolve, few safety systems can stand up to it.

On that occasion, two suicide bombers triggered their bombs to explode, one inside the port next to the fence (outer perimeter) and the other one outside. The explosions, which occurred almost simultaneously and were initially interpreted as the explosion of some fuel tank, left also some fifteen injured, three of them seriously. Ashdod is one of the two most important Israeli ports in the Mediterranean Sea. The main base for the Israeli Navy in the South of the country is also there, and due to this a high security level is in place, access being restricted by several checkpoints. Notwithstanding, the terrorists achieved, in part, their goal.

We may conclude that the best part of anti terrorism fight is centred on information very far away from the port, even further from the ship. But there is the obligation of creating as many barriers as possible, in order to prevent the problem reaching the ship or the shore from the ship by breaching the interface procedures. This should be achieved without disrupting or hindering port and maritime activities.

Currently, port safety as set forth by the Ship and Port Facility Security Plan generates all over the world procedures, standards and actions by security forces, both public and private. However, the general trend is covering safety with the lowest possible budget, and such shortness of funds affects equally the necessary technical resources and the human factor.

The only option for compensating for the lack of appropriate funds is to adapt in a non conventional way to the new situation, by applying integrated solutions to the usual port procedures. Existing merchandise and passenger control should be increased by radioscopy, but also with the detection of suspects by security personnel. Nowadays, appropriate security methods are available for creating secluded, constant flow areas for customers that do not compromise port operations. Port activities should not be disrupted by safety operational improvements that may mean excessive trouble and may hinder the normal development of port work.

The need for strong investment in port security, ship-port interface being the main priority, sets a number of implementation phases both for step by step investments and for the adaption of safety personnel, companies, crew and users to the new procedures.

It is evident that with the implementation of security plans on both, all have fulfilled verification requirements. Nevertheless, security approaches cannot be schematised in the same way as usual responses to the risks included in safety. Approaches are not related to physical or chemical variables, to structural strengths or to any measurable parameter. Now the problem is enlarged or human will (wickedness) is substantially changed for committing a criminal act, with the enormous variability in the possibilities involved.

The process becomes complicated when, besides, the event or conflict interacts with forces external to the ship, which generally do not know sufficiently the medium in which the maritime-port transportation activity develops, although they are based on better knowledge of technical and operating control procedures for such type of threats.

It should be mentioned that without a modern organisational system that includes a comprehensive implementation of the single command model, little will be achieved to reduce the risk of a terrorist attack, and even less to reduce losses should the attack become a reality. This has been widely demonstrated in the last massive attempts against cities all over the world by Al Qaeda.

The study presents a level of specialised knowledge on subjects included in security, both on methodology for procedures to detect risks related to the criminal action of human beings, involving identification of clues, signs, actions, behavioural patterns, response to certain control stimuli, etc., and from the ship's standpoint as an independent, autonomous unit integrally controlling safety.

The approach to contents is made based on the three main blocks composing the security process, namely:

> The ship; types, structural design and transits
> The port, as a filter of threats attempting to access the ship
> Personnel on both, besides criminals attempting to cause the damage

The ship is the great unknown, and in some way everything orbits around her, beginning with the ISPS Code itself, which is implemented to make her safe in the face of this new sense of a high risk threat and its consequences. The port plays an important role as the primary filter that prevents access of people and substances that may harm the ship; the ship applies her own measures, which are reasonably inferior in magnitude and resources; finally, there is the involved personnel that may hinder criminal actions, but they face activities that are not well known to them with low preparedness.

The result of this mix is uncertain by its own nature; there are many intermediaries, many ways of thinking and acting; although the code intends to cover the lack of synchronisation of all bodies and institutions that become involved in a threat, its contents and training development remain a set of traces too weak and inconsistent to represent a true barrier of effective measures for preventing and resolving the situations herein considered.

Objectives

Virtually to date, maritime-port activity has had as priority objectives a higher observance of regulations and requirements for achieving an acceptable safety level, while from now on, the firm and overwhelming inclusion of the security chapter finds the maritime transportation industry with scarce knowledge and no bibliographic references, which remain limited to sources from the Security Forces and the military.

In the extensive bibliography dedicated to safety, new criteria, viewpoints, organisational improvements, procedures and methodologies are still being added; however, the security field, when applied to a civil activity such as the maritime business, is void of any contents; only ideas, intentions and principles are presented, without any developments on how to achieve them, with what resources, in what manner, without proposing maximum and minimum limits for effectiveness and risk when any aspect is overestimated.

It is evident, therefore nothing to be surprised at, that in the future numerous publications, studies, analyses, research works and all types of contributions should be produced within the new knowledge area that security represents in its civil application by civilians; they should in turn result in an enhancement of prevention and the protection of life against foreign actions that are alien to the commercial, industrial and service activities with which maritime activities are related.

This study pursues the following objectives:

✓ To cover operational gaps in the control of crisis situations due to criminal actions as included in the ISPS Code, both from the ship and on her interface with the port.
✓ To improve the knowledge on the control actions that may be applied to the wide subject covered by the definition of security.
✓ To detail the aspects that produce, cause and culminate a security situation in ships, and their relationship with port safety in maritime transportation.

Schematic development of the study

Presentation and analysis of the various chapters of this work follow the diagram in Figure 1.

All sections are closely related to each other, with the common denominator of the figure of the ship, to finally converge in a line of conclusions.

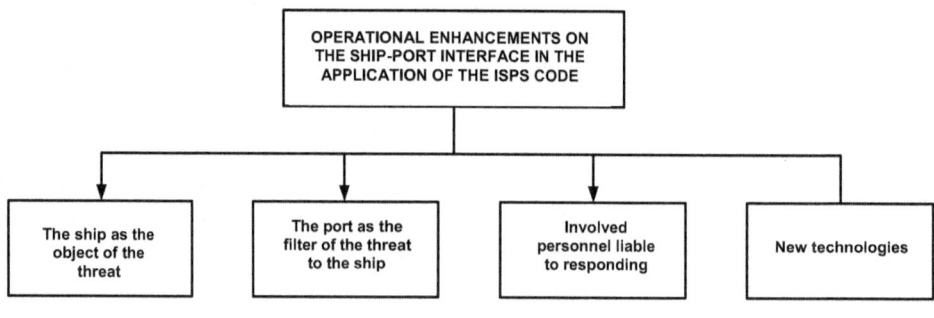

Figure 1

Overall, each of the blocks in the diagram constitutes a specific chapter addressing, in the depth and extent that may be required, the considerations and the identification of limitations and peculiarities that determine emergency plans in their application to a given ship and her interface.

Chapter 1. The ship as the object of the threat

1.1 Organisational means

Organisational means of a safety system should establish the risk levels and vulnerability of the facility to be protected. In the present case, complexity is accentuated as maritime environment is highly varied and changing, particularly in the ship-port interface, since the variety of ships and all the different actions that they may carry out at a port are enormous.

Evaluation of risks and vulnerabilities is something specific, with different procedures for each case. In this manner, it is understood that the specific level of risk for a container carrier loading at the port of Algeciras, bound for the U.S.A., and the level for a cruise ship berthing at the port of Barcelona, coming from a touristic crossing on the Mediterranean with mostly American passengers, are very different.

Nevertheless, both examples mentioned above have a high level of risk, but procedures used for their security will be totally different. Of course, should the threat materialise, loss reduction procedures would also be very different.

Establishing a safety system around the various processes of stowing, vehicle access to passenger ships, hydrocarbon unloading, etc., requires a specific study with a daily task schedule for safety personnel.

While airport activities allow flat management, since variables are passengers and cargo, and, furthermore, a type of very "clean" cargo, it is not the case with a port. Anyone attempting to adapt the experience of air safety to the maritime industry would fail dramatically.

Maritime safety requires solutions that, while respecting activities, may ensure safety and adapt to the following basic items:

- Type of ship
- Cargo
- The port: class and geographical location
- Operation to be carried out: mooring, berthing, collecting passengers, unloading dangerous substances, etc.
- Operations coinciding with those of other ships.

1.2 Ship related determinants

The ship has great significance, since it can even become a weapon if used for such purpose, or a vector for a massive destruction weapon, or the inadvertent means of transportation of a malicious cargo, unless appropriate measures are taken regarding maritime security and control[1].

Furthermore, the ship-port interface may be considered as the entrance of dangerous goods into the country, such as weapons, explosives, radioactive materials, etc., and also of people involved with terrorist networks, illegal immigration, or of criminals sought by the police who find in maritime transportation the ideal manner of moving between countries due to the low control exerted.

It is necessary to invest time on studying the threat that the ship represents as addressed and considered in isolation and independently from her environment, bearing in mind the vulnerability by type of ship, following Diagram 1.1. This will provide a very accurate idea of the kind of risk that each port activity may represent with that type of ship; these activities will be defined and analysed further on.

Contents as stated allow considering any security approach that may be intended for implementation at a port, as it will go unavoidably through considering the threat that the ship may represent as a direct or indirect, main or secondary objective, by addressing issues of public order, organised crime, terrorism, vandalism, brawls, etc.; otherwise, the criminal action might be applied indistinctly against the various on shore operators of any other transportation modality.

Items of the SSP that constitute the essential measures from which effectiveness levels may be defined in terms of ship security, as specifically detailed on Section 9.8 of Part B of the Code[2], are to be considered:

- ✓ Access ways
- ✓ Restricted areas
- ✓ Cargo handling
- ✓ Provisions supply
- ✓ Unattended baggage, and
- ✓ Ship security surveillance.

This scheme allows grouping them in accordance to the degree of structural vulnerability (type of ship), operating vulnerability (transits) and degree of rigor of the crew (skills), under the following criteria by blocks:

A. Passenger ships that according to Diagram 1.1 encompass ferries, cruise and Ro-Ro ships, based on the fact that they carry personnel on board other than the crew, may not be approached in the same way depending on which items are being considered, since there are significant differences in procedures and objectives between each type of maritime transportation.

---

[1] Communication from the Commission COM(2003)229 final, 2003/0089 (COD), proposal for a Regulation of the European Parliament and of the Council on enhancing ship and port facility security. Brussels, 2nd of May 2003.
[2] Virtually mandatory at EC level, under the regulation's prescriptions on Section 4.1.12 (Ship security plan review) of Article 3.

1 The ship as the object of the threat 17

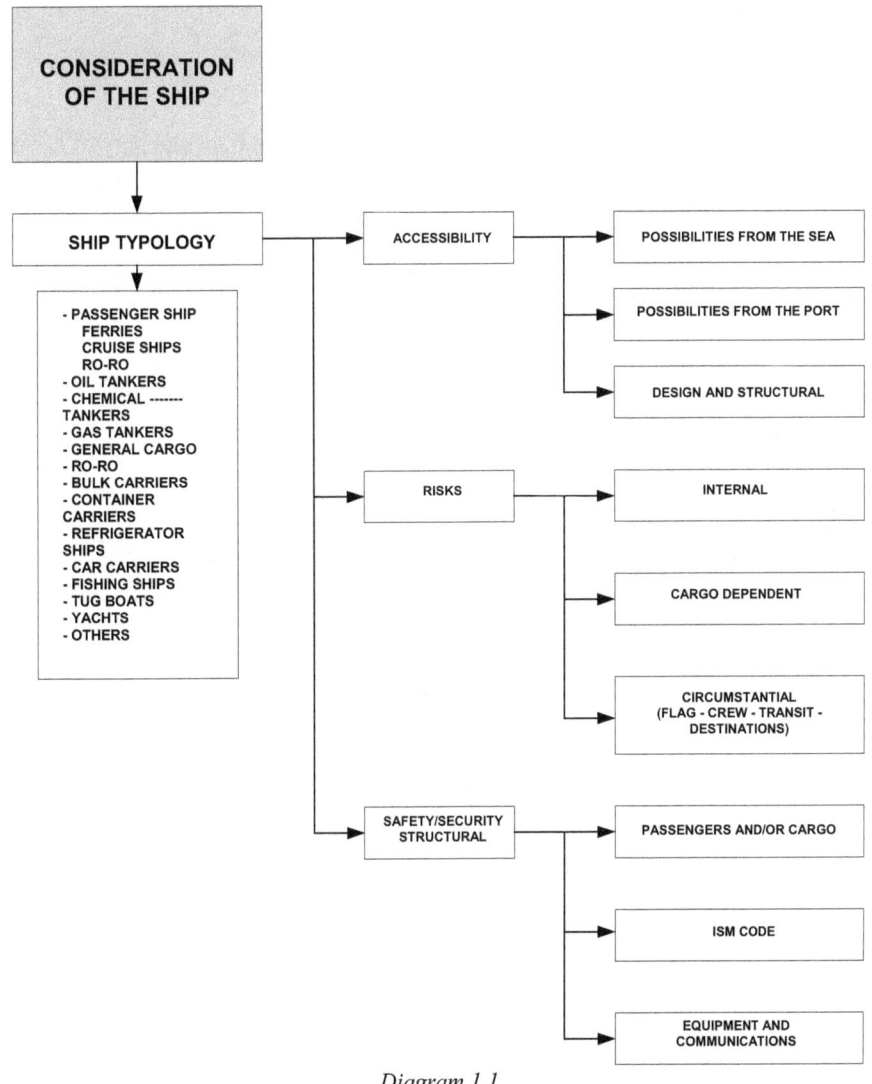

Diagram 1.1

B. Ships usually carrying cargo in tanks, like oil, chemical or gas tankers, will constitute a single group with similar approaches and considerations.
C. General cargo ships, refrigerator ships and bulk carriers will also be grouped within a category with unified approaches.
D. Ro-Ro ships without drivers or passengers, container carriers and car carriers compose a block with a similar approach.
E. Finally, types like fishing ships, tug boats and recreational vessels will be considered within a block of ships under port regime with a specific approach.

1.3 Ships in block "A"

Accessibility

At sea and from it, access to a ferry is difficult, given the height and the verticality of her dead works above the waterline. Access through the door ramps is only possible by opening from the inside; opening is always done in sheltered waters, with the ship at a standstill.

Assaulting from sea would only be possible if a previous occupation force existed to support boarding from within the ship, so that accessing outside decks could be done with the ship at a standstill or at a very low speed.

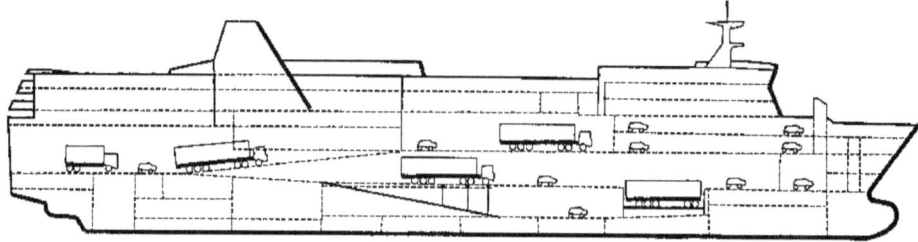

Figure 1.1

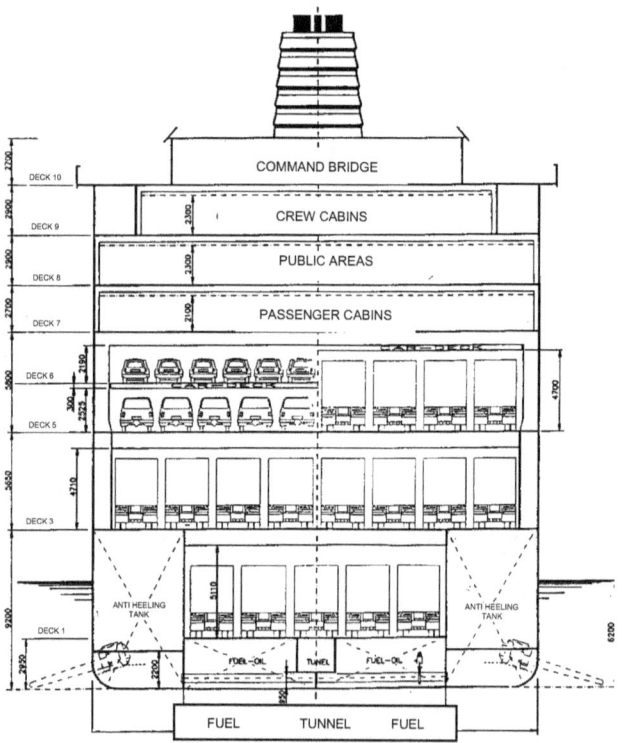

Figure 1.2

Accessing restricted areas on board

Except for cruise ships, on other ships in this block it is currently relatively easy to enter restricted areas that have special relevance due both to consequences internal to the ship and to external consequences for the port facility environment. Figures 1.1 through 1.3 show configurations of cargo and passenger areas, and how very easily they may interrelate.

ITEM	FERRY	CRUISE SHIP	RO-RO
Control areas and posts	Easy	Difficult	Easy
Areas with vigilance team	Easy	Difficult	Easy
Ventilation system areas	Easy	Difficult	Easy
Areas accessing potable water tanks	Easy	Difficult	Easy
Dangerous goods areas	N/A	N/A	Easy
Loading/unloading pumps	N/A	N/A	N/A
Crew accommodation	Easy	Easy	Easy

Table 1.1

The existence of security procedures in cruise ships means a remarkable breakthrough in this respect, since controlling such areas is, with a higher or lower effectiveness, aimed against intrusion and malicious handling of the equipment and services therein located.

Areas dedicated to dangerous cargo, due to their nature and classification in the IMDG Code, are not applicable to most passenger ships; occasionally, only very small quantities may be permitted, on a heavily controlled, very safe means of carriage.

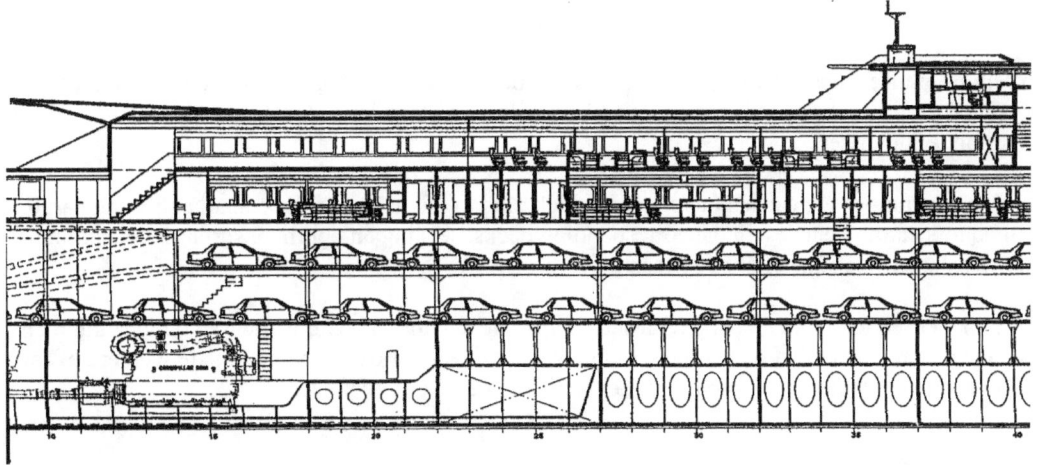

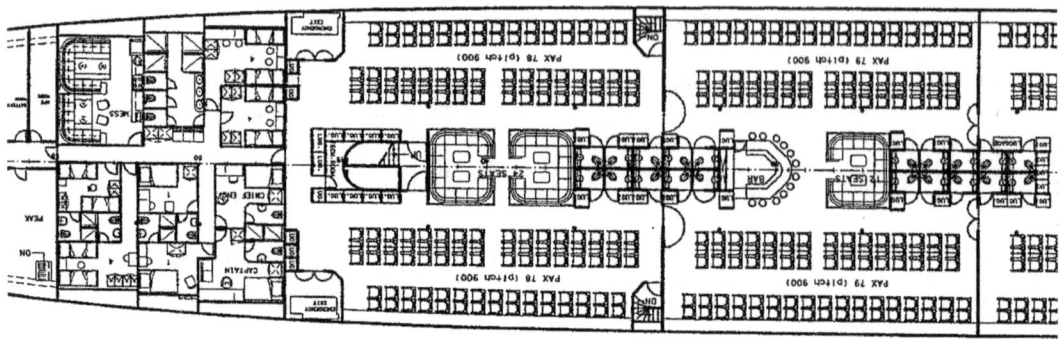

Figure 1.3

Cargo handling

ITEM	FERRY	CRUISE SHIP	RO-RO
Systematic inspection of the cargo	Normal	N/A	Normal
Inspection outside the port	Nil	Frequent	Nil
Verification of contents	Nil	Frequent	Nil
Vehicle search prior to boarding			
- Visual means	Scarce	N/A	Scarce
- Devices	Scarce	N/A	Scarce
- Dogs	Scarce	N/A	Scarce

Table 1.2

Except for cruise ships, on which this variable is not applicable (N/A), on ferry and Ro-Ro types cargo is accepted once it has gone through the checkpoints existing in the corresponding concession, and boarding is authorised.

Stowage operations are carried out aboard, which, due to the nature of the embarked rolling cargo, are limited to locating vehicles on the corresponding decks, seeking an optimum surface occupation based on the volumetric characteristics of each unit.

When palletised loads are embarked on such ships, the attention aboard is focused on locating them on the decks in a manner that they are not in the way and may not be harmed by the movement of rolling units, so that no damages are produced, neither is the vehicle flow hindered.

Provisions

Reception of all types of supplies may be considered as positive and acceptable in the manner it is done in most ship types in this block. Image and quality of received supplies have an appropriate priority, particularly on cruise ships; it is not good practice to accept items aboard that do not match the ordering specifications.

ITEM	FERRY	CRUISE SHIP	RO-RO
Packaging integrity	Yes	Yes	Yes
Reject without previous inspection	No	Yes	No
Undue handling	Yes	Yes	Yes
Only as requested	Yes	Yes	Yes
Order and delivery documentation	Yes	Yes	Yes

Table 1.3

Rejecting packages with loss of packaging integrity is a response in accordance with the degree of rigor that may be ruling aboard. A broken box can be accepted if the content is whole, without giving thought to the possibility of the labelling having been changed. The approach to security principles will have to change the philosophy of criteria application with respect to acceptation or reject.

Unattended baggage

ITEM	FERRY	CRUISE SHIP	RO-RO
Search prior to admittance aboard	No	N/A	No
Previous search at the port	No	N/A	No
Safety after inspection	No	N/A	No
Stowed in locked storeroom	Yes	N/A	Yes

Table 1.4

On cruise ships this variable is not applicable, because baggage is properly identified, owners being present aboard; otherwise, baggage is disembarked, since it is useless that it should remain on board. Nevertheless, baggage in such ships, which is never unattended, goes through each and every item in the table.

On the other two ship types, up to the present moment there is no control on board, baggage being admitted without further measures, in the confidence that any anomaly would have been detected by the on shore search procedures. Once baggage has been admitted, it goes into storerooms where it will remain stowed until unloaded on arrival at destination port. The safety of the locking system used for such storerooms is worth mentioning, as it leaves room for justified doubts regarding its effectiveness in terms of its strength and the technology applied.

Ship features with respect to risk variables

BY THE EXPECTED FREQUENCY OF THE VARIABLE			
ITEM	FERRY	CRUISE SHIP	RO-RO
Access ways: - At sea - At port	Difficult Easy	Difficult Easy	Difficult Easy
Restricted areas	Several	Many	Scarce
Cargo handling	High	Very scarce	High
Provisions delivery	High	Very high	Normal
Unattended baggage	Scarce	Very Scarce	Scarce
Ship security surveillance	Scarce/medium	High	Scarce
Degree of concealment	High	High	Medium

Table 1.5

While on tables 1.1 through 1.4 it is the routine procedure applied by the crew on this ship block that is being analysed, table 1.5 intends to address the opportunity offered by ships due to their specific construction, without the crew being the determinant, although it may become highly conditioned.

With respect to establishing a criterion in front of the possibility that the inside areas may make it easy to conceal unlawful materials, it is very high for all of them, depending directly on the number of areas that may be accessed by passengers.

1.4 Ships in block "B"

Accessing restricted areas on board

This variable has a routine fulfilment aboard the ships considered within this block. Specific, well defined characteristics of mostly all terminals and jetties, and the locations of the berthing lines, place them in the majority of cases in safe areas within port facilities, access being controlled by checkpoints and vigilance on their interface with the port.

Operations required by the specific cargoes for each ship type provide easy access to the crew, particularly to engine and deck personnel. Only outside access ways are under a strict monitoring to ensure that they remain closed, due to safety reasons related to cargo risks, in order to avoid the ingress of flammable or toxic vapours that the cargo may issue into accommodation and unsafe areas.

Most restricted areas on these ships should be easily accessible due to safety operating reasons. This will be the case with inside watertight doors, the role of which is isolating decks as fire barriers, which in any case do not have permanent, secure locks, but rather the opposite.

ITEM	OIL TANKER	CHEMICAL TANKER	GAS TANKER
Checkpoints and control areas	Normal	Normal	Normal
Areas with surveillance equipment	Normal	Normal	Normal
Areas with ventilation systems	Normal	Normal	Normal
Areas accessing potable water tanks	Normal	Normal	Normal
Areas with dangerous goods	Normal	Normal	Normal
Loading/unloading pumps	Normal	Normal	Normal
Crew accommodation	Normal	Normal	Normal

Table 1.6

Cargo handling

ITEM	OIL TANKER	CHEMICAL TANKER	GAS TANKER
Systematic inspection of the cargo	N/A	N/A	N/A
Inspection outside the port	N/A	N/A	N/A
Verification of contents	N/A	N/A	N/A
Vehicle search prior to boarding - Visual means - Devices - Dogs	N/A	N/A	N/A

Table 1.7

Due to the characteristics of the cargo and the enclosed transportation of the specialised products carried by ships in this block, none of the common applications to other ships apply to this case.

Provisions

For this variable, comments are the same as those already made for ferries, since the routine is the one accepted by the majority of the marine community. Provisions may or may not be the best or the desirable ones, but those coinciding with the request are always accepted, there not being any procedures in place alerting of criminal intents. Such criteria should change substantially by a training that is consequent with the purpose of the code and its implementation aboard.

ITEM	OIL TANKER	CHEMICAL TANKER	GAS TANKER
Packaging integrity	Yes	Yes	Yes
Reject without previous inspection	No	No	No
Undue handling	Yes	Yes	Yes
Only as requested	Yes	Yes	Yes
Order and delivery documentation	Yes	Yes	Yes

Table 1.8

Unattended baggage

Again, this variable is not applicable to either this or the subsequent ship type blocks, since the fact of not having embarked passengers makes it void; any baggage accompanied by the owners, i.e., the crew, may be inspected.

ITEM	OIL TANKER	CHEMICAL TANKER	GAS TANKER
Search prior to admittance aboard	N/A	N/A	N/A
Previous search at the port	N/A	N/A	N/A
Safety after inspection	N/A	N/A	N/A
Stowed in locked storeroom	N/A	N/A	N/A

Table 1.9

However, looking at security, sometimes part of the baggage of a crew member that has disembarked may be left on board, either because the crew member is soon to be enrolled and incorporated, or to be collected in a subsequent port. Such possibility should also be considered when security procedures are established, in order to ensure that such baggage is harmless and does not pose a threat to the ship when left aboard.

Ship features with respect to risk variables

Due to the characteristics of their freeboards, structures and superstructures, possibilities of being assaulted at sea are many, as recent piracy acts in identified maritime navigation areas of the Far East are demonstrating.

Due to the operating regime of ships in this block, and bearing in mind the specialised training and the awareness of their crew (in general terms), as well as their obligations derived from the requirements of the materials usually constituting their cargoes, it may be assured that industrial safety aspects related to their activity are largely complied with .

1 The ship as the object of the threat

BY THE EXPECTED FREQUENCY OF THE VARIABLE			
ITEM	OIL TANKER	CHEMICAL TANKER	GAS TANKER
Access ways: - At sea - At port	Easy Highly guarded	Easy Highly guarded	Medium Highly guarded
Restricted areas	None	None	None
Cargo handling	None	None	None
Provisions delivery	Normal	Normal	Normal
Unattended baggage	Nil	Nil	Nil
Ship security surveillance	Normal	Normal	Normal
Degree of concealment	Low	Low	Low

Table 1.10

Nevertheless, during their stay at port facilities, confidence in access control, vigilance and dedicated personnel causes security related preventative routine to become virtually nil, except, of course, when a specific warning is given that may call for adopting special measures by the crew; regarding code implementation, this would be considered as applying security levels 1 or 2, for which the crew should be specially trained and taught, this condition being applicable to all ships, whatever their type or cargo.

1.5 Ships in block "C"

Accessing restricted areas on board

Although the importance that is associated with the vital functions of the ship and what they represent for her own safety are specific, well defined and known, the pacific and civil purpose of the whole crew create a routine conduct and attitude that make this type of ship very vulnerable when applying security criteria.

Most restricted areas in such ships are often easily accessible due to an excess of confidence. Only inside watertight doors are of a marked interest, which have the purpose of communicating decks as fire barriers, or to prevent the entry of dusty concentrations coming from loading operations; in any case, they are not usually fitted with permanent locks that may hinder their being tampered with, but rather the opposite.

As berthings of these ships are often in port facility access ways that are not under close vigilance or are easy to access, crew members pay special attention to closing access ways to their cabins or areas holding goods, since thefts have occurred often, whether by stevedore brigades or people transiting the docks.

In any case, it cannot be said for this item that locks may also be included in the safety chapter, since forcing them would not oppose a great difficulty.

ITEM	GENERAL CARGO	REFRIGERATOR	BULK CARRIER
Checkpoints and control areas	Normal	Normal	Normal
Areas with surveillance equipment	Normal	Normal	Normal
Areas with ventilation systems	Normal	Normal	Normal
Areas accessing potable water tanks	Normal	Normal	Normal
Areas with dangerous goods	Normal	Normal	Normal
Loading/unloading pumps	Normal	Normal	Normal
Crew accommodation	Guarded	Guarded	Guarded

Table 1.11

It may be said with full conviction that implementing each SSP will turn confidence into interest, providing the required degree of tightness for the vital areas on the ship.

Cargo handling

ITEM	GENERAL CARGO	REFRIGERATOR	BULK CARRIER
Systematic inspection of the cargo	Medium	High	Low
Inspection outside the port	Normal	Normal	Normal
Verification of contents	Nil	Medium	Nil
Vehicle search prior to boarding			
- Visual means	Yes	No	No
- Devices	No	No	No
- Dogs	No	No	No

Table 1.12

The item focused on vehicle search should be understood as applied to the cargo related to each ship type.

Any criteria shown in the table as a response to the items are related to the cargo operational safety, not intended actions with a security purpose. When implementing security procedures, coincidence of safety and security purposes or the lack of it may be observed, as well as the substantial change that the clear differentiation and adaptation of routine methods to those prescribed by the code may mean.

If cargoes of refrigerator ships have a higher relevance with respect to control and register, it is due to their nature and the phytosanitary requirements, although these are not extremely different to the routine controls on other ship types.

For bulk carriers, the nature of bulk cargo, the means used for loading aboard, the closure of the holds and the danger to human life associated with their atmospheres point at a low incidence on security requirements.

On general cargo ships, any detected alteration is recorded as damage with a process for damage claims, otherwise they would be charged on the ship at the port of unloading.

Palletised and unitised cargo by any system allow detecting breakages on their wrappings: plastic, sackcloth, canvas, etc.; however, until now the focus was on the condition of the cargo rather than on unlawful contents, since in the officer's receipt, the safeguard is still the expression "unaware of weight and contents", the cargo being accepted and loaded.

Provisions

Criteria identified for any type of merchant ship are applicable to this block of ships, with procedures as mentioned above. In this respect, the crew act according to widely accepted routines that, without having been assessed objectively as the most appropriate, constitute normal practice in non imposition conditions; they are only modified when specifically required, and once normality is restored they return to their initial application.

ITEM	GENERAL CARGO	REFRIGERATOR	BULK CARRIER
Packaging integrity	Yes	Yes	Yes
Reject without previous inspection	No	No	No
Undue handling	Yes	Yes	Yes
Only as requested	Yes	Yes	Yes
Order and delivery documentation	Yes	Yes	Yes

Table 1.13

Unattended baggage

Again, the same discussion for all type of ships not taking passengers may be applied to this section, since baggage is attended by crew members at all times; exception is made of the specific, unusual cases already mentioned.

ITEM	GENERAL CARGO	REFRIGERATOR	BULK CARRIER
Search prior to admittance aboard	N/A	N/A	N/A
Previous search at the port	N/A	N/A	N/A
Safety after inspection	N/A	N/A	N/A
Stowed in locked storeroom	N/A	N/A	N/A

Table 1.14

Ship features with respect to risk variables

Due to the structural configuration of bulk carriers, closer to tankers in freeboard and their considerable length, they are easy to assault from smaller vessels, being very different with respect to the other two ship types considered within this block.

BY THE EXPECTED FREQUENCY OF THE VARIABLE			
ITEM	**GENERAL CARGO**	**REFRIGERATOR**	**BULK CARRIER**
Access ways:			
- At sea	Normal	Normal	Easy
- At port	Easy	Easy	Normal
Restricted areas	None	None	None
Cargo handling	Very high	High	Scarce
Provisions delivery	Normal	Normal	Normal
Unattended baggage	Nil	Nil	Nil
Ship security surveillance	Normal	Normal	Normal
Degree of concealment	Low	Low	Low

Table 1.15

However, while at port, methods and resources for bulk cargo handling, a lower need for personnel presence and the nature of the cargo itself, as aforementioned, grant bulk carriers a lower probability of security related events.

For the other items, no large differences may be seen between the manners of addressing security related threats on ships in this block.

1.6 Ships in block "D"

Accessing restricted areas on board

The same remarks made for the previous blocks are applicable on the items in this section, since these are still merchant ships with the same crew that, from one day to the other may be enrolled in one type of ship or another; therefore, unless it is a specialised ship, conduct at routine levels is aimed just at navigational requirements and at those associated with the nature of the cargo, without special measures being adopted, except in particular cases of ports and areas with known risks.

ITEM	RO-RO	CONTAINER CARRIER	CAR CARRIER
Checkpoints and control areas	Normal	Normal	Normal
Areas with surveillance equipment	Normal	Normal	Normal
Areas with ventilation systems	Normal	Normal	Normal
Areas accessing potable water tanks	Normal	Normal	Normal
Areas with dangerous goods	Normal	Normal	Normal
Loading/unloading pumps	Normal	Normal	Normal
Crew accommodation	Guarded	Guarded	Guarded

Table 1.16

Cargo handling

ITEM	RO-RO	CONTAINER CARRIER	CAR CARRIER
Systematic inspection of the cargo	Medium	Low	Low
Inspection outside the port	Normal	Normal	Normal
Verification of contents	Nil	Nil	Nil
Vehicle search prior to boarding			
- Visual means	Yes	Yes	Yes
- Devices	No	No	No
- Dogs	No	No	No

Table 1.17

Although the three ship types have been grouped in this block due to their external similarity, nature of cargoes and embarkment procedures differ substantially, which makes it easy to detect security related anomalies, although this was not the original intention.

Nevertheless, once the obtained results are analysed, whatever the method used, reality shows that no differences exist, and that the same vulnerability is present aboard, security depending on that existing at the terminals, at the level it may be exerted, there being no further steps for directly embarking on the ship.

Provisions

ITEM	RO-RO	CONTAINER CARRIER	CAR CARRIER
Packaging integrity	Yes	Yes	Yes
Reject without previous inspection	No	No	No
Undue handling	Yes	Yes	Yes
Only as requested	Yes	Yes	Yes
Order and delivery documentation	Yes	Yes	Yes

Table 1.18

The same remarks as for previous blocks apply to these items.

Unattended baggage

ITEM	RO-RO	CONTAINER CARRIER	CAR CARRIER
Search prior to admittance aboard	N/A	N/A	N/A
Previous search at the port	N/A	N/A	N/A
Safety after inspection	N/A	N/A	N/A
Stowed in locked storeroom	N/A	N/A	N/A

Table 1.19

Identical remarks to those already presented for previous ship blocks.

Ship features with respect to risk variables

Once again, ship features relevant to structural characteristics allow appreciating subtle differences, depending on whether the ship is considered to be at port or at sea; in turn, so do the nature of cargoes and the embarking operating procedures by the transit generated aboard, the number of personnel participating, the steps followed for controlling the cargo, etc.

For example, when considering cargo handling, the high frequency of movements in Ro-Ro ships and car carriers results in a higher probability of security events than in container carriers.

For the other items, no differentiating circumstances are identifiable between the three ship types composing this block.

BY THE EXPECTED FREQUENCY OF THE VARIABLE			
ITEM	RO-RO	CONTAINER CARRIER	CAR CARRIER
Access ways:			
- At sea	Difficult	Normal	Difficult
- At port	Easy	Normal	Easy
Restricted areas	None	None	None
Cargo handling	High	Scarce	High
Provisions delivery	Normal	Normal	Normal
Unattended baggage	Nil	Nil	Nil
Ship security surveillance	Normal	Normal	Normal
Degree of concealment	High	High	Medium

Table 1.20

1.7 Ships in block "E"

In strict compliance with the code application prescriptions, vessels considered to be in this block would not be contemplated, and therefore it would seem that they should not be addressed under security criteria; in fact, they would not be under the demands of any SSP, but they will be in the PFSPs.

However, such vessels produce a heavy transit in the inside waters of any port facility, which often goes past a minimum security control; even though they have been used for terrorist and other criminal acts, tug boats may be approached differently, since their operations are an indirect service within the port management, and therefore the port may control them at large, both the units and their crew, which are more or less stable and fixed in terms of their contracts.

However, due to their location within the port areas, they are all extremely accessible, therefore becoming easy to assault and used for actions that precisely the prescriptions of the code intend to avoid.

Therefore, taking such ships into consideration is not due to their owners, their objectives or their activities, but because of how easy they may be used by third parties with an intent of causing damage; it is evident that fishing ports and marinas are open to the outside of port facilities and have few control systems, and when existing, these are highly vulnerable in front of criminal actions.

It is deemed unnecessary to apply the procedure followed for the other ships, since if under a more strict operating regime, the items addressed appear to be precariously managed with respect to security related demands, in this block there are no positive items to be seen that may represent a barrier, control or filter to the first steps of piracy with terrorist objectives from within the port facilities.

Only the by frequency table is presented. Under the evaluations shown, little comment is needed; nevertheless, it should be taken into account for the general security at the port.

Ship features with respect to risk variables

BY THE EXPECTED FREQUENCY OF THE VARIABLE			
ITEM	FISHING SHIP	TUG BOAT	RECREATIONAL VESSEL

Access ways:
  - At sea
  - At port
	High
	High
		Easy
		Easy
			High
			High

Restricted areas	None	None	None
Cargo handling	Scarce	Nil	Nil
Provisions delivery	Scarce	Scarce	Scarce
Unattended baggage	Nil	Nil	Nil
Ship security surveillance	Nil	Normal	Nil

Table 1.21

Concealment aboard

Distribution of spaces, holds, storerooms, cabins, chambers, halls, workshops, allows that all ships, whatever their type, may offer a high number of possibilities for concealing unlawful materials, which may be used for smuggling, concealment of persons and, in relation to security, hiding weapons and explosives.

Concealment may be done by two groups of people; on the one hand, members of the crew, although the possibilities for this occurring are low; on the other hand, passengers or on shore work brigade members that participate in cargo handling, due to the easy access to concealment spaces.

On general cargo ships, the possibilities for accessing empty spaces in bulkheads, longitudinals and false bottoms will depend to a large extent on the level and effectiveness of (see Figures 1.5 and 1.6):

- ✓ Crew surveillance of the holds
- ✓ Control on embarked hand carried parcels
- ✓ Control on the contents of the loaded cargo

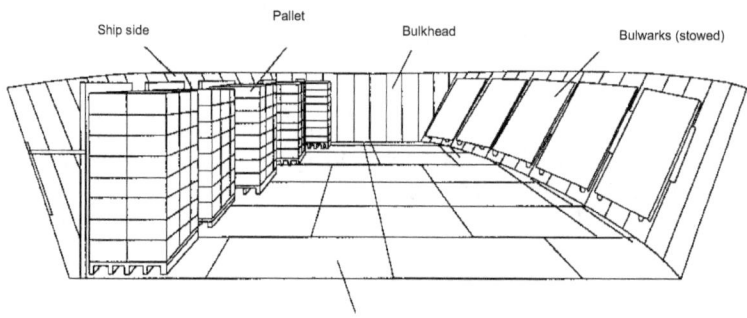

Figure 1.5

1 The ship as the object of the threat 33

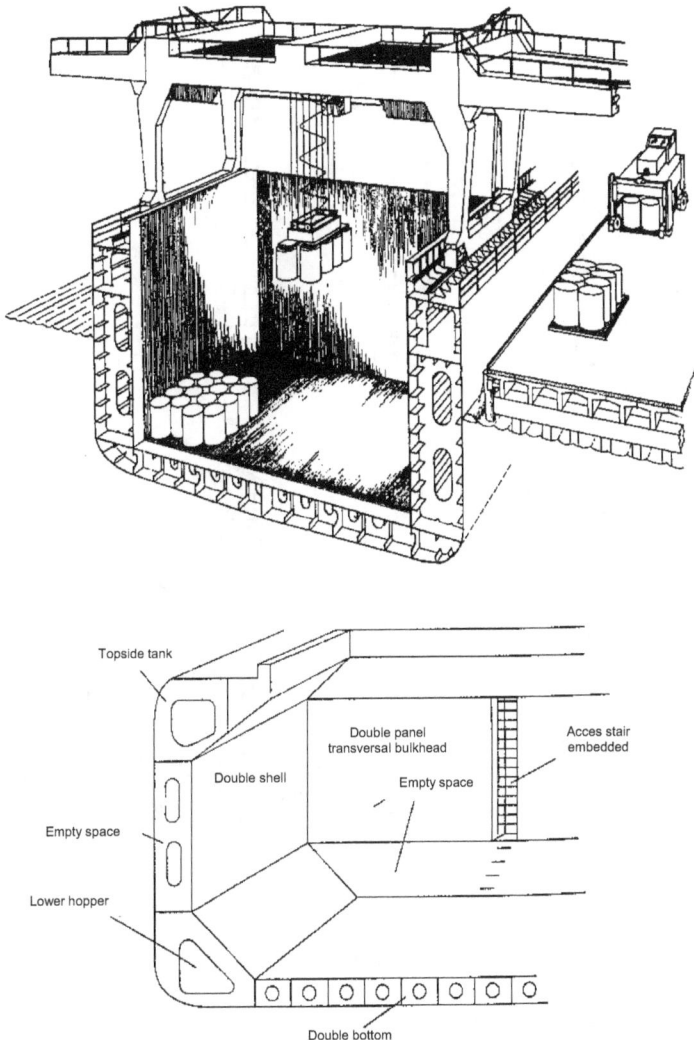

Figure 1.6

Container carriers offer other alternatives for concealment, although at first sight loading bays may not appear to allow or facilitate concealment; therefore, such areas should undergo more inspections than those carried out routinely (see Figure 1.7).

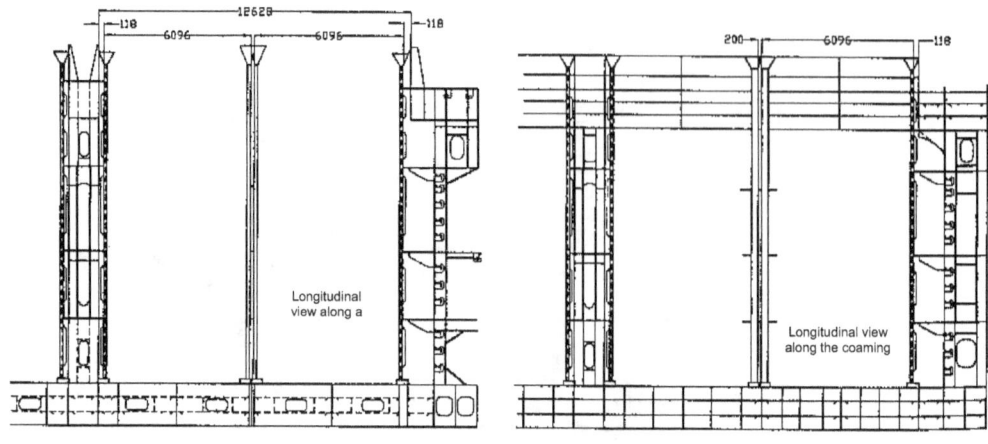

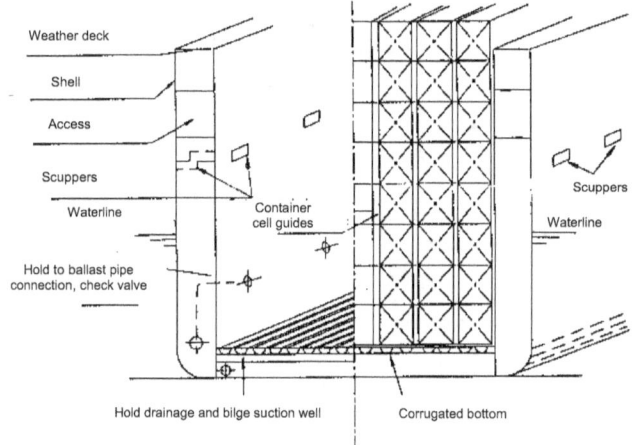

Figure 1.7

Ro-Ro ships offer easy access to spaces, some of them classified as restricted areas, but others freely accessible, which may be used as concealment locations (see Figure 1.8).

It is evident that in this case, access control to restricted areas should be comprehensive, although vehicles embarked as cargo may be what is mostly used for criminal purposes.

Areas dedicated to the crew, or those not freely accessible to passengers, but which at some point in time may be unoccupied, like bars and service posts, may also be chosen for concealment (see Figure 1.9).

1 The ship as the object of the threat

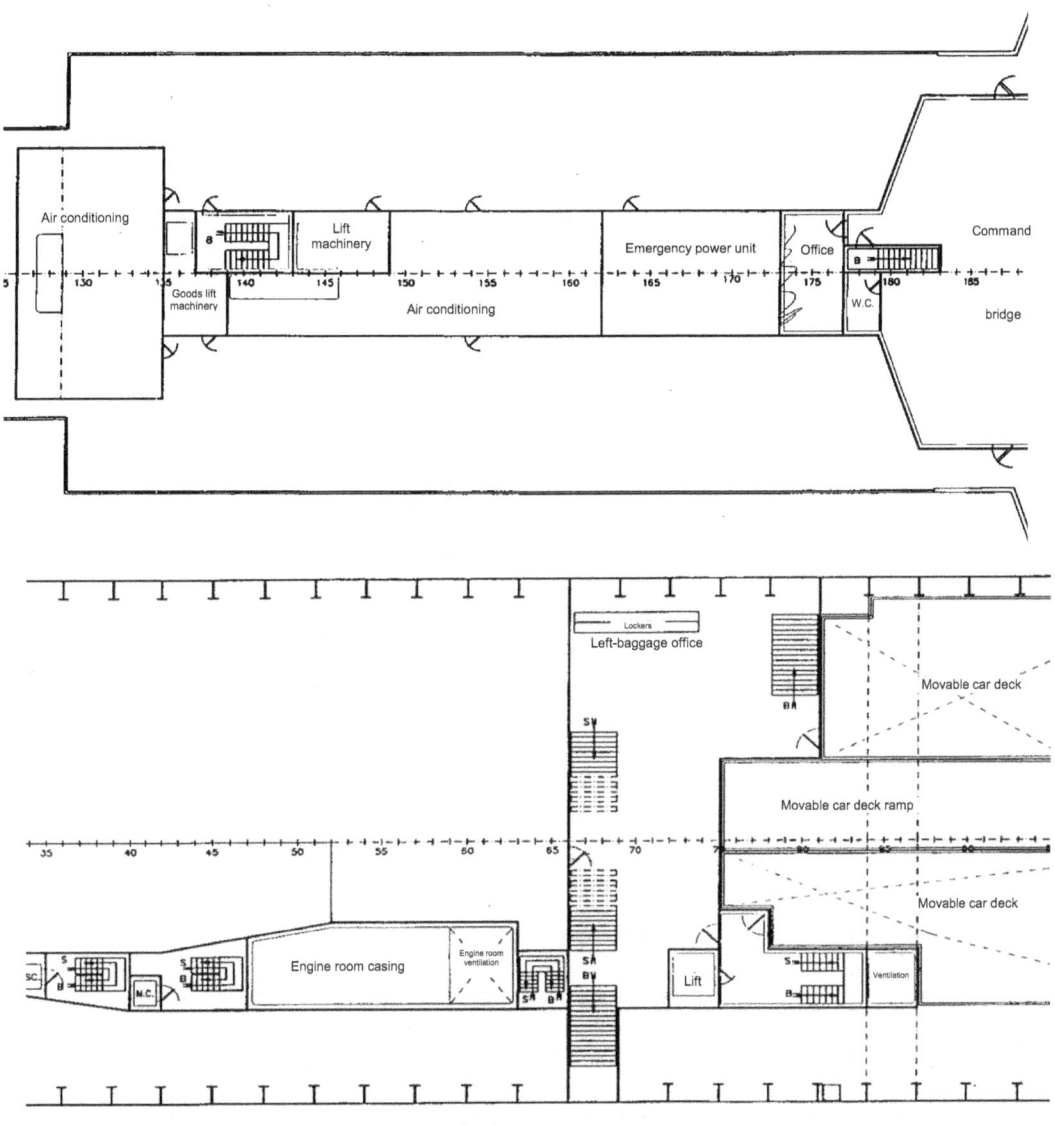

Figure 1.8

1.8 Ship related conclusion summary

On table 1.22, which has been divided into two parts due to its size, the summary by features is listed for each ship type, in a manner that they are identified by risk category according to the item in consideration; this allows to obtain a final evaluation (column on the right), which, in spite of the objectivity followed in this analysis, should be taken as an estimate, since under a terrorist intent any ship or vessel may be used, independently of the nature of the cargo, but rather by what they may take aboard, neither depending on the size of the ship, but rather on the opportunity to assault it or how easy it may be to use.

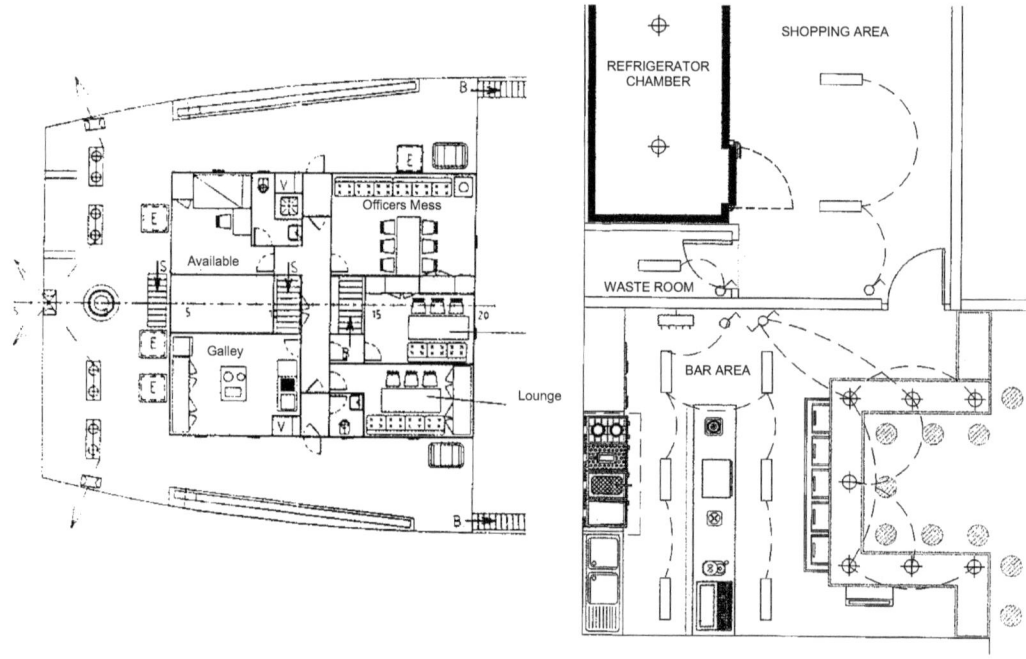

Figure 1.9

Once vulnerabilities of each ship type to risks as listed on the code are identified, three positive lines may be obtained:

> Assisting the PFSOs in their relationship with the SSOs.

> Providing the PFSOs with a reasonable knowledge of security related risks on ships.

> Assisting the PFSOs in implementing the PFSPs in those aspects directly related to ships.

Finally, the possibility should not be overlooked of having one of the most vulnerable locations of the ship while at port not on the pier side, where it is berthed and moored, but on the water side, where vigilance is always much lower, and where, unless activating level 3, there is no sufficient control to provide the required security; therefore, when the ship is at port, any such kind of threat should be detected, identified, controlled and neutralised by the security systems managed by the PFSP, counting for sure with the support, assistance and participation of specialised bodies, besides the electronic means that the port facility may have available for this purpose.

Coding: 1 Possible, 2 Scarce, 3 Normal, 4 High, 5 Very High

1 The ship as the object of the threat

RISK CATEGORIES (SHIPS) WITH RESPECT TO PORT							
	SHIP FEATURE			CARGO FEATURE		SHORE FEATURE	
Ship	Access from sea	Access from shore	Category	Cargo type	Category	Loading operations	Handling class
Cruise	N	S	2	N	1	N	N
Ferry	N	S	3	S	3	S	S
Tankers	S	N	2	S	5	N	N
Gas tanker	N	N	1	S	5	N	N
General	N	S	3	S	4	S	S
Refrigerator	N	S	3	N	2	S	S
Bulk	S	S	3	N	1	N	N
Ro-Ro	N	S	3	S	4	S	S
Container	N	S	3	S	5	N	N
Car carrier	N	S	2	S	3	S	N
Tug boat	S	S	4	N	1	N	N
Fishing	S	S	4	S	1	N	N

	SHORE FEATURE			CREW FEATURE		EVALUATION
Ship	Loading operations	Handling class	Category	Crew procedure	Category	Risk category
Cruise	N	N	1	N	1	1
Ferry	S	S	5	S	2	3-4
Tankers	N	N	1	N	1	2
Gas tanker	N	N	1	N	1	2
General	S	S	5	S	3	4
Refrigerator	S	S	3	S	2	2-3
Bulk	N	N	2	N	2	2
Ro-Ro	S	S	5	S	4	4
Container	N	N	4	S	4	4
Car carrier	S	N	2	N	1	2
Tug boat	N	N	1	N	1	1-2
Fishing	N	N	1	N	1	1-2
Ship	N	N	1	N	1	1-2

Table 1.22

Chapter 2. The port as a threat to the ship

2.1 Determinants associated with the port

Determinants associated with the ship are developed in diagram 2.1, based mainly on considering variables, accessibility, risks and structural approaches.

Since the IMO does not have the authority to tell Member States how to protect their ports, the concept of *port facilities* was created for referring to areas in which a ship under SOLAS convention security is serviced.

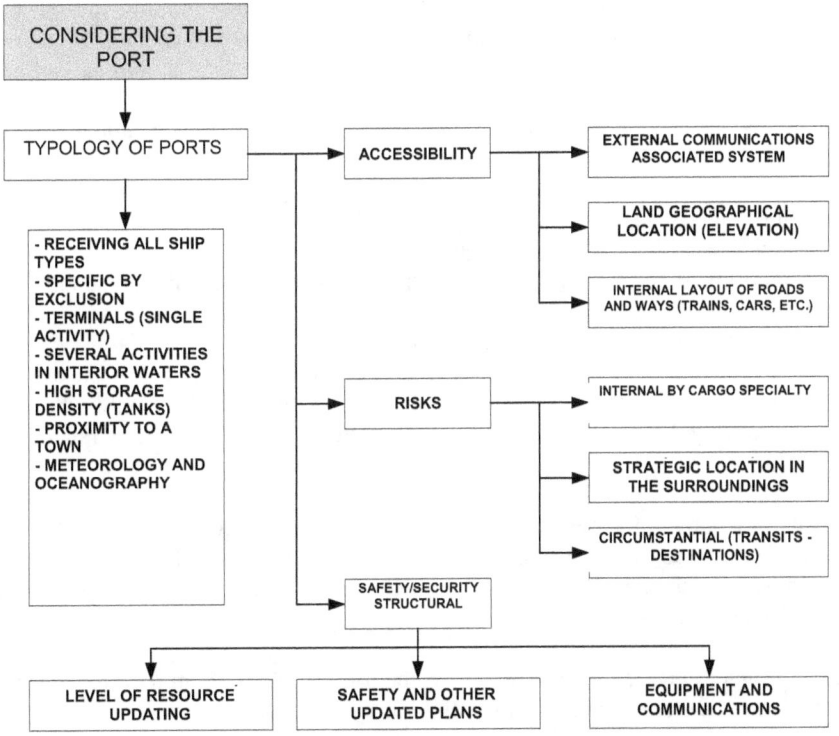

Diagram 2.1

2.2 Access control philosophy and principles

Port facilities lost the control on access ways they had formerly enjoyed, being a strategic part of a town, when opening their doors in the second half of the 20th century. In this manner, nearby towns found an area of recreation in which townsfolk could walk and carry out various recreational activities. The current situation generates a need to return to the former status quo as strategic areas. Nevertheless, in certain cases port management will allow defining a free transit area, in order not to disrupt the current situation in a traumatic manner.

The general philosophy applicable to the adopted measures for access control, both on personnel and on cargo, is that prevention and checks should be such that those flows are hindered to the least possible extent.

The main differentiating and risk multiplying factor at a port facility lies with its essential characteristic of its activity around the clock: 24 hours a day, 365 days a year. Furthermore, establishing a safe perimeter to create a protective bubble is virtually impossible with the currently available technical resources, besides budget limitations, rather common in most ports. This leads often to being short of personnel, who generally are not aware of safety related concepts, to a limited use, in terms of quantity and quality, of physical safety systems and, lastly, to a scarce allocation of resources for such concepts.

If facilities constitute the port's motor, their security should be initiated, at least indirectly, from the external perimeter, where a primary safe area should be established prior to the fence or the port access checkpoint. In this manner, active control systems are in place at an early stage, without them affecting the operating areas; for example, on adjacent roads.

From the above derives that access ways constitute sensitive locations, and should be reduced to the essential minimum:

A. Access of passengers and companions with or without vehicles.
B. Entry of vehicles with merchandise to be embarked.
C. Access of port workers, crew with leave, ships maintenance or supply personnel.

It would normally be inappropriate to limit any type of access within the area assigned to recreational activities of the townsfolk. Even potentiating such areas, in the same manner as the duty free areas in the airports, may report great benefits, since it would in no way justify people who do not belong there, staying in security areas. Such recreational areas should be protected with random controls and CCTV surveillance.

Access ways between operating areas and services area (except for common evacuation routes) are a very different matter. In any case, it is the access to such areas, in which vital facilities are located, where safety measures should be increased to the maximum; such control should be carried out through the various physical security systems.

Based on the configuration of a given port facility, the following minimum requirements are presented in order to attain a basic effectiveness in controlling its access ways:

1. Perimetric fence around port services, located objectively, having fully assessed the alternatives that may be applied in terms of construction and materials.
2. Defining restricted areas in the ship access facility, whether based on concessions, berthing lines, specialised cargo transits, or under any other consideration related to the risk and vulnerability of each area associated with ships.

The first item is conditioned by the superficial configuration of the public domain, the proximity of the external limits to the ship operating areas of the port, those determined by the town with which it may be closely related (engulfed), and by the current availability of port facility access.

The fence should clearly define and indicate a liability line, and in turn establish access determinants, and in particular its objective relationship with the ship-port interface. It would correspond to "P" in Figure 2.1.

Figure 2.1 shows an access control schematic for a port configuration, in which checkpoints are depicted:

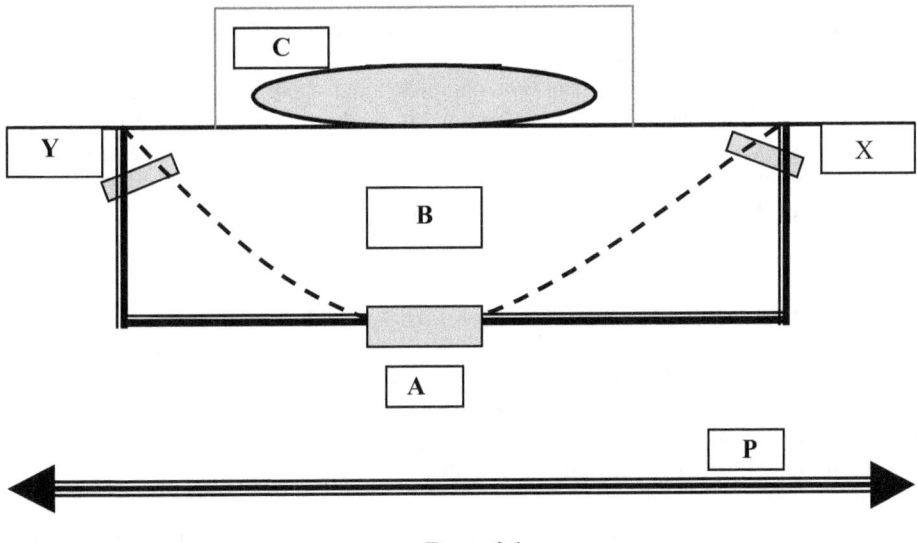

Figure 2.1

In turn, the second item constitutes the fundamental objective of the present study, since, independently of the existence of an outer fence defining the port facility itself, security control may only be possible if the main safety ring is appropriately defined, where filtering and dissuasive measures may be implemented.

    a. A restricted access and exit area should exist on the berthing line at which the ship is safely moored, bounding the ship's length on the shore side with sufficient clearance to include the operations and internal transit yard, as well as the mooring points (bollards) to which the ship is moored.

b. Such surface, "B", should be enclosed by a fence or by sufficiently solid, resistant materials with longstanding stability, low vulnerability, which are controllable to the highest possible extent.
c. It should have entry and exit access ways, as required by security operative measures, complying with the following mandatory items:
    i. It should be possible to close and keep them closed during situations as foreseen in Security Level 3.
    ii. Such ways should be differentiated between those for personnel use and those dedicated to the various types of services required by the ship.
    iii. Access ways may be in place to be operative only in case of personnel evacuation or to provide access to security operations.
d. If the ship is a passenger ship, access and exit ways should consist of (see Figure 1):
    i. A maritime station, "A", for normal use in Security Level 1.
    ii. An access, "X", for supply vehicle access, and others as considered in the PFSP.
    iii. An additional access, "Y", as an exit and evacuation way for use in the required situations, depending on the occupation of that area, ship included.
e. If the ship is a ferry or a Ro-Ro type, the approach is similar to that for a passenger ship, the difference being that access "X" would be used for vehicles boarding the ship or approaching the ship side for unloading supplies.
f. If the ship is a cargo ship, maritime station "A" would be an access gate equipped with the necessary means for controlling cargo, drivers and visitors, designed in a manner such that entries and exits would be carried out with complete safety both for people and for vehicles.
g. Finally, access from the sea, both to the ship and to the berthing line, should be a water surface with previously set boundaries, as defined in the PFSP, which may take the established security measures without significant difficulties; this would be area "C" of Figure 2.1.
h. The thick line, "P", would be a port boundary (public domain, etc.)

2.3 Access security control (personnel, vehicles and merchandise)

Firstly, safety standards at each port, which should depend on risk level, should be examined, in addition to the specific nature of the ship-port interface type that they generate (see Chapter 1: Application criteria). Since such risk level varies with time, it should be possible to increase security controls easily, without this interfering with port facility operativity.

In this item, the emphasis will be placed on access safety between the zones marked within the port. These areas have different security levels and the dealings with each individual, vehicle or merchandise will be more or less intensive.

2.3.1 Control zones

The *zone* concept includes all areas in a manner that each zone may contain the maximum number of services requiring an identical security level and the lowest possible number of zones and gates between them.

Denominations of zones are:

1. **Open zones:** General public circulation is allowed. Design should be aimed at allowing the public to carry out all their transactions and leave the area without accessing controlled zones. Intervention of security in such zones should be very cautious, but still should not be neglected, since most plans for committing an attempt will be done from this type of very much less exposed areas.

2. **Controlled zones:** These are reserved for passengers, crew, miscellaneous services and port employees. Each of these individuals has an access and security level allocated, but all should be identified while in the zone. Presence in the zone must be justified. Design should aim at allowing people, once identified, to move freely about; however, further identification and baggage control may be carried out if necessary.

3. **Restricted zones:** Exclusive for assigned people or for scheduled visitors. Additional security control is required. Procedure guide is detailed in Diagram 2.2.

4. **Prohibited zones:** Nobody may enter except those working there. Should the case arise that an unrelated person should access it, such individual should be escorted at all times by security personnel.

All devices and facilities that control access to each zone should be included in the security plan, so that their commissioning should be simultaneous with that of the remainder of the services. Procedures for each zone are as follows:

From the outside to the ship, the following zones are found:

1. Limiting zone outside the port perimeter

Vehicles parked close to sensitive areas, such as passenger terminals, fuel tanks, etc., should be watched.

Locations from which safety procedures may be observed or from which explosive artefacts, missiles, rockets or similar may be thrown should also be watched.

2. Zone of public access and passenger vehicle distribution, passengers on foot, carriers, crew and workers.

Security level for this zone is medium; actions are to be taken in the form of individual identification on any elements displaying an abnormal conduct. It serves also for effectively directing the flow of people, thus preventing mistaken intrusions in the following zones.

Another of the functions of this zone is to act as a barrier in case of a frontal attack at the port by a suicide striker or an armed group.

This first access control is very swift, allowing access with minimum intervention, but with very clear objectives. Personnel should be ready for intervention at all times, and should identify suspects and notify the next security step, acting as a filter.

3. Parking area for passengers and companions

This area should be separate from the terminals; if possible, at a minimum distance of 200 metres. Thus, the explosion of a car bomb would affect a reduced number of people, compared to the case of a closer location.

Permanent 24 hour surveillance should be in place, by means of CCTV and security personnel in the area. It is highly recommendable to use trained dogs in the area, on a random basis, for locating explosives.

4. Terminal area

Entry of passengers on foot makes it possible to place explosives inside the terminals. Therefore, the terminal should count on security personnel in civilian dress to control and frequently check usual or likely locations of placement.

Furthermore, armed personnel should be available in order to suppress eventual actions of suicide strikers or frontal attacks against passengers in the terminal.

Security personnel in the area should back access control personnel when required.

2.3.2 Access control to restricted zones

Access control protocol for restricted zones

In high risk terminals or during high alert periods, a previous control to the boarding control should be set up with interrogation experts, who should inquire from passengers and reveal suspect behaviours, contradictions between individuals that know each other when questioned separately, etc. A manual inspection of baggage should also be carried out.

Most interviews last 3 minutes at the most, some less, and only a few may last longer due to their complexity. Such interviews should be recorded and examined, and the next security level should be placed on alert.

Access control to boarding areas

Access control establishes that only people who are to board imminently may access the area. To that end, they should show their passes to the security personnel, as well as their identity document.

This first control may be carried out by the shipping company; passengers are registered in a list that will be delivered aboard.

Past this control, a baggage X-ray check should be carried out on all baggage accompanying passengers during the voyage. Passengers should be given the appropriate means to handle their baggage at the terminal in a convenient and safe manner. Passengers should go through a weapons and explosive archway detector.

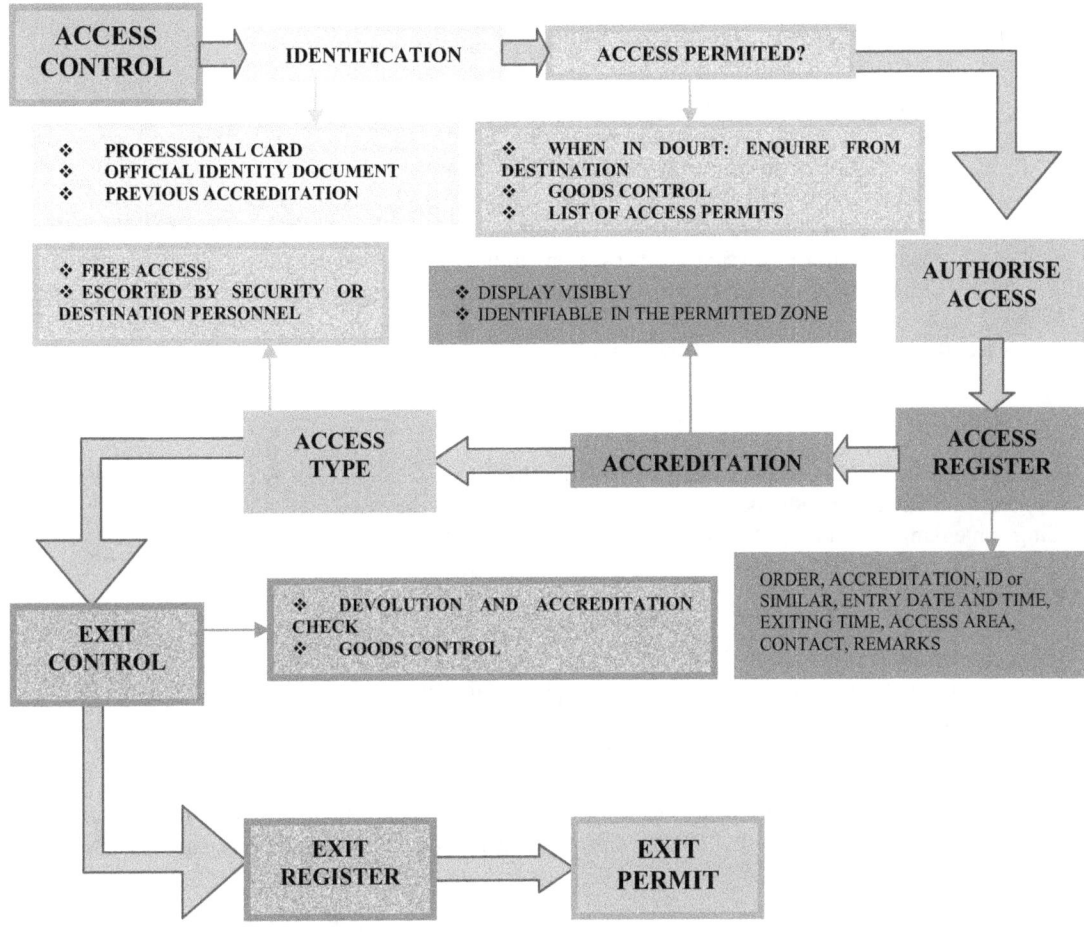

Diagram 2.2

All personal belongings of the passenger should be placed in a tray and X-ray scanned without exception. If a passenger causes the archway detector to set off twice, a search with a hand held detector and a manual pat down should be carried out.

Determination of the number of X-ray units for security control should be based on the following data:

    a = Number of passengers per hour originating at the terminal
    b = Non processed transits, for whatever reason
    y = Hourly package check capacity (reference: 600 packages/hour)
    w = Number of packages per passenger (reference: 2)

With these data, the number of units would be:

$$N = (a + b)w/y = \text{X-ray units}$$

If boarding periodicity is very high, calculation may be as follows:

- m = Number of places in the largest ship using the system
- y = Hourly package check capacity (reference: 600 packages/hour)
- w = Number of packages per passenger (reference: 2)
- $t1$ = Maximum waiting time for passengers in the pre boarding area
- $t2$ = Minimum waiting time for passengers in the pre boarding area

In this case, the number of X-ray units would be:

$$N = (60 \cdot m \cdot w)/y(t_1 - t_2) = \text{X-ray units}$$

Security controls should be concealed from people that are not embarking. A closed room should be provided for manual pat downs, for those cases when it may be suspected that a passenger may be hiding some dangerous item, even if it may not have been detected by the archway detector.

Pre boarding area

The departure area previous to boarding begins after the security control. Once in this area, no passenger may enter or exit without going through the aforementioned steps. This area should be a tight area, and nothing should enter or leave without going through the security control. It should be prevented that anyone may observe the area from outside or may throw any object inside it.

If there are cafeterias or shops in the area, both their personnel and the goods sold therein should be controlled. In maximum alert situations, level 3, a last manual control should be set up, if necessary at the ship access.

Vehicle boarding area

Vehicle reception at the dock should follow the protocols as detailed hereunder:

a) On vehicle arrival, the person responsible for its boarding should be present, with the vehicle's documentation and the transport contract.
b) Vehicles should be inspected at the boarding area by security personnel; with the owner or responsible person present at all time, they will request the opening of the boot or any inside space that might hold hidden explosives or weapons.
c) Search for dangerous goods may be random and more or less intense depending on the threat level. The use of trained dogs is recommended for searching for explosives.
d) Once the vehicle boards the ship cargo area, the area should be isolated from passengers, in order to avoid the eventual use of weapons that may have entered the ship hidden.
e) In the case of lorries carrying merchandise, contents should be listed and described in a packing list. This kind of transportation should be managed closely with the company, keeping in communication with it in order to confirm the identity of the carrier and the composition of the cargo.

Figure 2.1b

Merchandise access area

Once the public access and passenger and merchandise distribution area has been crossed, the carrier should proceed to the first control for identification and verification of vehicle documentation and cargo data.

When intending to embark aboard a mixed passenger and cargo ship, inspection should be carried out as in the vehicle boarding area.

Meanwhile, a random inspection should be carried out on lorries as it may be possible, checking, by getting in contact with the parties involved, the identity of the carrier and the nature of the cargo.

This area should be manned with a team of security agents trained for heavy vehicle and container inspection.

It is recommendable to use X-ray equipment for inspecting lorries and containers. If both containers and lorries should be inspected, the use of fibre optics and portable thermography cameras is recommended.

Given the complexity of heavy vehicles inspection, and the fact that this very circumstance make them the ideal means for a strike, due measures should be taken in order to ensure that when a lorry or a container comes on board, it contains no dangerous items.

2.3.3 Personnel control

The objective is that people stay at locations in which they have something to do, keeping excluded from the rest; furthermore, that they should not carry with them any dangerous item that might be used in a terrorist attack.

Maximum control extends to:

- passenger search
- hand luggage search
- baggage search

Control may be carried out in three non exclusive ways, which may reinforce each other should it be required.

- manual search
- manual hand luggage search and passenger search with a metal detector
- X-ray baggage search and passenger search with a metal detector

Manual search is carried out in closed premises, in which the passenger is searched, and on a table, on which the baggage is manually searched.

Access control procedures

a) Personnel
- Workers and crew: they should show their card to the security agent or warden and go through the transit lock and the metal detector; parcels or bags should go through the X-ray scanner; on exiting, the opposite process should be carried out.
- For crew arriving aboard, when the security inspection is carried out a copy of the Crew List with the required data will be requested from the Captain, including photographs, which may be taken on the spot with a digital camera; identification cards should be prepared as soon as possible, so that they may be issued to the crew against the corresponding receipt when coming on shore. Card validity should be exclusively for the time of the ship at port; for regular lines, validity will be as for the rest of the workers at the facility.
- Visitors, suppliers and occasional workers: they should show their ID to the security agent or warden and then go through the transit lock and the metal detector; parcels and hand baggage should go through the X-ray scanner. All this personnel is to be issued a self adhesive label that they should display during their stay at the facility; a photograph should be taken.
- VIPs will proceed according to the specific plan for them.

b) Delivered items and mail
- A person designated by the port facility management should collect the mail on working days; it should be checked on the X-ray scanner by the security agent or warden in charge, and then be distributed.

- On parcel deliveries, a representative of the destination department should be present at the access control in order to receive it after the parcel has been inspected on the X-ray scanner by the security agent or warden.
- Should any suspicion be raised upon the examination of the item, the plan against terrorist artefacts should be activated.

c) Vehicles
- A list should be available at the security control centre indicating the employees that are authorised to park their vehicles inside the port facility, as well as the relevant vehicle data; the vehicle should have an identification card on display behind the windscreen, visible while inside the premises.
- When accessing the port facility, both people in vehicles and the vehicles should be identified. If they do not hold an authorisation, a provisional one may be issued; the boot and its contents should be inspected. All this should be carried out by the security agent or warden on duty.

Anti intrusion security subsystem

Objective: Dissuading, detecting, delaying, verifying and reacting against any uncontrolled access of people, items, vehicles or crafts to the port facility and maritime area under charge.

Physical structure: Underground, fences, walls, windows, roofs.

Special intrusions: Battering ram, underwater, airborne and boarding.

Active and passive measures

a) Underground
- Closures with grating to UNE 108-142 in wells, water inlets and outlets, electricity, telephone and fibre optics, from the regulatory closure to a distance of ten metres inside the facility, built in on walls, floor and ceiling.
- Lighting every two metres in such tunnels with protected 100 W lamps.
- Four seismic detectors on walls, floor and ceiling, at about 2 metres from the closure.
- CCTV in each tunnel.
- Double curved pipe at every water inlet and outlet at the facility.
- Daily inspection by the security personnel of accessible tunnels, keeping a documentary record.
- Safety external locks in access ways inside the facility.

b) Open areas:
- Metal fence 2.5 metre high with barbed wire topping, with an associated inertial detection system. Should space availability allow it, a twin fence system, with a 4 metre gap, would be desirable; this allows the creation of a prohibited zone that delays intrusion and provides for reaction.
- Infrared barrier covering the whole perimeter.
- Microwave barrier covering the whole perimeter.

These three systems: inertial, infrared and microwaves, should be configured in pairs in "Y", in order to achieve a balance between alarms and false alarms.
- CCTV covering the whole perimeter with 360° scan capability.
- Lighting covering the whole perimeter.

In built areas (within the port facility), besides the infrared and microwave barriers, the CCTV and the lighting, the following should be in place:
- Seismic detectors on external walls, at equal distances depending on coverage.
- Windows on ground and first levels fitted with armoured glass level A-30.
- Inertial detectors on windows; this system linked to the infrared and microwave barriers, with the same configuration as detailed for open areas.
- Inside grilles on windows on ground and first levels to UNE 108-142.
- Unused doors bricked up, with seismic detectors as on an external wall. If necessary, keep a door operative for special cases, such as visits from VIPs, social occasions, etc.

Area with built decks (within the port facility):
- Microwave barrier.
- CCTV system.
- Lighting system.
- Magnetic contact systems at access ways.

2.3.4 Maritime area

In order to avoid uncontrolled access to the maritime area it is essential to have remote detection of ships and other vessels approaching the maritime area in charge of the port facility in terms of safety. Such space should be sufficient in order to allow their correct identification and prepare the suitable reaction.

This approach requires defining within the maritime space the zones as described for the access and stay control subsystem:

- Restricted
- Reserved
- Prohibited
- Anchoring
- A controlled zone should be added, within which every vessel should be detected and identified, their intentions enquired, or their entry at the protected port facility confirmed.

Obviously, this system should be linked, if possible, with the maritime transit control systems that may be available in the country where the port facility is located. At the same time, it is necessary to define and signalise the areas, which are security zones, given the State's responsibility over maritime areas; this requires in turn the associated regulations and their publication on nautical charts and even its physical marking with internationally agreed signals or those newly created, agreed upon by the relevant international organisations.

Underwater intrusion is a different matter. Even though the use of submarines may be discarded, it is not superfluous to establish the relevant detection measures.

Regarding intrusion by divers on their own or using small crafts, as considered in the section on special intrusions, the small range of actuation of this procedure becomes obvious, as it requires support from a nearby vessel; this would obviously be detected from the onset of the aggression by the system on the nearby coast; this requires integrating the port facility safety system with the relevant public safety system.

Maritime security zones

- Restricted zone: Maritime zone under the responsibility of the port facility.
- Reserved zone: Part of the restricted zone not included in the rest, including transit, berthing and manoeuvring zones.
- Prohibited zone: Maritime zone in which only maritime authorities in charge of security may act.
- Anchoring zone: Maritime zone in which ships that have to access the port facility place themselves for identification and inspection; this is located in the outer end of the restricted zone, and only such ships and the security maritime authorities with the required personnel may access it.

Human and material resources in the anti intrusion system

- Maritime patrols
- Thermal image cameras
- Surface radar
- Submarine hydrophones
- Signalling buoys

2.3.5 Criteria for establishing the water surface

- Identifying the initiating circumstances for shifting from one level to another, for each identified risk.
- Width depending on the port width dimension for each area.
- Establishing a minimum common width for all berthings.
- Establishing a minimum width by risks with categories higher than the common.
- Relationship with access ways (port entrances); increase for response times.
- Proposing alternative measures (solid floating barriers with props against the side of the ship).
- At level 1, unlimited patrols with regular frequencies, for dissuasion.

Controlling the approach of ships to the port entrance

- Speed from moderate to minimum steering speed.
- At level 3, stopping is mandatory, and then to minimum steering speed.
- Use AIS; otherwise, apply preventative doubt compensatory measures.
- Establishment of communications.
- Transit control (control tower), pilots, etc.

Special intrusions

➢ Battering ram

In front of the possibility that a land vehicle may be projected at high speed against a port facility access, it is necessary that barriers be set up in front of the access ways to force it to follow a curved (not straight) path, or that the control be located tangentially on a roundabout; this would force, in both cases, the vehicle to significantly slow down; in any case, tilting barriers should have the appropriate strength to stop a heavy vehicle at a certain speed.

➢ Underwater

As observed when addressing intrusion through the port facility maritime area, technology does not provide as yet adequate detection means performing similarly to terrestrial means, in order to detect an underwater intrusion of divers and react appropriately; this poses a serious problem, since hydrophone based systems do not ensure the detection of one or several divers intending to access a port facility or the ships moored therein.

In war conditions, this problem was addressed by closing the maritime zones with underwater nets, this being a costly and troublesome measure; occasionally, depth charges were launched periodically in order to get rid of potential intruders, this being in the current situation a totally unacceptable measure.

Regarding the reaction, this would require counting on the State Security Forces, specifically on the maritime service of the Guardia Civil that, according to the current Spanish legislation, would have a standby team of divers for carrying out periodic underwater reconnaissance, as well as for reacting in case of an intrusion.

Likewise, the measures proposed in the section on maritime zones are the only feasible ones in the current situation for controlling the possible attack launching points, and they would be executed by the corresponding Security Forces.

➢ Airborne

Intrusion using airborne means, usually light: paragliding, hang gliders, etc., has never been, to this date, used effectively, since it requires nearby heights and that the items to be carried by the intruder are light; in any case, the main countermeasure is a visual detection permitting a rapid reaction; as indicated when addressing other minor entity actions, response comes by remote detection; therefore, interconnection with the public safety system corresponding to the port facility location would be appropriate, in order to control potential attack launching points as part of their general services.

➢ Boarding

Boarding may be in two types of action; one would be launching a ship, with or without passengers, loaded or not with explosive, incendiary, nuclear, radiological, chemical or biological elements, or with a combination of them, against the port facility or against another ship, possibly carrying passengers.

The other type would be the boarding of a ship by a terrorist unit with the aim of kidnapping people or to carry out the above action.

When faced with the first type of action the only possibility is early detection as discussed when addressing maritime intrusion, in order to attempt a boarding by security forces where the threatened port facility is located, in order to gain control of the ship at any cost and abort the action.

Should this attempt fail, the only solution left would be sinking the ship by means of an air, naval or, what is considered to be the most appropriate, submarine attack, or with a combination of them; however, the difficulty of such action becomes clear due to the unlikelihood of counting on a submarine in the vicinity and, foremost, due to the responsibilities involved in ordering such an attack, if national and international legislations do not back it beforehand.

For the second case, each SSP should establish the specific procedure for this case, which, naturally, should be in coordination with the special plan against hostage holding on shore and/or aboard and, when required, against NRBC incidents, as detailed in the PFSP of each port.

2.4 Identifying and analysing risks at the port facility

The objective of identifying risks is to gather them in the widest extent possible, in order not to miss any aspects to be considered that may constitute system weaknesses.

In the basic handling and identification of risks, reference must be made to the analysis of the information available on the subject in:

- The bibliography on events related with the subject and the activity.
- Those consequential to the nature and classification of the activity.
- Those reasonably assumed by the expected effects and consequences (indirect methods).
- Those obtained from the knowledge of the State Security Forces and other expert sources.
- Those obtained from the Intelligence services, in real time.

Evidently, the best information, considering the confidentiality and the limits in data dissemination, should not come from the mass media (press, radio, TV) but from the State official organisations and bodies, through professionals and/or private experts, specialised in the subject.

At the same time, since the concept of *security* is one more block within integral safety, several inferable procedures that are characteristic to industrial risks (safety) are also applicable to a large extent. In such cases, when indirect methods are used from the assumed culmination of the criminal, unlawful act against which security is set, it allows to detect the weaknesses, and from then on to find the causes that might make it occur.

In this sense, by assessing and quantifying the level of damage and of caused or expected consequences, security measures may be classified in prioritisation strata; furthermore, by stating all of them and reaching comparison criteria in the nature of the variable, similar action blocks may be decided for different application points and aspects, which would mean an obvious simplification of the final handling of the security applied, and, doubtlessly, a reduction in overall cost.

Therefore, this being a subject with an enormous variability, since a strict cause and effect relationship may not be established, it generally depending on the criminal intentionality of minds whose owners will intend to evade all the established security measures, those that may finally be identified as main risks should undergo a constant assessment with respect to the potential changing evolution as required day to day and by the events.

In front of the need for implementing a safety system in a port facility it is necessary, previously, to determine and define those goods that should be the object of security, amongst which the following may be highlighted:

- Life and physical integrity of people: management, workers, visitors, crew and passengers.
- Ships located in the area of responsibility of the port facility.
- Cargo, both that stored at the facility and that stowed in ships berthed in the port facility.
- Vehicles and machinery used for the port processes.
- Vehicles and personal belongings of people that are in the facility and in the ship berthed therein.
- Those belonging to the port facility as a whole: buildings, warehouses, sheds, circulation routes, etc.
- Information and documentation belonging to the organisation, particularly the most sensitive one, both on hard copies (paper) and on magnetic and IT storage media.
- The securing of the industrial processes developed at the port facility.

Once goods are defined, it is necessary to identify the damages and the causing agents in order to better identify specific risks, thus proposing the appropriate safety measures in order to attain the highest possible safety level.

Types of damage

On people:
 - Death.
 - Injuries: serious, minor.
 - Illnesses: physical, mental.

On objects:
  - Total destruction.
  - Partial destruction.
  - Loss.

Risk assessment further comprises two factors:

- *Facility vulnerability*: This is defined as the possibility of it being *damaged*, this depending mainly on its structural and physical features: construction, materials, location, etc.
- *Threats to the facility*, since any facility may be the object of a variety of aggressions, theoretically numerous, but many of them unlikely; therefore, prioritisation criteria are required comprising two factors: highest likelihood and highest danger, which will evidently

be in the study of the terrorist and criminal ranking of the environment in which the PF is located.

In any case, all these actions, given the own features of a PF, will require a *zone* definition in order to better allocate security and safety measures.

2.4.1 Risk classification

A. Depending on the causing agents

Human risks deriving from antisocial activities:

Common offences:

- **Robbery:** Understood as defined in the Penal Code in force, i.e., including the factor of the exertion of force or intimidation on persons or force on objects, it is not deemed in its first meaning to constitute a typical risk for a port facility. In its second meaning, deriving from its typical activity involving the transit of passengers and merchandise, this type of risk has been traditionally one of the main problems for port facilities. Nowadays, the technical sophistication and the organisational complexity attained by some criminal groups, together with their international spread, has turned large scale robbery of merchandise and equipment goods into and actual threat for port facilities, having in many cases the connivance of carriers and even crew that seek in this way to improve their incomes. Therefore, a high level of risk is considered for port facilities.

- **Theft:** This kind of offence at a port facility, when not remaining a mere fault, has two kinds of sources; on the one hand, from personnel usually working there, who steal objects from their workplaces or from merchandises that transit through the facilities, normally being small in size since they are going to be "hand carried" by the thieve himself or sometimes in a private vehicle. The highest danger of this kind of offence, which occurs frequently, is that it may become usual, causing a real problem in the long term, this besides the "mimic effect" that it usually causes, as well as the damage to the image of the port facility.

The other kind of thief comes from outside the port facility. This is an action focused rather on passengers and their baggage than on merchandises, due to the difficulty in knowing the safety systems, storage, etc. It is deemed that a port facility has a medium level of risk in front of both kinds, but with a possibility for an increase if the number of passengers transiting through the port facility goes up significantly.

- **Fraud:** Two varieties may be found of this criminal activity: the fiscal fraud against the State that owners or receivers of goods originating from a foreign country with a non compatible fiscal system may attempt, in which case the State itself handles the control mechanisms it deems necessary, which obviously will integrate in the safety system; and the fraud or swindle using the port facility as a base for committing the offence between private subjects, mainly based on merchandise not complying with previously agreed conditions, this act being often allowed by the operating characteristics and structures of the port facility itself. Except for particular instances, risk for the port facility is deemed low.

- **Vandalism:** In some current developed societies there is a certain risk for damages on property done by rootless youths, who either wreck street furniture or paint graffiti on fences, walls or vehicles; it is considered that the port facility may suffer from this risk if such offences take place in its geographical area, damages caused being costly to remediate. Another more specific aspect are damages caused because of eventual labour conflicts at the port facility raised by some workers or external agitators, which in some cases may become acts of sabotage at the workplace. From the study, a low risk is derived for port facilities, except for the circumstances mentioned.

- **Kidnapping:** Economically driven kidnapping is not considered as a typical risk for port facilities.

- **Espionage:** In its industrial or economical version, it may be that the activities developed at a port facility may be the object of this kind of risk, given the vital importance and value that information has in the current developed world. In any case, the diversity of information channels allow in many cases to access it from other places than where it originates; therefore, this is considered a low risk for port facilities.

- **Narcotic Trafficking:** The significance of this kind of risk in its form of large consignments and the high probability of it happening in a port facility cannot be missed, since large quantities of such substances use seaways for transportation from the production areas to the traffic or consumption areas; they are usually hidden in objects that are cleared as normal merchandise. In this regard, the State Security Forces, within the aforementioned fiscal control, carry out drug detection tasks.

With respect to the smaller scale trafficking, it may be considered to be at a normal level within the country's framework; therefore, the risk may be considered as high for the first instance, and low for the second instance.

- **Aggression:** This type of event may occur anywhere where people come together; in the case of port facilities, they do not seem to be prone to such unless they are close to marginal housing, nightlife or prostitution areas. This may also change in case of labour conflicts that may occur between groups of workers or between them and the State Security Forces; in any case, this risk may be considered to be low under normal circumstances, unless the mentioned conditions occur.

Terrorism:

- **Firearm attempts:** This kind of action, always committed against people, is less and less used for indiscriminate strikes, due to its limited effectiveness in comparison to other means of aggression, being left only to selective actions, either with short firearms as they are easy to carry and conceal, thus allowing the aggressor to move about and approach the victim without raising any suspicions, their effectiveness being short ranged (less than 8 m for this kind of action), or with a long firearm with a telescopic sight, which allows distances ranging to 600 m. Neither case is considered as a typical risk for port facilities, except when a VIP visits the site or someone works at the facility who is under the threat of some terrorist organisation.

- **Aggression with an explosive device:** This action may be directed against people, goods, vessels, etc., given the great destructive power involved and the small size of the agent in comparison to other objects, so that it may be concealed in suitcases, bags, vehicles or any other object for transportation to the target. When the artefact is directed to people, it may contain shrapnel. This is a usual means for terrorist actions, as materials are easy to obtain due to their commercial or military use, or even making them. With respect to detonators, timers or radio controls are the most used, as they allow the executor to stay away. Another form of action is suicide bombing, by which the terrorist infiltrates in the target and actuates the device at the most suitable moment to cause the largest amount of victims or someone in particular. Port facilities have a high risk for this kind of strikes, due to the increase in passenger transit and to safety measures that are mostly below those at airports.

- **Aggression with an incendiary device:** This type of artefact is aimed at destroying material goods rather than at acting against people; usually characteristics are: low cost, simplicity and great destructive power, as long as weather conditions such as temperature, wind, humidity and those of the target, such as flammability, manner of storage, etc. are appropriate for an optimum result. Its use against facilities, goods, ships and cargoes at port facilities may be deemed as a medium risk.

Another aspect to be considered is the use of smaller devices of the Molotov cocktail type in low intensity terrorist actions, if the port facility is in an area where such risk may exist, and within there may be some specific target, or during riots due to labour conflicts or protests, such type of artefacts may be thrown against people and goods, the risk level depending also on the area history.

- **Aggression with chemical agents:** Amongst the risks being incorporated as action means of terrorist groups is the use of chemically loaded artefacts. Without going into further detail, such are directed against people, although they also affect animals. Based on their effects, they may be:

  - Dermotoxic, when acting on the skin
  - Hemotoxic, when acting on the blood
  - Pneumotoxic, when acting on the respiratory system
  - Neurotoxic, when acting on the nervous system.

Ideal dissemination of these products is as a gas or aerosol, this requiring the associated equipment, either sited at the target or nearby, or on a land, water or airborne vehicle that may disperse on it the substances, although the most effective use of these means is in confined spaces, as this avoids having to depend on weather conditions such as wind, temperature gradient, humidity, etc., which exert a great influence on the agent's effectiveness in open spaces.

Another form this type of aggressive substances may take are the so called binary weapons, in which two non lethal products become a toxic when mixed, although this process requires some system or mechanism to do the mixing and dispersion.

Regarding the risk of port facilities suffering this type of attack, wherever a large concentration of people is present within a confined space, like a cruise ship for example, the risk is present at a high level with respect to other special aggression means since, to this date, these have been used in various terrorist actions.

- **Aggression with biological agents:** Use of this means raises the great fear to human disease. These agents fall within two types:

    - Live beings: bacteria, viruses, etc.
    - Toxins: of animal or vegetal origin, etc.

The latter are used in a very similar way to chemical agents, effects being also very close.

Regarding the use of microbial beings, it is limited by UV rays, humidity and temperature conditions, which determine whether microbes may live and enter organisms in sufficient quantity to cause an infection. This involves an incubation period until the disease may be detected; once identified, it may be fought successfully by vaccination.

Regarding dissemination means, aerosols, release by sabotage or use of vectors (infected animals) are the most usual. The easiest elements to use are air conditioning systems, which show ideal conditions for life and diffusion of living agents.

From the above may be derived that risk of use at port facilities is limited to confined spaces, such as passenger terminals, public halls, ships, etc., where large numbers may gather; however, effects may take long to appear, so this could be deemed to be a medium risk, somewhat higher if used as part of a campaign to create panic or health issues within a ship, mainly a passenger ship, when required by another type of action.

- **Aggression with a radiological agent:** This type of action consists in disseminating radioactive materials with the highest activity level possible in order to contaminate people or neutralise a facility, ship or area; this may be done by using an explosive or an incendiary explosive charge in order to increase the activity. As with biological and chemical agents, influence of weather conditions is significant in determining contaminated areas, its use being more dangerous to people in confined spaces. In any case, this may be considered a low risk at port facilities, due to the low use to this date and to the difficulties for terrorist organisations in obtaining high activity radiological waste; furthermore, effects are on the long term, although it is yet another means for neutralising an area based on psychological impact.

- **Aggression with nuclear weapons:** At the present moment, excluding a war situation, it is not deemed probable that a nuclear weapon would be used, given the control exerted on them by the countries that have them. Indeed, their use would have terrible consequences on people and goods within their range, due to the combination of explosive, thermal luminous, radioactive and electromagnetic effects. As long as current estimates do not change, it may be therefore said that risk for a port facility is low.

- **Hostage holding:** This operation consists in a group of people holding another group of people by means of coercion, in order to achieve a political or economical goal, to have others freed, or to travel somewhere else. It is used both by terrorist organisations and during labour conflicts, although in the latter no firearms are used usually. When considering the two possibilities, i.e., that the act may be carried on shore or on waters under the responsibility of the port facility, clearly the latter appears to be the most likely and the most difficult to solve, due to the problems associated with simultaneously boarding and controlling a ship in order to preserve the hostages' lives.

This type of terrorist action represents a medium risk for port facilities with passenger transit, due to the lower control exerted to the present date with respect to airport terminals. In any case, the risk analysis on each ship and line carried out by each company should be known.

- **Boarding:** Directing a hijacked ship against another ship or the port facility is an extremely grave action, since it may be carrying passengers or dangerous goods, either from an industrial origin or from a terrorist origin in order to increase the effect. Such attack is deemed to be of low risk due to the low speed and manoeuvrability of vessels of a certain size, smaller vessels not being capable of causing significant damages.

- **Directed aeroplane crash:** Using an aeroplane as a missile against a building or facility, even a ship, involves prior hijacking of the aircraft.

From the standpoint of a risk study for a port facility, this may be considered as a low risk, as a port facility is not considered as a sufficiently interesting target due to the number of people it may concentrate, and because a ship is deemed as too small to be hit by a passenger aeroplane; furthermore, if it is a smaller craft, effects would not be significant, as the Japanese *kamikaze* showed in WW II.

2.4.2 Deriving from social activities

At work and in the activities at the PF, the following risks could appear:

- Risks when using machinery and tools.
- Risks when handling loading, carrying and storage equipment.
- Risks when handling power supply equipment.
- Risks when handling tanks and containers used for product storage.
- Risks when handling and using dangerous products and materials.
- Risks deriving from circulation and carriage.
- Risks caused by workplace environment and hygienic conditions.
- Risks deriving from navigation.

In this respect, it would be necessary to count on statistics for each activity and executing company when grading risks, in order to apply the relevant safety and industrial health plans, both for the tasks and at the PF.

Vulnerability level analysis

In order to know the vulnerability level for each identified zone within the port facility, it is necessary to know the risks to which it is exposed. Convenience and opportunity offered to the aggressor for committing the action should be analysed.

To that end, a number of circumstances should be quantified that, doubtlessly, will be the same ones that any hypothetical aggressor will take into account, whether consciously or subconsciously, when initiating the aggression.

Such circumstances may be defined as the opportunities that aggressors may have over the selected target:

- The possibility of observing the target, schedules, action protocols in routine and in emergency situations, etc.
- Access to the required information for carrying out the attack, by means of observation, the Internet, intrusion in port services such as safety, maintenance, etc.
- Knowing or identifying the selected area by any member of the aggressor group, at any time.
- Where damage may be most, and with what means, for each area.
- How easy it may be for an aggressor to approach the target.
- The most convenient place for waiting prior to executing the action.
- How easy it may be to carry out the action without facing any resistance.
- How easy it may be to escape, to leave the action scene, even when the action may not have been executed.

If this factor scale would come across to some response that would break the action sequence, probably the action would not be carried out. This is one of the basic preventative security measures that Port Safety would exert. It is essential to break the information sequence at all those points that are basic to the execution of acts of sabotage.

The great difference between the terrorist members of groups such as ETA or the IRA and the suicide integrist members of Al Fatah, Hamas or Al Qaeda is that while the former take into account all the aforementioned steps, the latter care very little about some of them, paying no importance to the traditional safety circles. The reason lies with escape not being an option and being able to carry out the action without taking into account any of the above.

Should the action be executed, terrorist success is the more warranted the easiest it becomes to achieve the objectives discussed. Conversely, the aggression will be the more difficult the highest the opposition created by port safety is for each of the aforementioned circumstances.

According to another type of analysis, very similar to the above, there would be:

- **Knowledge:** The target is known, close to the town, the action will have a large social impact on international public opinion, etc.
- **Observation:** Gather all information on the target. Correct data will provide accurate knowledge.
- **Analysis:** Review carefully the information gathered for verification and any eventual change.
- **Preparation:** This is the result of the above review.
- **Access/Contact:** This is the time for action, for the approach. It is the most critical moment for the terrorist, since the area is to be entered. If no detection takes place at this moment, it will be difficult for the safety system to react and neutralise the attack.
- **Exit:** This is the time of breaking access/contact.
- **Escape:** This is the time for concealment, after the action.

2.5 Vulnerability evaluation

Up to this point, an event analysis has been carried out; from now on, it is intended to provide parameters that may assist in carrying out an appropriate evaluation of vulnerability. Within the vulnerability evaluation, and as a guide for self analysis, the following parameters should be considered:

➢ **Observation**

The more discreet, distant and short the observation, the lower the possibility of detecting it.

Conditions of those assigned to collecting the required data for carrying out an attempt should be evaluated by the security service. Knowing the most suitable points for gathering information on port procedures will allow preparing a map of objectives to which the appropriate resources should be allocated, both technical and human. Detecting and identifying those people constitutes the active prevention that will permit to anticipate the aggression.

Access to the observation area should be controlled, not only from the sensitive area itself, but also from the zone in question itself.

Zone	Area safety classification	Time of stay in the area for observation	Conditions for observation	Possible damage caused
External safety perimeter	Public	Long term	Disguised	Scarce
Parking lots and internal roads	Public	Permanente	Justified	Minor
Concessions and loading jetties	Restricted	Discrete, brief	Not justified	Serious
Ferry maritime stations	Public	Limited time	Justified	Very serious
Cruise ship berthing docks	Restricted	Discrete, brief	Justified	Very serious
Container storage	Restricted	Long term	Not justified	Serious
Sheds and storage	Restricted	Long term	Not justified	Minor
Maritime transit control	Prohibited	Discrete, brief	Not justified	Very serious
Commanding and safety centre	Prohibited	Discrete, brief	Not justified	Serious
Docks water surface (concessions)	Restricted	---------	Not justified	Very serious
Docks water surface (cruise ships)	Restricted	---------	Not justified	Very serious
Docks water surface (?)	Public	---------	Not justified	---------
Anchoring	Public	Long term	Justified	Very serious

Table 2.1

Certain threats have a multiplication effect due to the effects they produce, since they are related with other facilities or activities (see Figure 2.2), as may be also seen on Figure 2.3, due to the effects of an action occurred at a port facility on a very sensitive storage area.

Approach/entry

Ease of access should be evaluated; speed reduction of vehicles within the premises should be actively carried out by placing mobile barriers in "L" configuration (see Figure 2.2) that may allow vehicles to transit at a steady but slow pace. Such systems will reduce the capability of intrusion of bomb cars driven by suicide attackers into the facility. This type of attempts forces strengthening the perimeters of port facilities; therefore, violent access points of the perimeter should be analysed, as well as sensitive zones such as maritime stations and hydrocarbon storage areas.

Particular attention should be paid to the water surface around the ship, including anchoring zones. The use of small craft as if they were torpedoes is a system that has been used in the past. Transit control on all vessels, irrespective of how small they may be, should be comprehensive.

Figure 2.2

Primarily, access to all critical zones should be considered restricted for unauthorised vessels, and those that are authorised should have the appropriate control measures in place to avoid being used by terrorists. Zones should be marked to prevent access by mistake of, for example, recreational yachts. In order to make such measures effective and preserve the safety of the port, the safety department should have patrols available to actively intervene against intrusions.

Figure 2.3

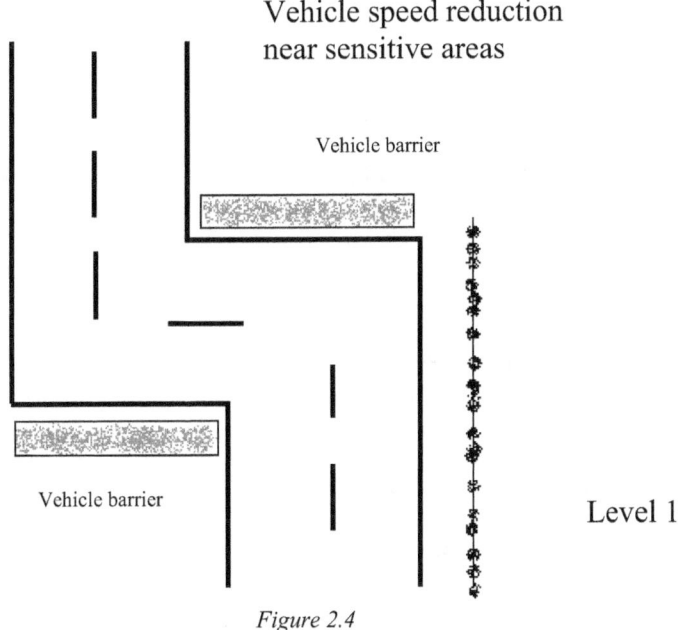

Figure 2.4

In anchoring zones and depending on circumstances, the following control procedures for ships should be applied:

SHIP CONDITION	SAFETY MEASURES	ACTIONS AT MAXIMUM ALERT LEVEL	RISK LEVEL
VERY CLOSE transit, not entering the port.	Following and watching direction and speed.	Activation of defences and blockage of port entrance.	HIGH
Seeking refuge from a storm.	Vigilance, watching direction and speed when setting sail.	Patrols on alert and defence systems ready for activation.	LOQ
Anchored, waiting for supplies or repair on board.	Ship surveillance and inspection jointly with the Port Authority.	Use of waterways to approach the port distant from the anchored ship.	HIGH
Waiting to enter, berthing manoeuvres.	Following and watching direction and speed, inspection and piloting.	Ship inspection by specialised forces.	LOW

Table 2.2

2.6 Execution of an attempt

The degree of effectiveness of an attempt is proportional to how easy it may be to obtain information on the target and to the lack of barriers. Setting up barriers in order to control access to the various areas does not prevent the normal vehicle and personnel transit. This contributes to a normal adaptation of users and workers to the new measures, without impacting on the operativity of the various services. Doubtlessly, however, this need will be taken advantage of by the aggressors.

The best safety systems should be constantly audited and adequately tested to prevent routine from diminishing their effectiveness. Precisely, the success of an attempt is based on another significant pillar, i.e., the slowness of safety services for shifting from routine to emergency. Assumptions made by the safety department, that a terrorist strike may not be possible, thus eliminating probability, are the initiation of an attempt. It should not be forgotten that every terrorist action has as its motto: "in the simplest way, with the highest damage".

Escape

It has been mentioned already that terrorist actions executed by suicide attackers do not consider this aspect. Even so, knowing how most cells of this type operate, it is worth mentioning as outstanding the observers accompanying the terrorists and ensuring that the action is indeed carried out; otherwise, they themselves trigger the explosives with a remote control or initiate the aggression (if it consists of shooting against a boarding area of a terminal).

However, in the type of actions executed by groups such as ETA, the following should be taken into account:

- Exits and subsequent itinerary.
- Public present at the scene and on the escape route.
- Exposition time from the time of execution to the closest safe location.
- Barrier/control set up after the action, to be overcome, and attitude of security agents.

2. The port as a threat to the ship

The atrocity of the terrorist act of 11th May, which occurred while the present study was being prepared, exposes the need for setting new control approaches, as the case should be for a maritime station, where currently entry and exit of people are free; it is important to clearly draw the line that marks the beginning of the interface with the ship, and therefore of the application of the PFSP; this outside area, which is adjacent to the interface, is a need covered and solved by the PSP.

2.7 Checklists

The effectiveness of checklists has always laid with the normalisation of the inspection procedure or compliance control, which allows identifying the evolution of security over time, both regarding deviations and in maintaining related aspects.

The following pages provide checklists for possible use on following on the PFSP.

IDENTIFYING VULNERABLE POINTS	YES	NO
Access to the port facility from the sea (berthings)		
Accessibility to anchored ships		
Access to the port facility from inland		
Structural integrity of the docks		
Structural integrity of the facilities		
Integrity of connected structures		
Existing security procedures		
Existing security measures		
Identification systems		
Infrastructure and port service processes		
Radioelectrical security and telecommunications		
IT system and network security		
Adjacent zones usable for an attack		
Agreements with private security companies		
Incompatibilities between safety and security plans		
Incompatibilities between security and facility tasks		
Personnel or execution limitations		
Deficiencies in providing training or during drills		
Deficiencies during daily operations		
Deficiencies after an event or alert		
Deficiencies on security reports		
Deficiencies in exerting control measures		
Deficiencies in carrying out an audit		

GOODS AND INFRASTRUCTURE SECURITY	YES	NO
Access ways, entrances and on shore approach routes		
Moorings and manoeuvring areas		
Berthings		
Loading facilities		
Storage areas		
Terminals		
Cargo handling equipment		
Electrical distribution systems		
Radioelectrical and telecommunications systems		
IT systems and networks		
Transit management and navigational aid systems		
Cargo transfer systems		
Bridges, railways, roads		
Service vessels (tug boats, barges, etc.)		
Security and surveillance equipment and systems		
Adjacent waters to the port facility		

IDENTIFYING POSSIBLE THREATS	YES	NO
Possible acts meaning a threat		
Damage or destruction of a facility or a ship (explosives, arson, sabotage or vandalism)		
* Hijacking or seizing a ship or the people aboard		
* Inappropriate cargo handling		
* Inappropriate equipment or system handling		
* Inappropriate handling of ship provisions		
* Unauthorised access or use, including stowaways		
* Weapon or equipment smuggling		
* Use of the ship for unlawful transportation of people		
* Use of the ship as a weapon or means of destruction		
* Blockage of port entrances, access ways, etc.		
* Chemical, biological or nuclear attack		
Consultation with the relevant authorities		
Execution methods		
Sufficient for determining vulnerability in the port area		
Sufficient for defining security measures and needs		
Sufficient for establishing prioritisation		
Sufficient to enable planning		
Sufficient for allocating resources		
Includes specific features of the port facility		
As above, for the maritime transit using it		
As above, for the likely consequences of an attack, such as loss of lives, damage to goods, economical alterations, disruption		
Capabilities and purpose of those who may attack		
Likely types of attack		
Conclusion between risk level and security measures		

2. The port as a threat to the ship

CLASSIFYING CORRECTIVE PRIORITIES	YES	NO
Depending on effectiveness to reduce probability		
Security reconnaissance, inspections and audits		
Consultation with owners and administrators of the facility and adjacent structures		
History of events impacting maritime security		
Operations carried out at the port facility		

PFSP CONTENTS	YES	NO
Organisation of security at the port facility		
Liaison with the competent authorities		
Liaison with ships		
Basic security measures for the three levels (I, II, III)		
Notification procedure with the Contracting Governments		
Analysis of the facility's physical and operating features		
Security functions and structure of the port organisation		
Tasks, responsibilities and training of the security personnel		
Specific training for armed personnel in dangerous goods areas		
Measures for assessing the effectiveness and performance of each individual		
Liaisons between the organisation and other national or local authorities		
Communication systems, uninterrupted and effective		
As above, between port facility, ships and authorities		
Guarantee of maintaining communications at all times		
Information safeguard procedures (hardcopies, computer based)		
Measure effectiveness assessment procedures		
As above, for identifying and resolving equipment failures		
Failure report assessment procedures		
Cargo handling procedures		
Ship provisions delivery procedure		
Dangerous goods inventory and location updated procedure		
Means for alerting patrols and specialised search		
Assistance to the SSO for identifying individuals (when requested)		
Procedures for crew leave, relief and visitors		

PORT FACILITY ACCESS CONTROL	YES	NO
Security measures in all means of access		
For each individual, restricted or prohibited locations depending on security level		
For each level, type of restriction or prohibition, and used means		
For each level, identification means for accessing the facility		
Permanent or temporary systems for personnel and visitors		
Coordinated identification systems, similar to those applied to the ship		
Passengers with boarding pass, etc., but without access to prohibited areas		
Identification systems regularly updated		

Disciplinary sanctions for misbehaviour		
Access denial if the individual does not wish to or cannot prove		
Reporting such cases to the PFSO		
Identified locations for searching individuals, belongings, vehicles		
Closed facilities, ready for continued use		
After search, direct access to restricted waiting areas		
Set up of separate areas for those having gone through control check and those having not		
Indicate control frequency, randomly or from time to time		
Level 1		
Determine restricted areas with fences or barriers		
Check identity of all people boarding the ship		
Vehicle control for accessing a ship		
Verify vehicles and identity of owners		
Limit access of those not working at the facility or unidentified		
Search of individuals, personal belongings, vehicles and contents		
Convenience of closing access ways that are not used regularly		
Level 2		
More surveillance personnel		
Limit number of access ways, closing them as required		
Enable barrier means		
Increase search frequency		
Deny access to individuals without verifiable justification		
Use patrol vessels for port waters security		
Level 3		
Cancel access in whole or in part		
Allow only security personnel access		
Cancel people and vehicle transit		
Cancel port operations in whole or in part		
Direct ship transit		
Evacuate port facility in whole or in part		
Increase patrols		

RESTRICTED AREA ACCESS CONTROL	YES	NO
Restricted area indication within the facility		
Restriction validity periods		
Access control measures and activities therein		
Area inspection measures before and after		
Individual, visitor and ship security complied with		
Protects the port facility		
Protects ships		
Protects vulnerable areas		

2. The port as a threat to the ship

Protects security and surveillance equipment and systems		
Prevents undue handling of cargo and ship provisions		
Controls access of people		
Controls vehicle entry, parking, loading and unloading		
Controls transit and storage of cargo and ship provisions		
Controls unattended baggage and personal belongings		
Restricted areas are clearly marked and objectives are signalised		
Automatic intruder detection devices with centralised alarms in place		
Areas on shore and adjacent waters to the ship		
Boarding, disembarkment, waiting, procedures and search areas		
Cargo and ship provisions loading/unloading areas		
Holding important secured information and protected cargo		
Area with dangerous goods and potentially harmful substances		
Maritime traffic planning control rooms, navigational aids		
Port control rooms, security and surveillance included		
Essential radioelectrical, communications, electrical and water stations		
Other locations where circulation should be restricted, etc.		
External areas from which the port facility may be observed		
Level 1		
Permanent or temporary barriers surrounding the area		
Access points manned with security wardens		
May be locked or blocked when not used		
Pass visibly displayed when authorised to stay in the area		
Vehicles authorised to enter the area clearly marked		
Set up patrols and watches		
Install automatic intruder detection systems		
Control vessel transit near ships		

UNATTENDED BAGGAGE	YES	NO
Identification measures and appropriate inspection, searches when required		
To be carried out prior to authorising access to the facility		
If equipment is available, the facility is responsible for inspection		
Level 1		
100% inspection and search, X-ray inspection when required		
Level 2		
100% X-ray inspection		
Level 3		
X-ray inspection from two different perspectives		
Unattended baggage restricted or held		
Unattended baggage not accepted		

SHIP PROVISIONS DELIVERY	YES	NO
Ensure packaging integrity		
Prevent ships from accepting provisions without prior inspections		
Avoid undue handling		
Avoid accepting unsolicited provisions		
Ensure delivery vehicle search		
Ensure vehicle escort within the facility		
For standard cases, procedure agreement, notification, documents.		
Level 1		
Inspect provisions		
Notify previously composition of sending, carrier data, license number plate.		
Search delivery vehicle		
Level 2		
Detailed inspections of ship provisions		
As above, for delivery vehicles		
Check with ship personnel that the delivery matches the order		
Escort delivery vehicle while at the facility		
Increase frequency and detail of searches		
Frequent use of examination equipment and trained dogs		
Restrict or prohibit delivery of provisions not sent on due date		
Level 3		
Close coordination, following instructions from those in charge		

CARGO HANDLING	YES	NO
Security measures to prevent undue handling		
Avoid reception and storage of cargo not for transportation		
Inventory control measures at access points		
Identification of cargo that went through control and is accepted for loading		
Restriction of cargo without confirmed loading date		
Level 1		
Cargo inspection, transportation units before and after handling		
Check cargo coincides with delivery note or equivalent		
Vehicle search		
Check seals on entry or storage		
Visual and physical check		
Check with mechanical devices or trained dogs		

For regular cargoes, agreement for inspection outside the facility		
In the above case, agreement with the PFSO		

Level 2		
Detailed inspection of cargo, units and storage area		
Increase checks, admit documented cargo		
Increase vehicle searches		
Increase seal check frequency		
Coordinate enforced measures with shipper and other responsible parties		
Level 3		
Close collaboration with security agents		
Limit or cancel cargo operations and handling		
Verify inventories of dangerous and other goods, checking locations		

Chapter 3. Ship's threats and risks

3.1 The ship as a threat receiver

In accordance to the contents of the tables in the analyses of the previous sections, the ship, as an indirect threat to the port, would suffer initially the first consequences becoming the target, means and object of the unlawful aggression that takes place against the port facilities, being used to enter them.

Diagram 3.1 references the aspects and variables affecting the ship.

At this stage, the ship acquires a fundamental role in the port system overall safety; the external assistance that may be provided by the State Security Forces and the logistic support that the port may provide should be managed under the ship security plan (SSP).

However, the ship may not be left alone to depend on her security capabilities on unknown, nor even friendly, waters, as it is generally accepted that she will always be the weakest point in the overall safety that would be implemented on maritime port activities; the ship is the least controllable element, even though means being implemented aboard (AIS, Traffic Control, etc.) increase in number and effectiveness.

The expression *alone to depend on* refers to the support that she may and should receive at all times from the shore, and the port should accept that, since it is in its highest interest that the ship should not come across any problems on her waters or at her facilities. On the one hand, the port should be made tight, and on the other hand, ships to be received should be made safer.

As it will be analysed in the chapter on port security, adopting preventative, dissuasive and control measures against the threat that the ship represents to the port will only become effective if those are based on a proper knowledge of the intrinsic risks that each type represents for the security sequence, effectiveness being higher to the extent to which it may adjust to each ship's case, to the probabilistic assessment and to the nature of the circumstances and conditions in which they are interrelated.

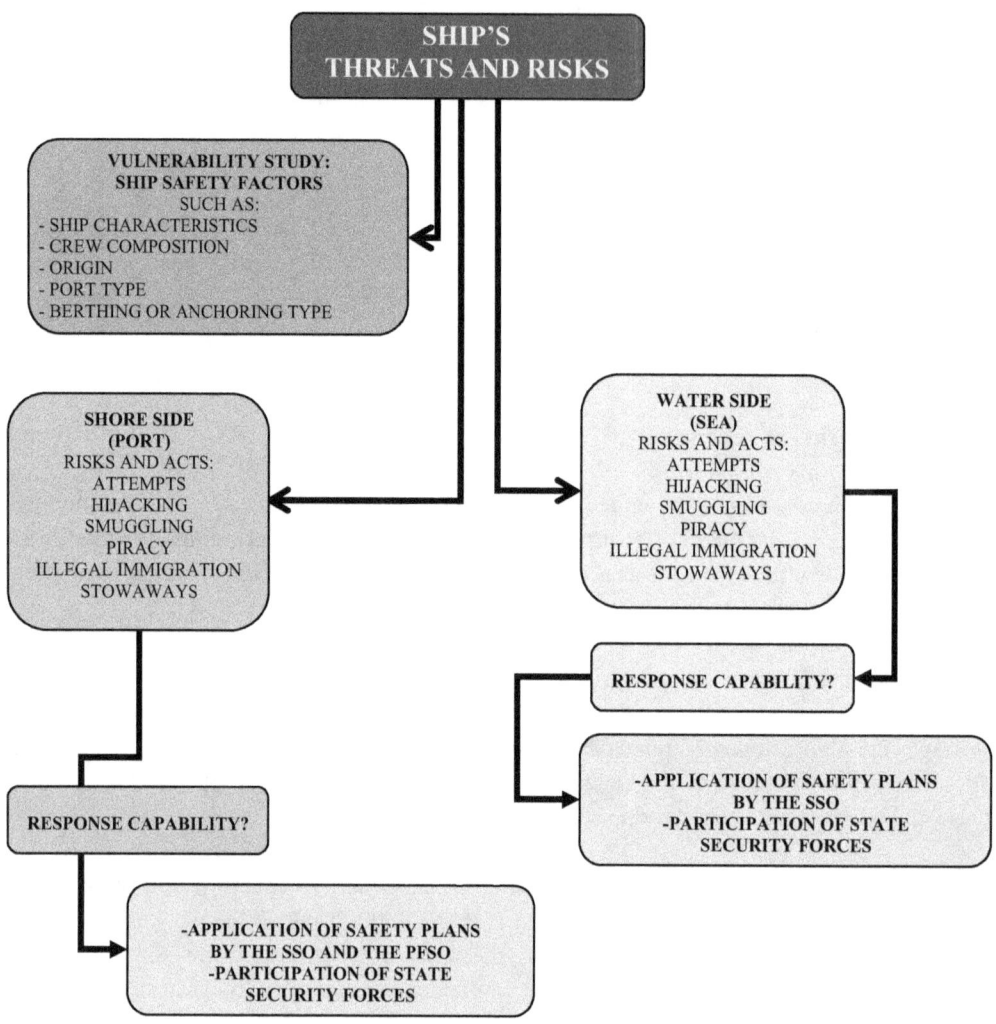

Diagram 3.1

Meanwhile, once the criminal actions have been completed on the ship, from then on she becomes the last link before the final objectives on the port may take place.

Diagram 3.2, which is the continuation to the previous diagram, shows the consequences as well as determining the affected parties in charge of decision making.

It may be observed that the weight of responsibility falls practically on the port, through its Facility Security Plans (PFSPs) and its Port Security Plan (PSP), since once the threat is known or the possibility of it becoming real is recognised, the application of the corresponding security levels is launched following a logical sequence, independently of the level of guarantees the ship security plan (SSP) may offer.

If the SSP is appropriate and everything humanly possible has been done from the ship in order to prevent her from becoming the criminal object, the threat will have been slowed down to the extent possible, and reasonable hope will exist that both efforts (the port's and the ship's) may provide a positive outcome of the security operations or may mitigate of the final consequences.

Knowing the ship vulnerability and the foreseeable consequences that she may cause to the port facilities, the PFSP should consider them in a balanced manner to cover security requirements.

Another factor to take into account would be the ship loading control systems. Effectiveness principles establish that nothing should remain without being looked into, and nothing should be looked into twice.

Therefore, inspections on ships coming from a safe origin would not be required. Furthermore, establishing safe origins will allow maritime traffic not to become paralysed, bearing in mind that comprehensive inspections at anchoring areas will become unnecessary, such actions being much more involved than inspecting cargo at port.

3.2 Security controls for cargo containers

In most cases, the problem will be external to the ship-port interface, and therefore more related to the PSP than to the PFSP. However, knowing the intermodality of this type of transportation and the high influence of containers as initiators of security incidents, it is deemed necessary to provide criteria and alternatives for improving control and identification.

Although this aspect may be addressed from the standpoint of terminal operation and effectiveness, the set of measures are directly and closely related to safety, and obviously, even under similar approaches, consequences at different levels of effectiveness will not be similar.

Therefore, the analysis will be carried out along the following aspects[1]:

- ✓ Incidents in container control and identification at the access points
- ✓ Consequences of queue build-up in access point jams

---

[1] With permission from Silvia Arilla Tomás, sections are used from her thesis, *Organización y gestión optimizada de una terminal de contenedores para aumentar su productividad* [Organisation and Management of a Container Terminal for Productivity Increase], 2002.

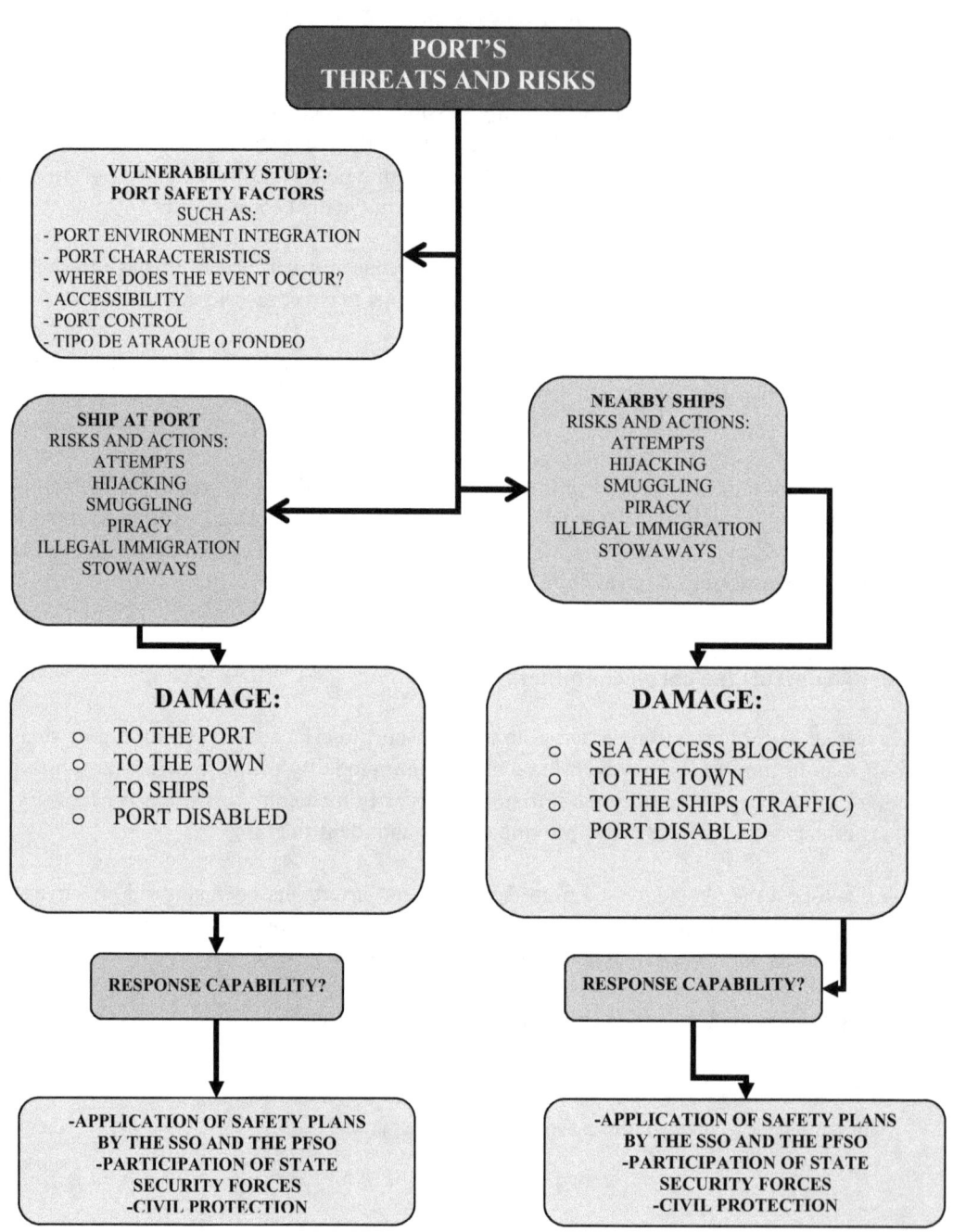

Diagram 3.2

3.2.1 Entry/exit operations

Although information handling at a modern terminal is computer based, much manual information is still being used. Indeed, manual databases were formerly used at the first terminals, but they have appeared again to compensate for cases in which IT systems are not capable of providing what is required or show numerous failures.

Gate operations are important since this is the departure point for export containers and the arrival point for import containers. Container reception or delivery times at the gate, which are important for terminal operations regarding the avoidance of peak hours, are not usually under the control of terminal operators, but it is rather the agents or the embarkers that fit the schedules to their convenience. This is the cause for the usual long queues of lorries at the gates at peak hours.

Furthermore, location at any terminal depends on the how containers are organised when arriving, and where to find them when leaving. This imposes two requirements on information systems:

- A unit follow up system should be in place; this should be done by recording yard coordinates; for example, block, lane, position within the lane, and height.
- Information should be available on the main characteristics of each unit. This should include the line to which it belongs, whether it is import or export, and any special feature (temperature, dangerous cargo, excess dimensions, etc.).

3.2.2 Gate operations analysis

There are two ways of organising waiting queues at the gates (see Figure 3.1):

- *Common style*: There are several entry lanes at the gate, but a single queue, so that the first in the queue gets to the first free entrance.
- *Separate style*: A separate queue is made for each entrance.

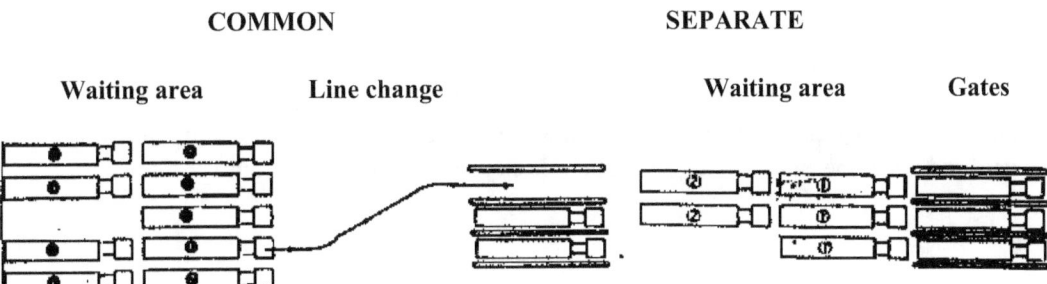

Figure 3.1

Vehicles driving through the gates may be classified as follows:

A. Entry

A1. Empty lorries picking up empty containers

In this case, only the booking number is the key to the whole procedure at the gate. The driver delivers a document to the gate operator. From the data obtained from this document, including booking number, the control centre decides which one is the empty container to be delivered, and advises the gate operator of the delivery location at the yard. Then, the gate operator issues a ticket indicating the location. This process may take from 1 to 6 minutes.

A2. Empty lorries picking up full containers

The lorry arrives at the gate with the container number and the bill of lading number. Based on the data in the delivery order produced by the driver, the control centre advises the gate operator where the lorry should go. The operator issues the driver a sheet indicating the situation, and a delivery order. This may take from 1.5 to 8 minutes.

A3. Lorries carrying full export containers

In this case, the booking number and the container number are the keys for all procedures at the gate. The container is weighed on the vehicle scale at the gate lane and weight is recorded. The gate operator takes the acceptance order and visually checks the container number; simultaneously, another operator visually checks container condition, its seal and number. The operator issues the driver the entry EIR[3] and the location sheet; location will have been previously advised by the yard controller. This operation has an estimated duration of 1.5 to 8 minutes.

A4. Lorries carrying empty export containers

In this case, the container number is the key for the procedure. The gate operator receives the acceptance order and the EIR from the driver, and visually inspects the container number while other operators visually check its condition. Then, the operator advises the driver about the destination at the yard and issues the entry EIR and a location sheet. Average duration is from 1 to 5 minutes.

B. Exit

B1. Lorry leaving with an empty container

---

[3] EIR: This is the document recording the visit, including operation times and other data.

When the lorry gets to the exit gate, the driver gives back the ticket to the gate operator. In this case, visual check of the container is not carried out at the gate; in most terminals, this is carried out prior to delivery. However, the terminal operator does confirm serial number and issues the driver the exit EIR. Average duration of these operations is usually from 1.5 to 5 minutes.

B2. Lorry leaving with a full container

The driver gives back the delivery order. The gate operator visually checks the container, while another operator checks that the seal and the container are in proper condition. The exit EIR and/or the release document (which facilitates customs clearance) will be issued to the driver. This takes between 1.5 and 5 minutes on average.

B3. Lorry leaving empty after entering with a full container

The lorry crosses the gate without following any particular procedure.

B4. Lorry leaving empty after entering with an empty container

The lorry crosses the gate without following any particular procedure.

3.2.3 Gate automation

In the section on gate operations analysis an overview has been given on the gate operations to be carried out. Here, a more technological view on the conduct of such operations is given, towards its optimisation.

Data collection

Containers arriving by road undergo a first control. At this point, container data are taken, such as identification, content, weight, characteristics, destination, etc.

In most terminals, these data are directly entered into the IT system. Advanced container information is entered into the system, so when the container arrives at the entrance, the container number is sent from the gate to the control personnel. If information has been entered previously, only missing data will be completed at the gate. If no prior information is available, it will be fully completed. Accuracy is critical at this point, since an inappropriate identification of container data at arrival may cause the temporary loss of the container. By decreasing the amount of times data are entered, errors are reduced.

Due to their differences, the involved parties in the transportation chain usually work independently from each other, in spite of the fact that there is an urgent need for integrating the different information flows and planning systems.

It would therefore seem logical that coordination between parties would optimise the overall process of transportation.

Currently, improving the development of information exchange modes at all levels, both internally (at the terminal) and externally (with all involved parties) is a significant challenge. In modern terminals, the gate is an important interface within the comprehensive concept of transportation, where all parties (agents, consignors, shipping companies, transport companies, customs...) play their specific roles within the information flow.

The distribution of cargo to the various systems in charge of its transportation to the interior determines the necessary infrastructure for clearing the containers. Road freight is still the main means of transportation used; therefore, the aim is to attain a stay time of the lorry at the terminal as short as possible.

Objectives

- Improving the productivity level of gate procedures by using IT, making both internal and external services more customer focussed.
- Homogenising and improving lorry stay times during the process.
- Integrating all activity groups (both internal and external) in the data exchange process.

Bottlenecks (saturation)

The main problem occurs between the terminal and the transport company. Thus, generally the main saturation situations are due to:

- use of equipment at the terminal
- waiting time at the gate
- incomplete information

As a consequence, both parties face problems when planning. On the one hand, if the port operator does not have accurate information on the estimated traffic, it will not be able to efficiently plan the use of the equipment. On the other hand, planning by transport companies is not optimum either, since it may be affected by external factors such as long waiting times at the gates, problems with documents, etc.

Vehicle planning is carried out based on the experience detected from past situations and on the expected traffic. However, this is not an ideal situation, since the lorries expected may be delayed due to various reasons.

Due to this, the most important for the terminal operator is having available the most detailed traffic information. In order to improve this situation, an information exchange system should be implemented, so that:

- it may allow transport companies to find information on ship arrivals and on expected road traffic, in order to plan the best arrival time at the port;
- consignors may send arrival notifications by electronic means;
- transport companies may send arrival notifications in order to make the terminal aware of lorry arrival planning and expected potential delays.

3.2.4 Various constituting processes of gate operations

Due to the fact that the complete container flow is being looked at, the following are considered:

Container arrival notification

An organisation may not be productive if it does not have appropriate, timely information available. Lack of information means lack of planning, which leads to errors in the subsequent operational process.

Since some time ago, various electronic messages were designed both locally and internationally to exchange information between the different participating parties. Focussing on the container flow towards the interior, the following may be mentioned:

✓ **Arrival notification instructions**

This message is sent by the agent to the terminal through EDI, and it may be used both for import and export containers; likewise, it is also used for collecting empty containers. It covers all the necessary information for full container delivery or empty container collection. The key of this message is the *space booking* at the terminal.

✓ **Collection instructions**

This message is consequential to a procedure that is used at the port of Amberes, where import containers may be delivered only to the person possessing a PIN code in combination with the container number.

This is a case in which the delivery process is sped up, avoiding as much document transfer possible; it also provides security against fraud. In order to carry out this communication, an agreement is reached between the shipping line and the terminal. This agreement states what means should be used for data exchange; it also includes the PIN coding, so that it may not be read by others. Once the message is received, the PIN code is decoded by the software. This application is completely protected from other system users.

When the appropriate person, the carrier in this case, accesses the terminal from the control point, it is only necessary to enter the container number, the prefix and the control digit together with the PIN number (up to three attempts); then the container may be collected. After three failed attempts, only an authorised person at the terminal may continue the process and deliver to the carrier, after checking as appropriate.

- ✓ **Lorry arrival (visit) notification**

In the transportation chain, transport duration time, and therefore associated costs, are very important.

At a terminal, most "visits" are caused by the delivery or collection of containers by lorry. Due to this, it is deemed necessary to launch a communications system between the transport companies and the terminal.

A high percentage of drivers still come across some problem during their *visit*, which lengthen throughput times above the average.

In a first phase, transport companies have the possibility of checking the system at the terminal (in a password protected web page). It is intended that later on the companies would have the possibility of carrying out administrative transactions directly on the terminal's system, with a clear aim to save time.

- ✓ **Administrative statement**

It has been already discussed that in order to ensure swiftness and the optimisation of the stay time it is important to provide advanced notice of operations, both from the agent's end and from the carrier's end.

This same procedure could be extended to customs transactions, which could be omitted in the same way as discussed for the delivery/collection instructions. However, given the fact that the terminal is a customs control point, the driver must still notify the customs officer, unless it is a free port where customs are located at the entrance of the port premises.

If the transport company prepares a number of preliminary notifications, the number of errors is reduced, and as a consequence the stay time decreases. When this advance notification system is run successfully, a reference number is allocated to the lorry and the driver may proceed directly to customs and complete the transaction. Conversely, if the process is not applied, the lorry data need to be verified in order to print an exit authorisation.

- ✓ **Customs establishment**

At a port that is not a free port, customs are located at each terminal. In consequence, customs registration is essential for the driver transiting the terminal.

In order to ensure an optimised registration, customs functions are integrated within the terminal's computer network. Both for import and for export containers, drivers need to notify the customs officer or their private customs broker. Depending on the nature of the cargo, the entry or exit authorisation issued by customs would consist of an electronic seal without which the lorry would not be authorised to go through the gate.

✓ **Technical inspection**

Nowadays, technical inspections carried out at the gate are still a time consuming activity, although some terminals have decided to drop it and assume the risks in exchange of an increased productivity and significant time savings. Of course, such inspections could be carried out more efficiently on dry cargo containers (amounting to an approximate 75% of the total), leaving aside empty containers, reefers and dangerous goods, on which inspections would be longer.

The various activities carried out at the gate include:

- Lorry identification
- Container damage assessment
- Seal inspection (placement/replacement)
- Container number (ISO...)
- Label inspection on dangerous goods
- On refrigerators: unit condition inspection and temperature

Thus, in order to reduce as much as possible the inspection point crossing time:

✓ **Entry lane division**

To achieve a more rapid flow through the gates, it is important to carry out an entry lane preselection, besides using IT. A possible distribution could be:

- Lanes segregated with barriers and an entry terminal, for collecting containers that, as discussed, have the appropriate reference number (customs cleared).
- Specific lanes for those types of containers that require additional controls, such as refrigerators, empty containers, dangerous goods.
- Lanes for the remainder.

✓ **Use of portable terminals**

Use of terminals that allow entering data into the system, which in turn offer wider autonomy and mobility.

✓ **Control time reduction**

Based on observations carried out at the gates of the port of Amberes, an estimate may be made of the necessary time for container check. Average times are:

Empty:	190 sec.
20/40', full:	230 sec.
2 × 20' (full /empty):	300 sec.

In order to improve these times, it seems necessary to identify the container and assess damages with video camera systems (OCR).

Advantages:

- Labour reduction at the gates
- Waiting time reduction
- Productivity improvement at the gates
- Vehicle flow increase.

In any case, a number of activities still need to be carried out manually, such as:

- Seal control[4]
- Temperature control for refrigerators
- Dangerous goods labelling
- Internal inspections
- Excess height, weight or length detection.

Thus, the above times become:

Empty:	50 sec. (without internal inspection)
20/40', full:	70 sec. (lorry identification, reference no.)
2 × 20' (full/empty):	115 sec.
Non standard:	300 sec.

The introduction of camera detection reduces times by about 33%, which means a time saving of about 2.5 minutes per lorry.

✓ **Transhipment area**

As soon as the driver enters this area, a code must be entered into a terminal. From then on, the system is activated for the transaction. Its execution is time dependent, and is based on the time of entry in

---

[4] The ISO attempted unsuccessfully to standardise a remote seal control system (ISO/TC 104).

order to select the equipment to be used. The system notifies the vehicle the transhipment area to which it should proceed and which container should be collected.

An important aspect for terminal efficiency is vehicle control and management, and more specifically, communications with them.

Each vehicle is fitted with a VDU and a keyboard connected to the main computer through a digital link; at the same time, vehicle control is carried out by a supervisor through the computer software.

The supervisor uses a screen with an updated list of all lorries. The system applies different colours to indicate their status (blue: in process; green: ready to process; black: not ready).

The computer issues the activity instructions as soon as the lorry data are entered into the system at the transhipment area.

In order to generate the vehicle activities, the computer considers the following:

- Task generation time
- Distance from the vehicle to the next task
- Container length
- Loading mode
- Total stay time.

✓ **Exit activity**

After loading or unloading, the driver proceeds to the exit. At this point, activities are related to the "visit" completion.

For exiting, terminal personnel codify the "visit number" and the container(s) number(s) loaded onto the lorry; the system checks for data matching, and if so, the interchange document is printed, to be signed by a terminal representative and the driver.

As a conclusion to this discussion:

Considering the various critical points during the arrival of the inspection to the containers entering or exiting on lorries, it is possible to derive that one of the first requirements for an adequate procedure on terminal activities is an appropriate flow of information. This allows the terminal to plan adequately and to provide their personnel with clear information. Communication between transport companies and the terminal is a must, which provides both parties with the possibility of prior planning. Transport companies should have the possibility of checking the terminal system for information on container arrivals, delays on ship arrivals and road traffic density. This would allow transportation planning and would avoid peak hours and waits. The terminal should also have information available on lorry arrival forecasts.

Waiting times for customs transactions are unavoidable, but may be significantly reduced by integrating them in the information flow. Vehicle flow through the gates and inspection points may be also improved by the use of detection and identification cameras.

Significant improvements are required on computer data safety when it comes to speeding up administrative and bureaucratic transactions.

3.3 Technological elements at the gates

The first aim in designing a modern gate is increasing operating efficiency. This involves two approaches:

a) Simplifying the gate process
b) Applying new technologies in order to speed up the process and reduce the required personnel.

Technology increases operational accuracy and reduces human interaction until it leaves no room for error.

Gate configuration will depend on terminal location, traffic, local regulations, and will include one or several entrances and exits, general and specific (specific for oversized containers, refrigerators). The following description covers further the technological elements currently used and developed for gate improvement.

3.3.1 EDI

Electronic Data Interchange (EDI) allows information transfer between terminal customers, drivers and other parties. Customers may use EDI to notify the terminal about bookings, to authorise empty container exit, to accept cargo, to receive IMO authorisations, to transmit import authorisations, as well as any other relevant information.

The terminal may use EDI to notify their customers about containers that have left or come in, together with bookings or other authorisations (see Figure 3.2).

Customs brokers provide the information required for processing their units through the gate prior to their arrival at the terminal. Information is collected and stored in a database file. When a unit arrives at the terminal, data may be accessed through the terminal computer network and electronically linked to the gate transactions.

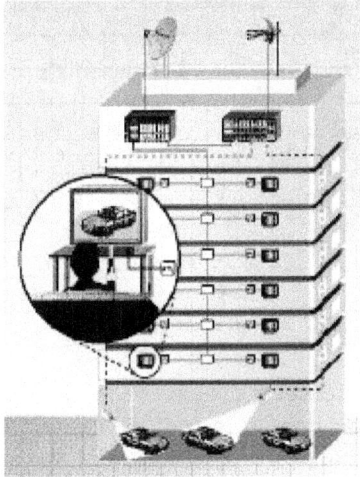

Figure 3.2

EDI is generally used by all the industry and its use will continue to expand with more users and additional types of transactions.

3.3.2 TOS (Terminal Operating System)

Medium and large terminals use TOS IT systems to support terminal operation. This IT system includes a gate operation component for the gate entry and exit processes (see Figure 3.3).

Figure 3.3

The system provides the gate personnel with previously entered data on the screen and captures information on every activity related to gate entry and exit. The software uses the data together with the bookings to verify activity validity, allocates and retrieves yard locations for delivered or collected goods, updates gate database activity and prints the corresponding forms.

Most software packages are capable of automatically retrieving the information captured during gate processes. These data allow verifying that the yard team is collecting the authorised container. Some TOS software packages connect to other processes in order to supply gate data and allow capture from other resources such as OCR, RFID labels and ID cards.

3.3.3 Video systems

Video cameras are used to visualize containers and chassis, and to create an identification set with the container number and the lorry license number plate at the gate on the gate personnel video screen. This system allows gate personnel to verify whether lorries leave the terminal with the correct container, and reduces human error in data entering. It is also used to check container damage when entering through the gate; when damages are present, they are recorded with the cameras.

3.3.4 Optical Character Recognition (OCR)

OCR is used to electronically capture container numbers and lorry license number plates, and to automatically connect to gate transactions and the database.

The system includes hardware and software components for direct installation on container handling equipment; a set of high performance camera units are mounted onto the crane structure. Cameras are configured to capture images for different container combinations and sizes while being handled by the crane.

While the container is unloaded by the gantry crane, a set of cameras records the crane from different angles. The container number recognition software analyses the images, determines and verifies the identification result, records the results and an image and sends them to the terminal's main computer. This information is used for container number follow up along various situations at the terminal.

System benefits:

- Container inventory automation capability
- Terminal efficiency and traffic increase
- Real time data processing
- Terminal management and follow up benefit enhancement

System features:

- Handles all standard containers
- Reads ISO code and checks control digit
- Real time follow up of containers handled with the crane
- Reads container number from both sides
- Simple configuration
- Minimum components
- Low maintenance
- Accurate reading

Since data are accurately captured and installation costs get lower and lower, the use of this technology is expanding.

3.3.5 RFID

Radio frequency identification devices provide capture of equipment characteristics and identification numbers. By using radio aerials and readers mounted onto the equipment that is used at the terminal, the radio transponders or the labels fixed onto the containers are interrogated.

Use of RFID to capture container numbers has not increased in the international market. Currently, RFID has a limited international application, and most maritime lines and charterers are not planning on labelling their containers. The large capital investment required for labelling and for handling the continuous database is a great obstacle for the development of this technology.

3.3.6 Magnetic Identification Cards (MIDC)

Magnetic identification cards may be used to provide identification of entries and exits of lorry drivers at the terminal (see Figure 3.5). Linked to a previously existing file, this technology improves gate operation. Cards with a magnetic strip, or Smati Cards, may be used for recording information about the delivered component, thus permitting to automate the data collection process. Use of MIDC technology is beginning to settle in. Currently, electronic cards issued by port authorities are used in some regions. Since this technology is more used in certain areas and is cheaper, it seems that its implementation tends to increase within the maritime industry.

3.3.7 Electronic gantry signs

Gantry signs are typically mounted across the entry or exit lanes to visualize messages or instructions for the entry or exit of lorries at the terminal. Modern electronic signs allow writing the desired messages and changing them as required by the terminal operator.

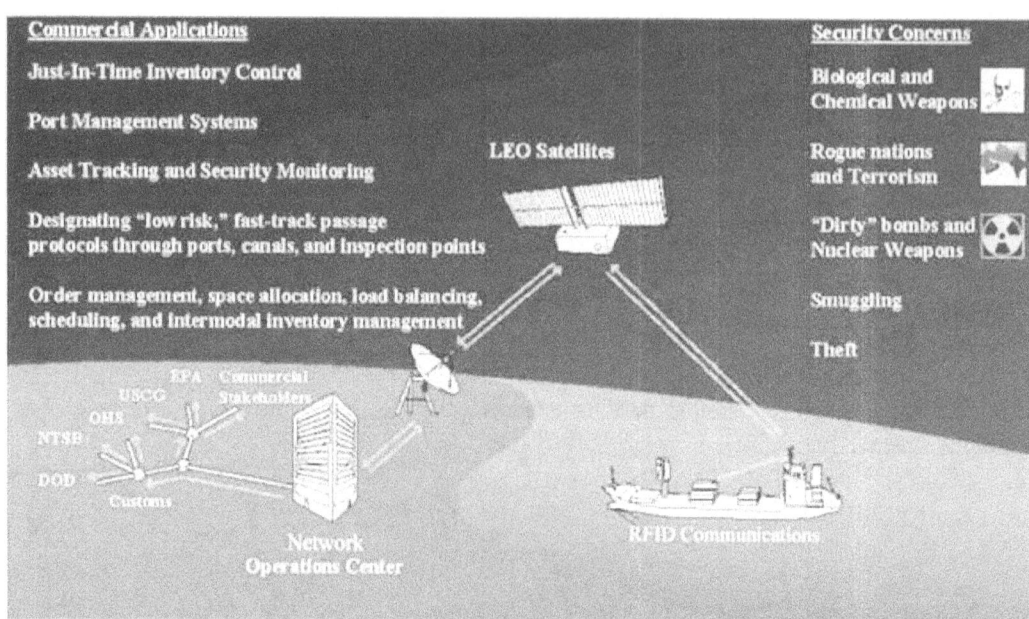

Figure 3.4

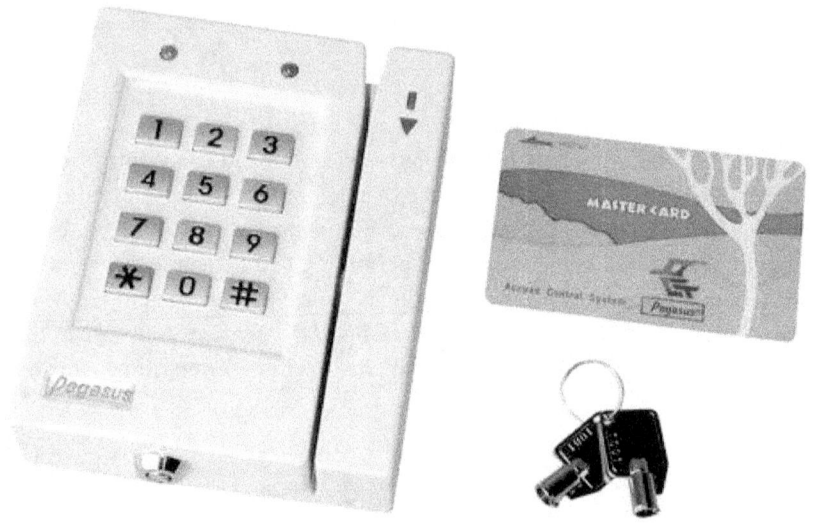

Figure 3.5

Signs written directly for each lane are used depending on the transaction or equipment type, and also indicate open and closed gate lanes, dedicated lanes for specific containers, etc.; i.e., signs are used both to show permits and restrictions to operations.

The use of gantry sign technology is applied mostly at terminals with reversible lanes and with traffic peaks that require such traffic control flexibility at the gate.

3.3.8 Intercom

Intercoms provide for verbal communication between lorry drivers and gate operators. Intercoms may be located inside and outside the terminal, at the various gate entrances and exits.

Information exchanged through the intercom is subject to significant mistakes due to the high background noise level and the loss of communication due to the various languages used. This technology may be easily integrated with any other technology, such as MIDC, in order to provide integrated solutions for gate processes. It may be used as a complementary system to other more sophisticated and precise systems.

Since the industry continues its efforts towards reducing the number of personnel located at the gate, the use of this technology will probably increase.

3.3.9 Electronic scale technology

Electronic scales provide an automatic connection between the scale entrance and the transaction area at the gate. The unit weight obtained at the scale is automatically sent to the TOS. With the tare data for the lorry or chassis, provided verbally or through EDI or RFID technology, the TOS computer system may calculate container gross weight and enter the information in the system database (see Figure 3.6).

3.3.10 Mobile Data Terminal (MDT)

Mobile data terminals are used at the gates to replace paper documents.

These mobile terminals provide a direct connection to the terminal's computers.

MDT allows the gate personnel to walk around the equipment during inspection, checking the seal and eventual damages while entering the data in real time. Once inspection is completed, a damage report may be printed subsequently and delivered to the lorry driver. This technology may be used also to record operational information.

Figure 3.6

3.3.11 Electronic seals at the gate

Electronic seals at the gate are beginning to be used on a trial basis. These seals may be recognised through remote control for integrity verification, using RF technology. The adoption of this technology should contribute to gate personnel downsizing.

3.3.12 Simulation models

Use of a simulator at the gate allows comparing and controlling several geometrical design options, with examples that simulate reality and applying theoretical models. Productivity volume, mixed traffic, entrance and exit geometries and functions may be modified. Data output from these models is used for measuring physical impact of each modification.

Analysed data and designed impacts are converted within physical design schematics that may be assessed together with the initial gate design objectives. Graphs simulate vehicle motions through the gate between the entrance and the yard buffer. The primary data introduction includes operating hours, arrival patterns at the gate and data traffic volume, vehicles mixed with data and processing times for each transaction type. The first data entry is in terms of vehicle time cycle, queues, etc.

Data tables are used for checking and comparing impacts of data entry modifications and to measure processing times, personnel labour, queues, costs and other factors that assist in determining possible solutions.

These data are translated into physical solutions in terms of number of entrances and exits, number of inspection stations, and decisions that will affect the technology that may be implemented in the gate design.

3.3.13 Automatic container code reading system

One of the solutions to the errors occurred during manual container number entry at the gate by entrance operators would be an automatic system for container number and lorry license number plate recognition that would process images with software architecture and algorithms for character and digit recognition.

The first task of some system applications is capturing an image of each vehicle crossing each access, retrieving license number plate and container characteristics from the image, recognising these characteristics and sending the result to a host computer for subsequent retrieval. Each control unit has several video cameras that are simultaneously controlled while lorries and containers are in motion. The system uses multiple cameras in order to check all container sides and to capture and analyse the lorry license number plate.

The advantages of this system in front of manual data entry are:

- Comprehensive automated process
- Increase of lorry and container traffic processing at congested gates
- Traffic history collected by data system
- Simultaneous identification of container and lorry while being handled
- Real time views of gate traffic

The system provides also the following advantages over other automated solutions:

- Simple configuration (few cameras)
- All containers covered (20', 40' and combinations)
- Recognition in motion (no need for the container to stop)
- Simple computer integration within existing resources at the port
- High recognition index (2-3 redundant views of each container)
- Simple operation
- System safety
- 24 hour operation
- Fast response (within seconds)
- Low cost solution

The main purpose of the recognition system software is taking container images, retrieving alphanumeric characters from the image (by software image processing), accuracy verification (by using the container control digit in a final check analysis) and sending the identification and, optionally, the image files.

Currently, the system software reduces enormously the information amount. It converts a 512×512 pixel photograph into an ASCII character string (a total of 10 bytes, control digit excluded).

The total reduction ratio from the raw (unprocessed) image to the extracted string is of 1 to 261144. Thus, the system optimises the subsequent transmission and processing when sending simply a string instead of the full photograph.

Furthermore, the system sends only the identified string when detecting the container sides, thus reducing the need of sending multiple images of different markings and positions. This enhances to a large extent the decrease in raw image transmission and storage. This is the system's essence.

The system may combine with a similar lorry license number plate recognition system. It would then reduce and automate to a large extent the recorded traffic processing, normally done manually, thus increasing processing speed at the gate.

Operation

When a vehicle crosses a terminal gate entrance, an invisible light beam between two sensors is interrupted. There are two such sensor sets at each entrance, a front set and a rear set.

The front set is the first sensor set at which the light beam is interrupted, and the first one to be restored. The moment the rear set light beam is restored, the exact position of the vehicle becomes known, and image acquisition begins. As with vehicle identification, light sensors play an essential role in the accurate location of the container within a Container Code Recognition (CCR) lane. The system will capture side and rear images when the container breaks and restores a specific light beam. Depending on requirements, images of the container rear doors, left side, front side, chassis code number and license number plate may be captured while the vehicle is transiting the lane. Multiple image units should be strategically located in order to ensure that the desired information falls within the recognition system visual field.

Once the image is captured, the first step is finding the target characteristic area within a large amount of similar objects surrounding the image. Likewise, a large number of codes and license number plates may be seriously damaged, faint or soiled. The system includes algorithms developed to notice basic size and proportion traits and, in general, attributes to distinguish the target area amongst the other image objects.

The first reading task is locating, isolating and identifying each of the aforementioned fields. Once one of the fields is located, image data from that area will be magnified using a magnification contrast algorithm, and characteristics will be separated from the background.

The shipping company is indicated by four characters assigned by the ICB at Paris. Therefore, characteristics read on this field may be verified against a list of predetermined codes. Furthermore, more checks are carried out, like, for example, on size and type codes, which may be checked in the same manner as the owner code, based on an ISO code standard list. Possible verifications depend only on the previously available information on the containers of the various maritime companies involved. Owner code and serial number are used in combination to calculate the control digit. If the reading and the control digit calculation coincide, a high confidence degree will be allocated to the reading.

However, if a disagreement takes place, it does not always mean that there is an error, since some companies purchase containers and change the owner code without modifying the control digit. Furthermore, the code will be read from at least two different images. By combining the results of these multiple readings, the degree of confidence in the results will increase.

3.4 Railway

At railway terminals, additional problems exist regarding data. The main problem with boarding containers coming from railways is waiting for the data. Except in those cases where trains carry a cargo exclusively for one maritime line, it is difficult to obtain from the railway advance information on the containers.

Due to this, the containers may arrive with no information, and therefore bureaucracy comes after the train. Likewise, a confirmation of destinations over the phone may not be obtained immediately. The sophisticated systems used for container handling may not be used until the information on the containers arrived by train is available.

Similar problems may occur with containers arriving by boat. These problems are less critical due to two reasons:

• Most lines are careful to provide all manifests in advance to the ship arrival, so that all data may be entered by the time the ship arrives.
• Import containers do not need as much follow on as export containers, since liabilities lie with the receiver.

In any case, often very basic information such as number of containers to be unloaded or loaded is unavailable, due to last minute decisions made by the maritime line and to modifications in the cargo at the last port. Although not always, these "surprise" containers are empty containers that are handled differently to full containers (since the value of their cargo is nil). If there is a high occupation level at the terminal, it may be that there is no space for empty containers to be unloaded. Even in the most modern terminals control systems lose their effectiveness if key data do not come in timely.

The industry attempts to face this problem by creating links between terminal, shipping company and consignors information systems

3.5 Result verification

Container and lorry license number plate images are sent together with the generated ASCII text string to the yard control computer.

The data merger will be determined with the yard personnel, with a clear understanding of the information existing in the system, like, for example, the online databases that may be used for checking the code reading and other possible transactions, such as:

• When a container is unloaded from the ship, the terminal operator will automatically obtain the numbers of the containers in the system. By comparing with the cargo list, squaring up with the ship will be done with a higher accuracy and speed, providing the container owner with a more precise container control.

• When containers are loaded onto a ship or a train, the system will read the number and automatically create a cargo list with fewer errors, more rapidly than with the manual squaring that would be done without the system.

• At the gate's internal and external limits, terminal operators may identify when containers have entered and exited from the port facility. This information, combined with the lorries' license number plates, allows operating personnel to ensure that the assigned cargo has been transferred to the appropriate transport company. By using time and electronic data, the unloading process may be followed on.

The software at the workstation where results will be verified will receive data from the image processor and its display. Results will be measured by the number of license number plates and container codes properly read, together with some detected reading errors. The operator should be alert when the system determines that a reading is not correct. The operator has the opportunity to correct the container code reading for transmission. When the data report is sent to the yard control system, the original and the corrected data may be saved together with the image.

A client application also collects the data from the message and writes them to a text file. Additional applications would also use the message information for other purposes. A specifically designed network product may broadcast the message through the network to the central processors and databases.

The main display is a window with a predefined format that is displayed on the screen and operated as a console. The user needs not to select any subwindow; the display shows that the system is operating; recognition results, together with condition and history, are displayed.

The main display is composed of several subwindows:

• Menu system: includes several user selectable options
• Displayed images: the camera shows the container, lorry and chassis/wagon images
• History window: shows the history of the identified container
• Condition: shows condition.

The container code recognition system shows that intelligent recognition technology is integrated in a recognition system that has already proven terminal operators a threefold productivity increase, a more efficient use of personnel and a capability for directing company management and reducing time cycle.

3.6 Conclusion

An optimum gate design solution does not exist. Numerous protocols are in place that may be examined, numerous variations that may be tried in the various processes, and numerous technologies that may be used. Finding the ideal combination at each terminal requires a good comprehension and assessment of the factors that may be examined.

By using the simulation model, a process may be designed that will be specifically tailored for rational gate productivity at a given terminal.

In any case, procedures, methods and means (infrastructure) used at container terminals, which lately have experienced significant progress, answer to operational and management criteria related to fluidity in yard handling and stowage.

Individual container identification functions have experienced a significant particular increase, this aspect matching the purpose of security, since it allows either clearing or raising suspicions regarding origin, contents, and to a great extent the threat that a container may pose to the port facility in question, or to the ship to which it is due to be embarked, this representing a risk for the next port of call.

Beyond the positive aspects that accurate, immediate identification of units may represent, the only verification that excludes risks and threats would be inspection of contents; nowadays this is being done with powerful, sophisticated equipment using penetrating technologies (X-rays, gamma rays and eventually others), which will enhance control on any type of unlawful merchandise, even on the use of containers for illegal immigration.

Therefore, this section could be extended with the information on such specialised equipment, which manufacturers and distributors promote and offer to ports that should comply with the ISPS; however, it is not deemed necessary to go into further detail, their effectiveness having been recognised, irrespective of the criticism that may be made to the random process applied in sampling containers for contents inspection.

Chapter 4. Merchandise transfer enhancements

4.1 Introduction

Escalation of terrorist acts, as well as of other crime typologies associated with marine activities (smuggling, piracy, sabotage, boarding, illegal immigration, etc.), caused the IMO International Assembly, held in November 2001, to unanimously resolve the adoption of new measures relevant to port facility and ship safety, to be adopted by the countries undersigning the SOLAS 1974 convention, starting from the firm decision sealed in December 2002. This established new provisions with respect to SOLAS 1974, in addition to the implementation of the ISPS Code.

The new requirements served as the foundations for the new international structure, within which ships and port facilities should cooperate towards the detection and neutralisation of risks that might threaten the safety of the maritime transportation industry.

Taking into account that currently all first category port facilities that adopted SOLAS 1974 have a multimodal transportation system (with at least four of the following traffic types: air, motorway, railway, public road network, piping and maritime), and that a safety increase involves unavoidably a cost increase (as reflected in the application of new safety procedures in air transport after the events of 11th of September 2001), measures should be adopted directed at optimising the cost-benefit ratio, which should be easily adaptable to the multimodal system, so that the increase in safety may benefit maritime activities by diminishing criminal actions associated with such activity.

With the arrival of the current intermodal transportation systems, which are integrated within port infrastructures, a permeability issue appears. Every transfer process from one transportation mode to the other demands checking, in order to avoid risks during handling. If requirements set forth for merchandise loading and unloading are duly complied with, a satisfactory safety level is attained. Notwithstanding, when receiving or transferring merchandise from or to any transportation mode, cargo lists should be verified again.

Merchandise bulk handling should be kept to the least possible; use of containers increases handling safety, even though it may hinder those inspections using non-electronic means or that do not require seal violation.

Likewise, such measures should accept short term implementation, without these increasing costs. Process implementation requires effective cooperation between all parts related to the activity, such as users, shipping companies, shipyards, port authorities, State Security Forces, on board personnel, on shore personnel, passengers, managers and anyone that, in one way or another, may participate in activities that interact with maritime safety processes. In this manner, responsibilities are established that should be mandatorily assumed by the companies in the industry, so that they become integrated within the common safety plans, as set forth by the ISPS.

Processes already in use should undergo review and revision; those not providing the required safety level should be replaced or updated.

The purpose of this document is to present, within the implementation of the ISPS at the facilities under the State's ports authorities, procedures and a proposal of systems that may enhance the existing safety level in merchandise transfer between port facilities and ships, considering even the reception of merchandise from the outside to be part of the port facility processes.

Amongst those, action protocols are presented for documentation checks, suspect recognition, container contents control, freight owner identity verification, shipping company identity transparency, creation of a registry of authorised companies and transportation means identification through an IMO code (which should be displayed on the sides of the ships anyway), databases to ensure ship traceability, automatic identification systems, antipanic system implementation and enhancement on ships for swift alerting of task teams, and stay time reduction by stowage and unstowage process optimisation.

To that end, procedures for merchandise arrival at the port will be divided between two cases: when coming from the shore and when coming from the sea; specific procedures will be applied to each case.

The aim, therefore, is to promote at the various access control points (even considering ship inspection as such) suspect detection and implementation of enhancement processes for personnel and merchandise identification; not so much for the detection of dangerous elements in the cargo, this corresponding to a second level of priority.

4.2 Registry of companies authorised at the PF

One of the critical points to port safety is the existence of various services rendered by companies external to the Port Authority, to which no enhanced training or operation control procedures have been applied, particularly on personnel executing the contracted services, other than those relevant to compliance with the respective contracts and with safety at work regulations.

With respect to airport safety, it has been shown in numerous occasions that the main risk comes from internal management personnel and subcontractor personnel.

Due to this, in order to improve control and information systems on personnel involved in port activities (stowage and unstowage, maritime operations, procurement, external and internal transportation, waste management, IT systems, catering, etc.), a classification registry for participating companies should be created for each Port Authority, including not only those with facilities within the Port Authority scope, in order to endow them with responsibilities and involve them in safety matters, and have them increase personnel contracting procedure rigorousness.

Following are some requirements for classifying a company as authorised, in addition to the accreditation requirements for an authorised company employee.

4.2.1 Obtaining an authorisation

Any company holding either a direct contract with the Port Authority or a contract with the various companies operating within the facilities under the Authority will be considered an authorised company. In order to become authorised to operate, the company should be registered in a dedicated database; the registration record should include a contact person (CP), who will be at all times the person to communicate with the corresponding safety manager.

If the company is a supplier or a customer of a shipping company, a subcontractor or any other company, it will be the company's CSO who will establish contacts with the CP. Registration of authorised companies is the Port Authorities' responsibility, after the proposals by the companies.

For activities not requiring a CSO, it will be the Port Authority who, through the PSO office, will establish contacts with the CPs.

Registration requirements will be, as a minimum but not limited to (so that they may adapt to the characteristics of each Port Authority):

- Company registered name
- Trade name (for self employed workers or one person companies with a different name to the registered name)
- Mother company nationality (in such cases, the same data should be provided as for the company applying)
- Registered office address (updated as required)
- VAT number
- Address of the regional office corresponding to the Port Authority (branches)
- Addresses of warehouses or other buildings related with the company's activity
- Telephone number
- Fax number
- Email address
- Integrated in the Port Authority's Intranet?
- Number of employees. Percentage breakdown of contract types (indefinite, part time, seasonal, fixed term, by days, even through temporary employment agencies)
- Number and type of vehicles, ships and other means related with the activity within the Port Authority.
- Highest ranking company representative at the branch (ID or passport number and all data therein contained, 24 hour contact telephone number, name of position)
- Contact person for safety related matters (ID or passport number and all data therein contained, 24 hour contact telephone number, name of position)
- Type of relationship with the Port Authority scope
- Date of initiation of services in the Port Authority scope
- Expected service duration
- Direct contract with the Port Authority? If so, contract file number.

- Detailed description of services provided in the Port Authority scope
- Offices located within the Port Authority premises?
- Related subcontractors
- Former safety related events
- Remarks

The form should include due reference to data security in accordance with the LOPD[1], and an acceptance of investigation by the State Security Forces Information Services.

Once the form is submitted, the Port Authority should evaluate it and issue a decision.

A sanction regime will be imposed for maintaining the authorisation, based mainly on the eventual occurrence of safety related events.

Once authorisation is granted, companies are obliged to report immediately the eventual contract termination of any worker; the company is responsible for collecting and returning the worker's accreditation, for access permit cancellation purposes. The Port Authority may at any time request the company's National Health worker registration statements for verification purposes.

Failure of the company to return the accreditation card will constitute a safety related event.

The PSO should send to the various CSO and CPs (authorised contact persons for safety related matters in the various authorised companies) lists with the required documentation in each case for providing access to or allowing departure from the facility; receipt of the lists should be acknowledged, and they should be attached to the safety plans as records. Should the established requirements not be complied with in full, the non compliant item should be put on hold until the issue is solved. The lists should be issued in Spanish, in the official language of the Autonomous Community and in English. Eventual need or requirement for translation to other languages will be on each company's charge.

4.2.2 Authorised company personnel accreditation

Once the relevant evaluation has been carried out and the authorisation has been issued to the applicant company, personnel accreditations will be issued.

In this respect, the creation of identification credentials for authorised company workers will be considered. Employees, particularly those having access to restricted areas or without dedicated surveillance, will be subject to carrying an authorised company worker identification credential. Such credential, which in the USA is contemplated within the TWIC (Transportation Worker Identification Credential) program, should have an extended operating scope, so that it may be used for the identification of all authorised company workers. Current IT systems allow storing in the credential sufficient information as to even include an individual biometric map, besides the IMO coding.

---

[1] *Ley Orgánica de Protección de Datos* — The Spanish Organic Law for Data Security.

The credential further allows reducing personnel identification documentation and adds a safety plus to access ways for external personnel to the Port Authority. This identification system may be implemented also for Port Authority personnel.

Worker registration data should be:

- Name and surnames plus all data contained in the ID, passport or residence document. In no case may a driving license be accepted as an ID, as they are easy to forge. If current address does not coincide with that in the document, it should be stated through an accrediting document; such modification should be introduced in the ID.
- Accreditation of worker registration in the National Health system, both for company employees and for self employed workers.
- Company certificate stating worker's job description, including job category.
- Brief worker CV, signed by the worker in proof of veracity.
- For transport agents, copies of the operating licenses.
- Extract from the judicial record.
- Type of relationship with the Port Authority scope.
- Expected date of initiation of services in the Port Authority scope.
- Expected duration of services.
- Detailed description of services provided in the Port Authority scope.
- Type of relationship with the authorised company (direct contract, subcontractor, temporary employment agency).
- Former safety related events.
- Remarks.

In order to preserve confidentiality and not to disseminate information, labour contracts and organisational regulations should include clauses requiring from personnel not to provide information relevant to port security, security training, access control systems, security and communication equipment location, or routine activities and port matters, to individuals that do not actually need to know.

Once the Port Authority preliminary evaluation is passed, biometric data will be taken from the worker, to include them in the credential.

One is aware of the difficulties that the proposed system creates for short term replacements and temporary workforce upsizings (usually covered by temporary employment agencies), but it is precisely with such type of contracts where safety control may create weaknesses.

Presentation of the credential alone will not cause the worker to be admitted; besides comparing at the entrance credential data with those in the Port Authority's database, the following process should be applied in order to avoid damages caused by computer viruses eventually present in the credential (viruses may be created that cause false data to be entered into databases in real time):

1. Credentials should be read by a reader that is not linked to the general information network. The database of this reader should be updated daily. The reader will give a result of "Known" or "Unknown" and "Active" or "Inactive".

2. Verification against the general database. In order to speed up the process, this second check may be used when the credential reading fails, because the real time general database is more up to date.

This independent data crosscheck provides a higher safety level.

4.2.3 Transportation means accreditation

For the accreditation of road transport means that belong to an authorised company, which may need to transit within the Port Authority scope, the same process as for cargo inspection should be followed, i.e., vehicle identification and inspection, a previous sending of information being required from the authorised company.

This information will produce an electronic credential that may be read by terminals at access control points.

It will be mandatory also to indicate the chassis locations for each vehicle where identification numbers are found. This practice is aimed at speeding up the inspectors' task and reduce waiting times; however, these numbers will not be necessarily accepted as authentic, since, in case a strike was being plotted, false numbers could be shown in the indicated locations, while real numbers would be in other points of the vehicle.

Presentation of the credential alone will not cause the vehicle to be admitted; besides comparing at the entrance credential data with those in the Port Authority's database, vehicle documentation should be requested. The following process should be applied in order to avoid damages caused by computer viruses eventually present in the credential (viruses may be created that cause false data to be entered into databases in real time):

1. Credentials should be read by a reader that is not linked to the general information network. The database of this reader should be updated daily. The reader will give a result of "Known" or "Unknown" and "Active" or "Inactive".

2. Verification against the general database. In order to speed up the process, this second check may be used when the credential reading fails, because the real time general database is more up to date.

This independent data crosscheck provides a higher safety level.

4.3 Merchandise road transport

Introduction

An analysis of the multimodality of transport systems that coincide at port facilities allows making the statement that one of the highest risk points when evaluating risks at port facilities is related to road transport delivering merchandise.

With the creation of current intermodal transport systems, which are integrated within port infrastructures, a permeability issue appears. Every transfer process from one transportation mode to

4. Merchandise transfer enhancements 105

another requires a process check to avoid risks during handling and in transport system and personnel access. If requirements indicated at access control and cargo inspections, as well as at unloading and loading supervision, are duly observed, a satisfactory safety level is achieved.

The volumes that this transport system allows to handle make it particularly necessary to consider terrorist attack risks, both at ports and on ships once the cargo is loaded.

Therefore, a meticulous procedure is presented here for access control and merchandise and vehicle inspection coming from outside and with destination to the freight transfer elements.

4.3.1 Merchandise entry from road transport

4.3.1.1 Previous operations to arrival at the PF

- Admission of the transport company in the authorised company register.
- Reporting to the Port Safety Officer the inscription of the vehicle occupants in the authorised personnel database by the authorised company, for carrying out the tasks corresponding to the company's activity.
- In order to admit and authorise an individual in the register, the following conditions should be met:
    o Void criminal record; not being indicted in criminal or civil suits.
    o Having identification undergone preliminary examination by the State Security Forces Information Services.
    o Not having participated formerly in safety related events at the Port Authority.
    o Holding a labour contract in force with the authorised company. In case of self employed workers or workers subcontracted by the authorised company, all documentation requested by the Port Safety Officer, duly accrediting the labour relation with the authorised company, should be submitted,
    o In case of handling transportation means, holding the required administrative licenses. Particular attention should be paid to dangerous goods transport licenses (ADR).
    o Creation of IMO codes through mathematic falsification-safe algorithms.
    o Posting IMO codes on vehicles intending to access the port facility.
    o The Port Safety Officer should be notified about the operation: vehicle to carry out the service, occupants and freight (freight documentation should already include all required information). This information should be submitted 24 hours in advance.

To summarise, authorised company worker credential and vehicle accreditation will be required, which would contemplate the aforementioned items.

4.3.1.2 Reception inspection procedure

On an arrival at the port facility, the inspector checking vehicle and identity for access control will proceed as follows:

- With the digital image acquisition systems as proposed, a first plane of the vehicle and occupants should be taken. These data should accompany the declaration of whether the vehicle is carrying cargo (although it is more important to include the freight merchandise entry receipt).
- Evaluate the possibility of responding to a violent action. Depending on this, the vehicle should be detained at some location.
- In order not to lose sight of any of the vehicle occupants, it would be ideal to have two agents manning access controls.
- In *no case* will it be assumed that either the vehicle or its occupants represent no threat, even if occupants are children, pregnant women, senior citizens, religious ministers or mentally or physically handicapped persons. Although the individual or individuals may be known, they may be carrying out some action under duress. *No unauthorised person shall enter the facility.*
- The possible appearance of secondary and tertiary threats should be evaluated. A row at an access control may be a diversion manoeuvre.
- Initiative and control over the procedure at access control should be kept at all times, so that it should be the agent challenging the individual, and not the other way round. It is the individual who is interested in crossing over the access control, so it is up to him/her to observe the relevant rules.
- It will be requested to stop the vehicle and the engine. This is important, since it provides a quieter environment that will assist the inspection tasks; furthermore, if the engine is started before permission is given, it may be considered that some action is going on.
- Once the vehicle is stopped, the following documentation should be requested from the driver:

Freight documents

- In case of container freight, container IMO code. This number should be shown on all container sides. To that end, placard holders should be available for locating plastified cards. Only containers with the latest admissible safety measures at the moment of inspection should be admitted, this being certified by the code inclusion. Each container should be identified by its serial number, by a three character code that identifies the manufacturer, and by its IMO code for that particular freight.
- Merchandise in container or not in container. Gross and net weights. Merchandise characteristics. Check registration in dangerous goods register (ADR). In case of dangerous goods, check for accreditation placards at the locations established by the regulations.
- Freight seal inscriptions (in case of containers) should be verified and checked for consistency with the documentation. Seal condition (integrity) should be checked. If the seal is found to have been forced, damaged, tampered with, etc., the vehicle should not be admitted. The event should be reported to the Port Safety Officer for notification to the Company Safety Officer, who should in turn include it in the daily safety related events report, a copy of which is to be sent to the State Security Forces upon request. Full data relevant to the vehicle involved in the event should be provided to the State Security Forces, for accreditation verification.

Vehicle documents

- o **Electronic accreditation by the Port Authority**
- o **Vehicle registration:** In the face of any doubt about its authenticity, it should be checked against the pattern provided. It should not be damaged, amended or scratched. In case of a provisional registration provided by an agent for a limited term, a comment should be included in the "remarks" field in the vehicle database register, for future date comparison of eventual forged documents. The vehicle registration includes the vehicle chassis number, which should be checked on the vehicle itself; if chassis numbers do not match, the vehicle should be detained immediately, as a response to a potential action. The occupant should be questioned on this respect, while taking every precaution.

MOT certificate requirement should be checked against the vehicle licensing date.

Chassis number location points

In the engine compartment, on a plate riveted on any of the beams that make the compartment cage.

Stamped on the chassis, on the vehicle structure itself, possibly visible from the right front wheel arch.

Under a flap of the inside garnishing, next to the passenger seat, on the vehicle floor or under the passenger seat.

- **Technical inspection certificate:** This reflects the vehicle's technical characteristics. Faced with any doubt about its authenticity, it should be checked against the pattern provided. It should not be damaged, amended or scratched.

The most important part to examine during an inspection is dimensions, in order to detect eventual false bottoms for concealment of dangerous items or persons for unauthorised access. Maximum weight and tare should be checked for correspondence with those indicated in the cab and container markings.

- **MOT inspection test certificate**

If MOT inspection is overdue and the certificate is not available, the vehicle should be detained for an in depth inspection. This should be reported to the Port Safety Officer, who should in turn take the appropriate measures regarding the transport company' authorisation.

If the certificate is produced, but it indicates "Unsatisfactory", clearly it will not be accompanying the registration document. It should be checked that the limit date stated by the MOT for solving vehicle non conformities that caused the "Unsatisfactory" inspection has not been exceeded; if it is overdue, the vehicle should be detained and the Port Safety Officer notified.

In any case, the driver should be advised that the authorisation provided by the MOT station is only to drive to the workshop for solving the non conformities, not for continuing to work with the vehicle.

- **Mandatory insurance**

The insurance certificate should be requested for the complete vehicle, i.e., including the trailer; the following should be checked:

- fee receipt date is within validity
- certificate data matches the vehicle arriving at the access control.

The valid fee receipt should include the following information, and accompany the underwriter's contract (for coverage check purposes): validity initiation date, validity expiry date (for quarterly or half yearly receipts, check that the period matches), contract number, insurance company, coverage.

- **Waste carrier documentation**

If the cargo consists of materials legally classified as toxic or hazardous waste (THW), either by the national legislation or by the autonomic legislation in those communities with environmental competences, THW carrier registration accreditation should be requested. If this is not produced and validated, the vehicle should not be admitted to the facility, because there will be reasonable doubt on the vehicle appropriateness for the transportation of such substances; thus, the risk of an accident at the facility will be avoided; or it may be considered as the detection of an eventual action.

Together with the TWH carrier accreditation, the waste control and monitoring document, the waste admission document and a copy of the waste collection advance notification document should be requested, in addition to a copy of the waste management facility accreditation of the company receiving the waste. If these requirements are not fulfilled, admission to the facility should be denied, and the security forces environmental agents should be notified (local police or the Nature Protection Service from the Guardia Civil).

- **ADR**

If goods carried are classified as dangerous goods (not waste), the transport company authorisation for carrying such goods should be accredited with the relevant administrative permit.

The vehicle should be checked for the appropriate placards and for the certification enabling it for the carriage of such goods or substances.

Packages, containers, portable tanks and tank containers not fully compliant with ADR provisions relevant to packing and packaging, group packaging, package marking and labelling or sign attachment and orange panels, but in conformance with the IMDG Code instructions or with the ICAO Technical Instructions, may be admitted for transportations including marine or air transit under the following conditions:

a) Packages, when not marked and labelled according to the ADR, should be marked and labelled according to the provisions of the IMDG Code or the ICAO Technical Instructions.

b) Provisions of the IMDG Code or the ICAO Technical Instructions will be applicable to single package group packaging.

c) For transportations including marine transit, those containers, portable tanks and tank containers not fitted with label placards and orange panels in accordance with ADR 2005, Annex, Chapter 5.3, should bear label placards and markings in accordance with the IMDG Code, Chapter 5.3. In this case, paragraph 5.3.2.1.1 of ADR 2005 would be applied only to vehicle markings. For unwashed empty portable tanks and tank containers, this provision is applicable until taken to a tank wash. This exception will not be valid for merchandises classified as dangerous in classes 1 to 8 in the ADR and as non dangerous according to the applicable provisions in the IMDG Code or the ICAO Technical Instructions.

Use of portable tanks approved for maritime transport

Portable tanks not compliant with provisions of Chapters 6.7 and 6.8, but built and approved before 1st of January 2003 in conformance with the provisions of the IMDG Code, amendment 29-98 (transitory provisions included), may be used until the 31st of December 2009 on the condition that they comply with the applicable provisions on tests and checks in the IMDG Code, amendment 29-98, and that the instructions of columns 12 and 14 of Chapter 3.2 of the IMDG Code, amendment 30-00, are fully complied with.

They may be used after the 31st of December 2009 if they comply with the applicable provisions on tests and checks in the IMDG Code, on the condition that the instructions of columns 10 and 11 of Chapter 3.2 and Chapter 4.2 in the ADR are respected.

Entry to the facility will be denied to vehicles that:

- do not have the registration document, or it is damaged, forged or not matching with the vehicle;
- do not have the technical inspection certificate, or it is damaged or not matching with the vehicle;
- have not passed the MOT inspection test or, being obliged to pass it, may not prove having passed it with the relevant certificate;
- do not hold the documentation relevant to dangerous goods or toxic waste;
- have any markings forged or altered.

Occupant documents

- In summary, an ID should be requested as a must (Spanish DNI, passport, residence card, etc., but not a driving license or similar), in addition to the authorised company worker credential.

4.3.1.3 Inspection and examination

Any vehicle may be subjected to inspection when entering the port facilities. At level 1, random inspections should be primarily carried out (random but intensive), including a comprehensive characterisation of occupants and cargo.

Workers should not take vehicles inside. Vehicles should exhibit the relevant accreditation, which will be issued for duly justified service vehicles. Internal bus services may be set up at port authorities, covering routes in a manner to make private vehicle access unnecessary.

Canine detection systems should be considered a priority, both for detection and for challenging possible suspects. If the animal (should it be the case) or the access control personnel would detect any type of materials listed as prohibited goods for boarding, the vehicle will undergo physical inspection and will not be permitted to embark or disembark or to access the embarkment or disembarkment area. If the driver refuses inspection, access to the previously mentioned areas will be denied; vehicle data will be recorded, as well as occupant data if possible, for subsequent examination and report to the State Security Forces.

- State Security Forces vehicles (except for those specifically allocated to the Port Authority, which will have restricted exit), should hold a special accreditation, as well as civil servants (in this respect, they should be considered as an authorised company); this should be carried visibly, and should be produced when requested. Interiors should be shown to access control inspectors, with the purpose of reducing the possibility of security vehicles being used by impostors for accessing the facilities.

- Suspect detection systems through nonverbal language should be applied at all times. This is the more significant when considering the examination of a lorry that is carrying a sealed container which makes inspection more difficult.

- It may be the case that the driver of the vehicle being inspected is not conscious of the cargo being carried, which would hinder or prevent identifying him/her as a suspect, as his/her behaviour would not be such. It is for this reason that support means are applied, and fundamentally a cargo check during inspection.

- First plane photographs and video recordings should be taken from the vehicle and its occupants. Special attention should be paid to document state, keeping always at hand a list with the specific characteristics of each one of them, for comparison purposes with those produced by the personnel intending to go through access control. Identification documents should always be kept readily available, as they may be requested at any time by the Port Authority security agents.

- No weapons or artefacts of any type that may deflagrate or may be incendiary will be admitted in any area of the facility, passenger terminal included.

- It should be requested that vehicle keys are left on the dashboard.

- Occupants should be requested to keep hands visible at all times, and to place on the dashboard mobile telephones or any other communication equipment that they may carry.

- Primarily, an inside and outside visual inspection should be carried out on the vehicle and the cargo compartment. Interior inspection should be directed by one of the access control inspectors, so that one of the occupants, preferably the driver, would be opening the various vehicle compartments and occupant luggage or bags.

- Since most inspections will be carried out on lorry cabs, given their height, security agents should be equipped with mobile devices to lift them to the level of the opposite door to that of the occupant who is participating in the inspection, in order to control the occupant's hands and face. Such devices should have the appropriate mobility and stability.

- Even serving as support means, electronic detection devices (scanners, metal detectors, mirrors) should be considered for each Port Authority and, as mentioned above, animals.

- For vehicle inspection, a layby should be available prior to the access, not in an inside area. It should be out of users' vision field, and with a closure with such characteristics that may dampen an eventual explosion.

- Inspections will be carried out at three levels.

Type 1 inspection: random inspection

The outside will be examined, including a detailed inspection of underbody, motor compartment, wheel arches, and boots if any. If no seals are used, the cargo compartment should be examined also. Interior inspection will be more aimed at challenging occupants.

Type 2 inspection: in depth inspection

Level 2 should be applied on vehicles matching some supplied description, or when during a type 1 inspection some suspicious attitude or object is observed. It will be like a type 1 inspection, but with higher attention on the search for specific objects.

Type 3 inspection: comprehensive inspection

It should be carried out when there are high chances of some dangerous or prohibited element being concealed.

When anything suspicious is observed

- The individual should be reminded of the obligation of keeping hands visible.

- Information should be requested on the fact or object raising suspicions. It should be kept in mind that on occasions it may be convenient not applying this item and continuing the inspection pretending to have neglected the item. This may serve for keeping a high safety level for the team, but it should be discreetly communicated (through some established code) to the inspection colleague, who should in turn report it to the PSO by some antipanic system.

- The occupant will be requested to leave the vehicle; suspects should be watched at all times.

- Documentation will be double checked, paying special attention to its eventual forging, to service entry dates for that personnel, and to the area where they are supposed to have worked previously.

- Report it to the PSO, who should in turn notify the authorised company contact person.

- Under the PSO's permission, the State Security Forces should be alerted.

- The PSO should attend the location.

- A comprehensive vehicle and occupant inspection (level 3) should be carried out.

- *The other vehicles should not be overlooked at any time.* This will be aimed at avoiding secondary or tertiary threats. It should be kept in mind that such a safety related event may not be definitive, and may constitute a diversion to distract the attention from the arrival of the true problem, or it may be also a safety system testing operation.

- Include company, vehicle and occupant data in a database, to be supplied to the State Security Forces for study by their Information Services.

4.3.1.4 Stevedoring

Every loading operation on a ship with a risk should be inspected throughout by a Port Authority inspector, who should check and, if required, provide container seals, should supervise cargo lists and should issue the ship departure proposal. Cargo operations should be examined depending on cargo nature (containers, bulk solids, liquid bulk, Ro-Ro, passengers, etc.).

PFSP levels 2 or 3 should be applied on ships defined as risk ships, as established by the Ministry of the Interior.

Nevertheless, when receiving or transferring merchandise to or from any other transportation mode, cargo list checks should be carried out again. Merchandise bulk handling should be kept to the least possible; use of containers increases handling safety.

Simultaneous loading on other transport means should be avoided if independent watch on each loading may not be ensured. After loading, cargo lists should be verified. All merchandise handling should be carried out in restricted areas.

Since the ISPS implementation is an international process, a general program should be initiated not only to develop container scanners (fixed, and also portable on lorries to set up provisional yards for inspection of ships with doubtful safety or not to disrupt safety systems when current yards are redistributed), but also for the insertion of anti sabotage identification chips, containing container and freight information, etc.; special electronic seals should be available also, that would allow, besides ensuring seal inviolability, to include information relevant to Port Authority inspections and eventual safety related events that may occur in relation to them. They should allow adaptation to new inspection systems.

Within available budgets, inspection systems not requiring container opening should be acquired (heat sensors for stowaways, explosive detectors, Geiger counters, various chemical detectors, personnel and container scanners).

Merchandise usually stowed in containers:

- Parcels, medium size parts, and general sendings
- Power related (crude oil, fuel oil, diesel oil, petrol and others, petroleum gases, natural gas, coal)
- Steel (iron, scrap metal,...)
- Metallurgical (metal ores, others, ...)
- Fertilisers (phosphates, potassium salts, natural fertilisers,...)
- Chemical
- Building materials (tar, cement, clinker, others)

- Farming and livestock (cereals, flour, soya beans, fruit, vegetables, wine, drinks, preserves, tobacco, cocoa, coffee, oil, fats, frozen fish, fodder)
- Miscellaneous (cork, wood, salt, paper and pulp, machinery, tooling)
- Special transport (cars and spares, lorry platforms, Ro-Ro, containers, transiting containers).

4.3.2 Merchandise departure by road transport

Previous operations to ship arrival at port

- Compare with the port of origin identities of crew and passengers (if any).

- Check ship identifier on the lists of risk ships (the European Community have such lists[1]). The list shows ships that have been detained after an inspection, and are classified depending on their risk. All such ships should be mandatorily inspected prior to entering the port. Inspection results and measures adopted in each case should be checked[2].

- Grade ship risk level in at least five segments.

- This list should be checked at the time of inspection, in order to have it as up to date as possible. The referenced web pages should be used; therefore, web accessibility should be ensured at all times; to that end, an Internet access point should be permanently available even when main offices may be closed.

- A program should be created for on board inspections prior to entering the port on ships exceeding a threshold risk (level 4 is advisable for a high seas inspection).

- For risk level classification, data on the ship's previous operations should be considered, her classification in the aforementioned list, silences of radio and beacon (which should be considered as mandatory to ensure traceability), and any information that may point at "contamination".

As a base for this circumstance, mandatory installation of a sealed location beacon should be considered, which could be analysed by an inspector prior to ship entry at the port. The beacon could record ship stops and their duration, as well as data collected from the panic button that it includes so that eventual covert attacks may be recorded. In the same way that the pilot regulates ship manoeuvres at the port, the port safety inspector boarding would be a mandatory measure for data collection from the safety beacon.

- Requesting from the Captain of the ship the International Ship Security Certificate. If the certificate is not produced, once the limit date for applying the measure is exceeded, the ship will be denied entry to the port.

- Full application, under the highest rigor, of the integrated procedure for ships' port calls in general interest ports.

---

[1] http://europa.eu.int/eur-lex/pri/es/oj/dat/2003/c_272/c_27220031113es00160016.pdf
[2] http://europa.eu.int/comm/transport/maritime/safety/index_en.htm

To that end, the maximum information should be gathered through the DUE[1] and through annexes that each Port Authority may require to issue. These annexes do not require the DUE itself to be modified (since it is covered by a regulation, it may only be modified through a ministerial order). Such modifications or new annexes will be reported to the Ministry of Public Works, for the purpose of documentary enhancement and eventual regulatory modifications covering all Port Authorities.

Despite the operational difficulty in advancing presentation by 24 hours, the possibility should be examined of having it mandatorily delivered 36 hours in advance in case of ships that are considered as suspects under any of the established criteria (the relevant list should be of general use between port authorities and major entities, such as the European Community and the USA), in order to enable planning a comprehensive inspection of such ships at quite a distance from the port, even in international waters if possible. This should be an essential requirement. In order to study the feasibility of this measure, the percentage these ships represent over the total traffic in general interest ports should be considered, and particularly for each individual port, since some will be receiving a significantly higher quantity of potentially dangerous traffic, or the destination ports (in the USA) may require that ships coming from our ports are clean.

Conversely, it should be possible to request from the USA safety systems (amongst which are military satellite follow on and ship intelligence) to provide as much information as possible. A solution for traceability, below the level provided by military information and intelligence systems, would be the aforementioned mandatory requirement for a traceability beacon.

According to the integrated procedure ministerial order, internal traffic ships, recreational vessels and national fishing boats are exempt from presenting the DUE. In the new Royal Decree 91/2003, the exemption is extended to warships, auxiliary vessels, wooden ships of primitive construction and non commercial, State owned ships. As by law this procedure is not required on such, they are susceptible of becoming risk ships due to eventual merchandise exchange in high seas. There are recreational or internal traffic vessels that are big enough as to hinder large ship manoeuvrability at a port. The law authorises the Port Authority to request DUE compliance; its implementation should be considered, or at least the collection of sufficient data in order to examine the risk that such vessels may represent.

- The above item on widening suspicion to any ship type may be extended to the application of Article 5.3 of the Royal Decree 91/2003, since it underlines that a ship having undergone inspection in the past six months by any Member State may not be inspected except when: she is listed in the annex I of the Royal Decree, or she has been reported due to deficiencies, or *there are justified reasons to do so* (this is the text on which the inspector should base the selection, since this is the framework within which risk criteria may be established by Puertos del Estado[2]; in the same manner, 5.4 may be applied, which allows the application of any operational control as provided by the application of international conventions undersigned by Spain; and, of course, the ISPS with reference to the SOLAS is the case providing for a widest margin of manoeuvre). In such cases it should be possible to inspect them, since, although they may not be within the obliged types, this does not exempt them from posing a certain risk. Regarding ships flying a foreign flag, Port State Control inspections are defined by the MOU and analysed by Maritime Authorities.

- A study should be carried out on which ships are covered under clearance by time.

---

[1] *Documento Único de Escala* — Unified Berthing Request Document
[2] *Ports of the State* — The Spanish Government Agency that manages port facilities.

4. Merchandise transfer enhancements   **115**

- The DUE electronic transmission system (known as EDI) through a BERMAN message (Berth Management) should be completely safe. The external sender to the Port Authority should be unable to access the system; therefore, any sending should be fully surveilled for embedded trojan software that could allow system intrusion. It is the Port Authority who should impose the communication system. DUE reception IT systems should be as tight as possible (like with the other ship-port interface systems), so that the various IT controls may not be avoided. In this manner, anti intrusion controls are enabled for each procedure, while increasing certainty that DUE transmission to the Merchant Marine Authority and Puertos del Estado will be clean and safe.

- Ship identification codes (as proposed in the applicable IMO Codes to activities within the Port Authority, such as vehicles entering the Port Authority for collecting merchandise) should be created through control systems that may make irregular sourcing extremely difficult. Coding algorithms should be replaced periodically. Two codes should be produced: a provisional code until ship inspection, and a final code, both completely different and unmistakable. Identification code allocation should not mean call number allocation, and even when a call number is assigned, it should not mean that berthing is authorised; this would be confirmed when a final identification code is granted after a satisfactory inspection prior to port entry. The ministerial order includes a berthing authorisation form.

- After a port call and having satisfied the requirements for ship departure authorisation, the departure document should be verified, which should be sent to the presumed destination port. This document ensures ship traceability; in no case should a ship be admitted at a port covered by the SOLAS convention if it is not the destination port as stated in the departure document. The ship will only be admitted at a different port after a comprehensive inspection ensuring operational safety and recording reasons for destination change. A report should be issued, containing the whole process, to be stored in the Convention members' joint database. Such destination change will mean in any case that the ship will be a "risk ship" in subsequent voyages, and she will be considered as such, even when declared "clean" upon departure from the port of origin.

- One of the items to be included by the PFSO in the proposed annexes to the DUE is the collection of information on a special sheet that may assist in classifying the ship as a potential attack weapon.

- A large scale, supra national database should be created. One step towards this would be the EU's black lists. These lists and the en route follow on systems (in international waters) would reduce the risk of boarded ships, or ships with dangerous cargo stowed in high seas, entering the port.

- If a suspect or risk ship arrives, task teams should be called, both local and those at the Port Authority. An alert level code system should be established with these teams for resource optimisation.

- Personnel leaving ships prior to entering the port should be limited. Those in charge on the ship should request leave in writing; nobody not on the list should be authorised to leave the ship. The list should be part of an extended document (including a large amount of information on safety, comprehensive of personnel or passenger medical ailments, prepared in recent dates), which should accompany the DUE. As with the latter, this document should be sent 24 hours in advance; this time is used for collecting information on personnel and, depending on the risks they may pose, prevent the ship from entering the port.

4.3.2.1 Ships to be inspected with priority

Irrespective of the selection factor, inspection of the following ships will be a priority:

- Ships with respect to which the pilot or the Port Authority may have reported deficiencies that may be diminishing navigational safety.

- Ships that may have been reported by another Member State (particularly those included in the aforementioned lists).

- Ships that may have been reported on safety issues by their Captains, a crew member or any individual or entity without doubtful interests, unless the Port Authority may consider in a justified way that such reports are groundless. The identity of the reporting individual may not be disclosed to the Captain or ship owner under any circumstance.

- Ships that have been boarded, or have stranded or grounded while sailing to the port, or that may not justify appropriately a stop recorded by the traceability beacon.

- Ships that have been charged with uncontrolled or unregistered unloading of noxious or dangerous substances or with any other registered spillage or with having thrown overboard materials, merchandise, etc.

- Ships having carried out erroneous or unsafe manoeuvres, without applying traffic safeguard measures as approved by the International Maritime Organisation (IMO) or other safe navigational practices.

- Ships having carried out actions endangering persons, goods or maritime environment.

- Classified ships having had their classification suspended or withdrawn for safety reasons in the past six months.

- Any ship that, not falling within the above items, may be suspect of risk.

- Ships calling for the first time or after an absence of twelve months or above at a port of a State undersigning the SOLAS 1974.

When applying these criteria, Member States should also take into account inspections carried out by the Paris Memorandum members. When suitable information for fulfilling this requirement may not be available, Member States should base themselves on data available in the SIRENAC database and inspect ships that are not registered therein from the entry into force of the database on 1st of January 1993. Likewise, all ships requesting entry to the port and not producing the International Ship Security Certificate.

- Ships not inspected by any Member State during the past six months. Even when inspected, this should not prevent a new inspection if suspicions are raised. This modification is to be considered.

- Ships for which mandatory construction and equipment certificates in accordance with conventions and classification certificates have been issued by a non recognised organisation.

- Ships flying the flag of a State included in the black list as published in the Paris Memorandum annual report.

- Ships allowed departure from a Member State port under certain conditions such as:

    a) Solving deficiencies prior to departing.

    b) Solving deficiencies at the next berthing port.

    c) Solving deficiencies within a fortnight.

    d) Anomalies for which other conditions may have been specified.

The adoption of ship related measures and the solution of all anomalies should be taken into account.

- Ships on which a previous inspection may have found deficiencies, depending on their number.

- Ships detained at a previous port.

- Ships flying the flag of a country not having ratified all expected relevant international conventions.

- Ships classified by Collaborating Entities of the Administration with a deficiency percentage above average.

- Ships older than thirteen years of age.

With respect to the aforementioned ship types, the competent authority should determine inspection priority by using the general selection factor indicated in the SIRENAC information system. The higher the factor is, the higher the priority. The general selection factor equals the sum of the applicable selection factor values.

4.3.3 List of certificates and documents to be examined

1. International Tonnage Certificate (1969).

2. Safety certificates:

    a) Passenger Ship Safety Certificate

    b) Cargo Ship Safety Construction Certificate

    c) Cargo Ship Safety Equipment Certificate

    d) Cargo Ship Safety Radioelectrical Certificate

    e) Cargo Ship Safety Radio Certificate

f) Exemption certificate, including, where appropriate, the list of cargoes

g) Cargo Ship Safety Certificate

h) International Ship Safety Certificate.

3. International Certificate of Fitness for the Carriage of Liquefied Gases in Bulk; Certificate of Fitness for the Carriage of Liquefied Gases in Bulk.

4. International Certificate of Fitness for the Carriage of Dangerous Chemicals in Bulk; Certificate of Fitness for the Carriage of Dangerous Chemicals in Bulk.

5. International Oil Pollution Prevention Certificate.

6. International Pollution Prevention Certificate for the Carriage of Noxious Liquid Substances in Bulk.

7. International Load Line Certificate (1966); International Load Line Exemption Certificate.

8. Oil Record Book, parts I and II.

9. Cargo Record Book.

10. Minimum safety manning document.

11. Certificates issued in accordance with the STCW Convention provisions.

12. Medical Certificates.

13. Stability Information.

14. Copy of the Document of Compliance and Safety Management Certificate issued in accordance with the International Management Code for the Safe Operation of Ships and for Pollution Prevention (SOLAS, chapter IX). If toxic and hazardous waste as contemplated within the European regulations and directives is being transferred, acceptance, delivery pre alert and control and follow on documents should be included, as well as the Hazardous Toxic Waste Carrier authorisation, whenever within the scope of such regulations.

15. Certificates on hull resistance and machinery condition, issued by the relevant classification society (only to be requested if the ship maintains its class with a classification society).

16. Accreditation document for compliance with special prescriptions as applicable to ships carrying dangerous goods.

17. High Speed Craft Safety Certificate and Permit to Operate High.

18. Manifest or special list of dangerous goods, with a detailed stowage plan.

19. Ship's log book with respect to the records of tests and drills and the log for records of inspection and maintenance of lifesaving appliances and arrangements.

20. Special Purpose Ship Safety Certificate.

21. Mobile Offshore Drilling Unit Safety Certificate.

22. For oil tankers, the record of the oil discharge monitoring and control system for the last ballast voyage.

23. The muster list, fire control plan, and for passenger ships, a damage control plan.

24. Shipboard Oil Pollution Emergency Plan.

25. Survey Report Files (in case of bulk carriers or oil tankers).

26. Reports of previous port State control inspections.

27. For Ro-Ro passenger ships, information on the A/A-max ratio. List with vehicle data, license number plates and chassis numbers, number of vehicle occupants when boarding and their identities.

28. Document of authorization for the carriage of grain.

29. Cargo securing manual.

30. Rubbish Management Plan and Rubbish Record Book. If registered toxic and hazardous waste is generated, a special location within the ship should be in place for their storage. A dedicated record book should be produced.

31. Decision Making Support System for captains of passenger ships.

32. For passenger ships operating on fixed routes, a plan for co-operation with SAR services.

33. For passenger ships, list of operational limitations.

34. Bulk carrier booklet.

35. Loading/Unloading Plan for bulk carriers.

36. Certificate of financial insurance or any other financial security in respect of civil liability for oil pollution damage (CLC, 1992).

37. International Ship Security Certificate.

38. Continuous Synoptic Record.

39. Security related deficiencies record.

4.3.4 List of clear grounds for a more detailed inspection

- Not having appropriately completed the Oil Record Book.

- Finding inaccuracies during certificate and documentation review.

- Inspectors detecting suspicious behaviours among crew members. Inspectors should apply suspect recognition techniques following usual procedures and observing body language.

- Indication of crew members being unable to fulfil their roles due to a low training level on maritime jobs.

- Evidence of cargo and other operations not being carried out safely or in accordance with IMO guidelines, such as, for example, when the oxygen content in the inert gas system for cargo tanks is above its maximum prescribed level.

- Failure of the Captain of an oil tanker to produce the record of the oil discharge monitoring and control system for the last ballast voyage.

- Not finding aboard an updated crew muster chart, or lack of knowledge of some crew members of their duties in case of fire or ship abandoning.

- The issue of a false distress alert, not followed by the appropriate cancellation procedures.

- Not finding aboard basic equipment as prescribed by the conventions, or the texts of such conventions.

- Excessively insalubrious conditions aboard.

- The inspector's impression or observation of indications of hull or structural damages or serious deficiencies that may pose a risk to the ship's structural integrity, water tightness or weather tight integrity.

4.4 Ship control procedures

- Principles of Safe Manning
- International Maritime Code provisions for the transport of dangerous goods.

4.4.1 Ships subject to expanded inspection

- Chemical and gas tankers older than ten years of age, as determined on the basis of the date of construction indicated in the Ship Safety Certificate.

- Bulk carriers older than twelve years of age, as determined on the basis of the date of construction indicated in the Ship Safety Certificate.

- Oil tankers with a gross tonnage of more than 3000 Tm and older than 15 years of age, as determined on the basis of the date of construction indicated in the Ship Safety Certificate.

- Passenger ships older than fifteen years.

The information to be reported to the competent authority is everything contained in the DUE and/or, as a minimum:

    a) Name
    b) Flag
    c) IMO ship identification number, if applicable
    d) Deadweight
    e) Ship construction date, as determined on the basis of the date of construction indicated in the Ship Safety Certificate
    f) For tankers:

        1° Configuration: single hull, single hull with SBT, double hull
        2° Cargo and ballast tank condition: full, empty, inerted
        3° Cargo volume and nature

    g) Estimated time of arrival at the port of destination or pilot station, as required by the competent authority
    h) Expected duration of port call
    i) Planned operations
    j) Planned statutory survey inspections and substantial maintenance and repair work to be carried out whilst in the port of destination.

4.4.2 Expanded procedure for certain ship categories

To the extent if may be feasible, and taking into account eventual limitations due to the safety of persons, ship and port, expanded inspections should address, as a minimum, the following items. Inspectors should keep in mind that safe conduct of certain operations aboard, such as loading, may be endangered if tests having a direct impact on them are required during their execution.

1. Ships in general (all categories in Section A):

- Electrical supply shutdown and emergency generator startup; emergency lighting inspection.

- Emergency firefighting pump inspection, with two houses connected to the main header.

- Bilge pumps operation.

- Watertight doors closure.

- Lowering a lifeboat.

- Emergency remote shutdown system test of, for example, boilers, fans and fuel pumps.

- Steering gear test, including the auxiliary.

- Radio installation emergency power supply inspection.

- Inspection and, to the extent possible, test of engine room separator.

2. Chemical and gas tankers:

Besides the items in 1, for chemical and gas tankers the following items should also be considered as part of the expanded inspection:

- Cargo tank monitoring and safety devices relating to temperature, pressure and ullage.

- Oxygen analysing and explosion-meter devices, including their calibration.

- Availability of chemical detection equipment (bellows) with an appropriate number of suitable gas detection tubes for the specific cargo being carried.

- Cabin escape sets giving suitable respiratory and eye protection for every person on board (if required by the products listed in the International Certificate of Fitness or Certificate of Fitness for the Carriage of Dangerous Chemicals in Bulk or Liquefied Gases in Bulk, as applicable).

- Check that the product being carried is listed in the International Certificate of Fitness or the Certificate of Fitness for the Carriage of Dangerous Chemicals in Bulk or Liquefied Gases in Bulk, as applicable.

- The fixed fire fighting installations on deck, whether they are foam or dry chemical or other, as required by the product carried.

3. Bulk carriers:

Besides the items in 1, for bulk carriers the following items should also be considered as part of the expanded inspection:

- Possible corrosion on deck machinery seats.

- Possible deformation or corrosion of hatch covers.

- Possible cracks or localised corrosion on transversal bulkheads.

- Cargo hold access ways.

- Verification of the following documents being available aboard; document review and confirmation of endorsement by the flag State or by the classification society:

a) Structural inspection reports
b) Ship condition assessment reports
c) Thickness measurement reports
d) Descriptive document as contemplated in IMO's resolution A.744 (18).

4. Oil tankers:

Besides the items in 1, for oil tankers the following items should also be considered as part of the expanded inspection:

- Fixed foam firefighting system on the deck.

- Fire extinguishing equipment in general.

- Inspection of engine room, pump room and crew accommodation fire dampers.

- Inert gas pressure and oxygen content control.

- Ballast tanks: at least one of the tanks in the cargo area should be inspected, initially from the manhole or from the deck access; if the inspector decides that further inspection is required, the tank should be entered.

- Verification of the following documents being available aboard; document review and confirmation of endorsement by the flag State or by the classification society:

    a) Structural inspection reports
    b) Ship condition assessment reports
    c) Thickness measurement reports
    d) Descriptive document as contemplated in IMO's resolution A.744 (18)

5. Passenger ships not covered by directive 1999/35/CE (Royal Decree 1907/2000)

Besides the items in 1, for passenger ships the following items should also be considered as part of the expanded inspection:

- Fire detection and alarm system test.

- Fire door closure.

- PA system test.

- Firefighting drill, during which, as a minimum, all fire brigade equipment should be checked; part of the catering personnel should participate.

- Proof that crew members with a significantly important role are aware of the damage control plan.

- If deemed appropriate, inspection may be continued while the ship is sailing to or from a Spanish port, under the Captain's or shipping company's approval.

- Inspectors should not hinder ship operations; neither should they cause situations that, in the Captain's opinion, may endanger passenger, crew or ship safety.

4.4.3 Ship detention criteria

Prior to determining whether deficiencies revealed during inspection justify ship detention, the inspector should apply some criteria.

When the detention cause is an accidental technical failure suffered by the ship while sailing towards the port, no detention order should be issued as long as:

a) SOLAS provisions have been duly fulfilled regarding the reporting of the relevant certificate issue to the Administration of the flag State, the destination port and the Recognised Security Organisation (RSO) designated inspector.

b) Prior to port arrival, the Captain or the shipping company have provided the Spanish Maritime Authority with accident and suffered damage details, in addition to information on the mandatory reporting to the Administration of the flag State.

c) Appropriate corrective measures have been taken on the ship to the satisfaction of the Maritime Administration, which, having been notified about corrective measure completion, guarantees that clearly hazardous deficiencies are remediated.

1. Main criteria:

Prior to issuing a professional judgement of ship detention, the RSO inspector should apply the following criteria:

a) Ships which are unsafe to proceed to sea will be detained upon the first inspection in which the deficiencies are revealed, irrespective of the time the ship will stay in port. If this may be suspected of being a stratagem to facilitate ship entry at the port for carrying out some action (terrorist strike, landing of persons not registered in crew lists or boarding lists, or even of such persons when a specific disembarkment leave has not been given), the preliminary inspection should be carried out prior to entering the port.

b) The ship will be detained if the deficiencies are sufficiently serious to merit a new visit from the inspector to satisfy himself that they have been rectified before the ship sails.

The need for the inspector to return to the ship classifies the seriousness of the deficiencies.

However, it does not impose such an obligation for every case. The Authority will verify, preferably by a further visit, that the deficiencies have been rectified before departure.

Main criteria application

When deciding whether the deficiencies found in a ship are sufficiently serious to merit detention, the inspector will assess whether:

a) The ship has relevant, valid documentation.

b) The ship has the crew required in the Minimum Safe Manning Document.
During inspection, the inspector will further assess whether throughout the forthcoming voyage the ship and/or the crew are able to:

    a) Navigate safely.
    b) Safely steer, conduct and control ship condition.
    c) Operate the engine room safely.
    d) Maintain proper propulsion and steering.
    e) Fight fires effectively in any part of the ship if necessary.
    f) Abandon ship speedily and safely and effect rescue if necessary.
    g) Prevent pollution of the marine environment.
    h) Maintain adequate stability.
    i) Maintain adequate watertight integrity.
    j) Communicate in distress situations if necessary.
    k) Provide safe and healthy conditions on board.
    l) Provide the maximum of information in case of accident.

If the result of any of these assessments is negative, taking into account all deficiencies found, the ship will be strongly considered for detention.

A combination of deficiencies of a less serious nature may also warrant the detention of the ship.

4.4.4 Deficiency reference list

To assist the inspector in applying these criteria, following is a reference list of deficiencies, grouped under relevant Conventions and/or Codes, which are considered of such a serious nature that they may warrant the detention of the ship involved.

However, the detainable deficiencies corresponding to the STCW 78 application scope are the only grounds for detention under this Convention.

1 General deficiencies:

The lack of valid certificates and documents as required by the relevant instruments. However, ships flying the flag of States not a party to a Convention (relevant instrument) or not having implemented any other relevant instrument, are not obliged to carry the certificates provided for by the Convention or other relevant instrument. Therefore, absence of the required certificates and/or documents will not by itself constitute reason to detain these ships; however, in applying the *no more favourable treatment* clause, substantial compliance with the provisions must be required before the ship sails.

2 Deficiencies within the SOLAS 74 scope:

a) Failure of proper operation of propulsion and other essential machinery, as well as electrical installations.

b) Insufficient cleanliness of engine room, excess amount of oily-water mixtures in bilges, pipe lagging including exhaust pipes in engine room contaminated by oil, improper operation of bilge pumping arrangements.

c) Failure of the proper operation of emergency generator, lighting, batteries and switches.

d) Failure of the proper operation of the main and auxiliary steering gear.

e) Absence, insufficient capacity or serious deterioration of personal lifesaving appliances, survival craft and launching arrangements.

f) Absence, non-compliance or substantial deterioration to the extent that it cannot comply with its intended use of fire detection system, fire alarms, fire fighting equipment, fixed fire extinguishing installation, ventilation valves, fire dampers, quick closing devices.

g) Absence, substantial deterioration or failure of proper operation of the cargo deck area fire protection on oil tankers.

h) Absence, non-compliance or serious deterioration of lights, shapes or sound signals.

i) Absence or failure of the proper operation of the radio equipment for distress and safety communication.

j) Absence or failure of the proper operation of navigation equipment.

k) Absence of corrected navigational charts, and/or all other relevant nautical publications necessary for the intended voyage, taking into account that electronic charts may be used as a substitute for the charts.

l) Absence of non-sparking, mechanical exhaust ventilation fans for cargo pump rooms.

m) Serious deficiency in the operational requirements.

n) Number, composition or certification of the crew not corresponding with safe manning document.

o) Failure to carry out the enhanced survey programme.

p) Absence, failure of the proper operation or non operation, handling aspect, broken seals, etc., of the Voyage Data Recorder (VDR), when its use is compulsory.

4.5 Deficiencies in the IBC Code scope

a) Transport of a substance not mentioned in the Certificate of Fitness or missing cargo information.

b) Missing or damaged high-pressure safety devices.

c) Electrical installations not intrinsically safe or corresponding to code requirements.

d) Sources of ignition in hazardous locations.

e) Contraventions of special requirements.

f) Exceeding of maximum allowable cargo quantity per tank.

g) Insufficient heat protection for sensitive products.

Deficiencies in the IGC Code scope

a) Transport of a substance not mentioned in the Certificate of Fitness or missing cargo information.

b) Missing locks in cabins or service spaces.

c) Bulkhead not gastight.

d) Defective air locks.

e) Missing or defective quick closing valves.

f) Missing or defective safety valves.

g) Electrical installations not intrinsically safe or not corresponding to code requirements.

h) Ventilators in cargo area not operable.

i) Pressure alarms for non operating cargo tanks.

j) Gas detection plant and/or toxic gas detection plant defective.

k) Transport of substances to be inhibited without valid inhibitor certificate.

Deficiencies in the Loadlines International Convention scope

a) Significant areas of damage or corrosion, or pitting of plating and associated stiffening in decks and hull effecting seaworthiness or strength to take local loads, unless proper temporary repairs for a voyage to a port for permanent repairs have been carried out.

b) A recognized case of insufficient stability.

c) Absence of sufficient and reliable information, in an approved form, which by rapid and simple means, enables the Captain to arrange for the loading and ballasting of his ship in such a way that a safe margin of stability is maintained at all stages and at varying conditions of the voyage, and that the creation of any unacceptable stresses in the ship's structure are avoided.

d) Absence, substantial deterioration or defective closing devices, hatch closing arrangements and water tight doors.

e) Overloading.

f) Absence of or impossibility to read draught mark.

Deficiencies in the MARPOL Convention, Annex I scope

a) Absence, serious deterioration or failure of proper operation of the oily-water filtering equipment, the oil discharge monitoring and control system or the 15 ppm alarm arrangements.

b) Remaining capacity of slop and/or sludge tank insufficient for the intended voyage.

c) Oil record book not available.

d) Unauthorized discharge bypass fitted.

e) Inspection report file missing or non conforming.

Deficiencies in the MARPOL Convention, Annex II scope

a) Absence of the P&A Manual.

b) Cargo is not categorized.

c) No cargo record book available.

d) Transport of oil-like substances without satisfying the requirements or without a duly amended certificate.

e) Unauthorized discharge by-pass fitted.

Deficiencies in the STCW scope

a) Failure of seafarers to hold a certificate, to have an appropriate certificate, to have a valid dispensation or to provide documentary proof that an application for an endorsement has been submitted to the flag State Administration.

b) Failure to comply with the applicable safe manning requirements of the flag State Administration.

c) Failure of navigational or engineering watch arrangements to conform to the requirements specified for the ship by the flag State Administration.

d) Absence in a watch of a person qualified to operate equipment essential to safe navigation, safety radiocommunications or the prevention of marine pollution.

e) Failure to provide proof of professional proficiency for the duties assigned to seafarers for the safety of the ship and the prevention of pollution.

f) Inability to provide for the first watch at the commencement of a voyage and for subsequent relieving watches persons who are sufficiently rested and otherwise fit for duty.

Deficiencies in the ILO Conventions scope

a) Insufficient food for voyage to next port.

b) Insufficient potable water for voyage to next port.

c) Excessively unsanitary conditions on board.

d) No heating in accommodation of a ship operating in areas where temperatures may be excessively low.

e) Excessive rubbish, blockage by equipment or cargo or otherwise unsafe conditions in passageways/accommodations.

Deficiencies that may not warrant a detention, but where, for example, cargo operations have to be suspended

Failure of the proper operation (or maintenance) of inert gas system, cargo related gear or machinery will be considered sufficient ground to stop cargo operations.

Publication of information related to detentions and inspections at Member State ports

Published information will include the following:

- Name of the ship.
- IMO number.
- Type of ship.
- Tonnage.
- Year of construction as determined on the basis of the date indicated in the ship's safety certificates.
- Name and address of the company of the ship.

- In the case of ships carrying liquid or solid cargoes in bulk, the name and address of the charterer responsible for the selection of the vessel and the type of charter.
- Flag State.
- The classification society or classification societies, where relevant, which has/have issued to this ship the class certificates, if any.
- The recognized organization or organizations and/or any other party which has/have issued to this ship certificates in accordance with the applicable conventions on behalf of the flag State, stating the certificates delivered.
- Port and date of the last expanded inspection stating, where appropriate, whether a detention was ordered.
- Port and date of the last special survey and the name of the organization which carried out the survey.
- Number of detentions during the 24 previous months.
- Country and port of detention.
- Date when the detention was lifted.
- Duration of detention, in days.
- Number of deficiencies found and the reasons for detention, in clear and explicit terms.
- Description of the measures taken by the competent authority and, where relevant, by the recognized organization as a follow-up to detention.
- Indication, where relevant, of whether the recognized organization or any other private body that carried out the survey has a responsibility in relation to the deficiencies which, alone or in combination, led to detention.
- Description of the measures taken in the case of a ship which has been allowed to proceed to the nearest appropriate repair yard, or which has been refused access to any Community port.
- If the ship has been refused access to any Spanish port, the reasons for such measure in clear and explicit terms.

Information concerning ships inspected will include the following:

– Name of the ship

– IMO number

– Type of ship

– Tonnage

– Year of construction

– Name and address of the company of the ship

– In the case of ships carrying liquid or solid cargoes in bulk, the name and address of the charterer responsible for the selection of the vessel and the type of charter.

– Flag State.

– The classification society or classification societies, where relevant, which has/have issued to this ship the class certificates, if any.

– The recognized organization or organizations and/or any other party which has/have issued to this ship certificates in accordance with the applicable conventions on behalf of the flag State, stating the certificates delivered.

– Country, port and date of inspection.

– Number and nature of deficiencies.

4.6 Inspection report

The inspection report should include as a minimum the following:

I. General information:

1. Competent authority preparing the report

2. Inspection date and location

3. Name of ship inspected

4. Flag State

5. Ship type

6. IMO number

7. Call signal

8. Tonnage

9. Deadweight, if applicable

10. Year of construction as determined on the basis of the date indicated in the ship's safety certificates.

11. The classification society or classification societies, where relevant, which has/have issued to this ship the class certificates, if any.

12. The recognized organization or organizations and/or any other party which has/have issued to this ship certificates in accordance with the applicable conventions on behalf of the flag State.

13. Name and address of the company of the ship.

14. In the case of ships carrying liquid or solid cargoes in bulk, the name and address of the charterer

responsible for the selection of the vessel and the type of charter.

15. Final date of inspection report issue.

16. Statement indicating that the detailed information related to inspections or detentions may be published.

Information related to the inspection:

1. Certificates issued under the application of the relevant international conventions, Authority or organisation issuing the relevant certificate or certificates, stating issue and expiry dates.

2. Ship areas or elements subjected to inspection (in case of more detailed or expanded inspections).

3. Type of inspection (inspection, more detailed inspection, expanded inspection).

4. Nature of deficiencies.

5. Adopted measures.

Supplementary information in case of detention:

1. Date of detention decision

2. Date of detention lifting

3. Natures of the deficiencies justifying the detention decision (making reference to conventions when applicable).

4. Information on the previous intermediate or annual visit.

5. Indication, where relevant, of whether the recognized organization or any other private body that carried out the survey has a responsibility in relation to the deficiencies which, alone or in combination, led to detention.

6. Adopted measures.

4.7 Data provided in the context of monitoring implementation

1. Every year the Spanish Maritime Administration must provide the Commission with the following data for the preceding year by 1st of April at the latest.

1.1 Number of inspectors acting on their behalf in the framework of port State control.

The information should be sent to the Commission using the following table model:

4. Merchandise transfer enhancements 133

Port /Area	Number of full time inspectors	Number of part time inspectors (1)	Conversion to full time
Port X			
Port Y			
Total			

(1) Where the inspections carried out in the context of port State control represent only part of the inspectors' work, the total number of inspectors must be converted to a number equivalent to full-time inspectors.

This information must be provided at a national level and for each port considered. A port is taken to mean an individual port and the geographical area covered by an inspector or team of inspectors, comprising several individual ports where appropriate. The same inspector may be required to work in more than one port or geographical area.

With respect to the total number of ships that entered their ports at national level, the Spanish Maritime Administration must:

a) provide the Commission every six months with a detailed list of movements of individual ships, other than regular ferry services, that entered their ports, containing for each movement of the ship its IMO number and its date of arrival;

or,

b) provide the SIRENAC with the IMO numbers and dates of arrival of individual ships, other than regular ferry services, that entered their ports daily.

Furthermore, the Spanish Maritime Administration must provide the Commission with separate lists of regular ferry services each time changes take place in such services.

4.8 Procedures relating to refusal of access at Community ports

1. If the conditions described in Article 9 are met, the Authority of the port in which the ship is detained for the second or third time, as appropriate, must inform the Captain and the owner or the operator of the ship in writing of the access refusal order served on the ship.

The Maritime Authority must also inform the flag State administration, the classification society concerned, the other Member States, the European Commission, the Maritime Affairs Administrative Centre and the Paris Memorandum Secretariat.

The access refusal order will take effect as soon as the ship has been authorised to leave the port after remediation of the deficiencies leading to the detention.

2. In order to have the access refusal order lifted, the owner or the operator must address a formal request to the Maritime Authority that imposed the access refusal order. This request must be

accompanied by a certificate from the flag State administration showing that the ship fully conforms to the applicable provisions of the international conventions. The request for the lifting of the access refusal order must also be accompanied, where appropriate, by a certificate from the classification society which has the ship in class showing that the ship conforms to the class standards stipulated by that society.

3. The access refusal order may only be lifted following a re-inspection of the ship at an agreed port by inspectors of the Maritime Authority that imposed the access refusal order and if evidence is provided to the satisfaction of this Authority that the vessel fully complies with the applicable requirements of the International Conventions.

If the agreed port is located within the European Community, the competent authority of the Member State of the port of destination may authorise, with the agreement of the Maritime Authority that imposed the access refusal order, the ship to proceed to the port of destination in question, for the sole purpose of verifying that the ship meets the required conditions.

If it would be evident that the risks of taking the ship to port were greater than those intended to avoid, the Captain will be notified of the necessity of carrying out the intervention on open seas.

The re-inspection shall consist of an expanded inspection.

All costs of this expanded inspection will be borne by the owner or the operator.

4. If the results of the expanded inspection satisfy the Member State, the access refusal order must be lifted. The owner or the operator of the ship must be informed thereof in writing.

The competent Maritime Authority must also notify its decision in writing to the flag State administration, the classification society concerned, the other Member States, the European Commission, the Maritime Affairs Administrative Centre and the Paris Memorandum Secretariat.

5. Information relating to ships that have been refused access to ports within the European Union will be made available in the SIRENAC system.

4.9 International and European Community minimum requirements related to Voyage Data Recorders

1. Ships in the following classes must, inasmuch as they call at a port of a Member State of the Community, be fitted with a Voyage Data Recorder system:

a) Passenger ships built on or after 1st of July 2002.

b) Ro-Ro passenger ships built before 1st of July 2002, not later than the first survey on or after 1st of July 2002.

c) Passenger ships other than Ro-Ro passenger ships, built before 1st of July 2002, not later than 1st of January 2004.

d) Ships other than passenger ships, of 3000 gross tonnage and upwards, built on or after 1st of July 2002.

2. Ships in the following classes and built before 1st of July 2002 must, inasmuch as they call at a port of a Member State of the Community, be fitted with a Voyage Data Recorder system meeting the relevant IMO standards:

a) Cargo ships of 20 000 gross tonnage and upwards, not later than the date fixed by the IMO, or, in the absence of a decision in IMO, not later than 1st of January 2007.

b) Cargo ships of 3000 gross tonnage and upwards but less than 20 000 gross tonnage, not later than the date fixed by the IMO, or, in the absence of a decision in IMO, not later than 1st of January 2008.

4.10 Manoeuvring within port premises

- Interior of the port includes also external jetties, such as crude oil tanker unloading areas, etc.

- Although it may seem obvious, port preparedness for receiving ships of such characteristics should be certified. In saying this, it should be kept in mind that during ship manoeuvres or stays, accidents or attacks may occur that, depending on the characteristics of the ship or the cargo, will make it necessary to ensure that resources, training and response capability for a primary and secondary intervention are in place to face any contingency. If this is not the case, the ship should be inspected outside the port or redirected to another port the facilities and resources of which may provide for an optimum response.

- An area should be prepared at the port for risk ships, as far as possible from inhabited areas and at a distance from the port entrance. Such area would be under the highest level of surveillance and isolation from other port areas. Access to this area should be possible with a minimum number of manoeuvres, so that even crew members without a great experience on the ship may work it in case of emergency.

- During ship entry to the port, no other ship should be carrying out the same operation, so that at least an entry and exit way may be safeguarded in case the ship would ground or would attempt a port blocking manoeuvre.

- Transfer zones should be created for controlling risk ship merchandise.

Ship victualling:

Ship victualling comprises of supply operations of provisions and others, electrical power, fuels (petrol, kerosene, fuel oil, diesel oil, gas), water, ice, spares, equipment, etc.

This item includes also the removal of rubbish, all kinds of waste, including THW, and waste water.

The procedure should ensure that no reverse flows may occur (i.e., from ship to facility, except when removing waste) when transferring power, fuels and water, particularly for the latter. In order to ensure the prevention of vulnerabilities of the water public network supply, recycled water should be used whenever possible for non hygienic and non alimentary purposes; surveilled recycled water tanks should be in place (one at each berthing point), independent between themselves, fitted with non return valves.

During the victualling process, the crew aboard should be recorded and compared with the personnel entry and exit record list. For electrical supply, the new automatic systems should be used whenever possible, as they include the adequate protection level.

Regarding fuels, they should be handled in a manner so as to reduce to a minimum the risk of making use of victualling for hazardous actions. If possible, tanker lorries should be used, since fixed installations are more vulnerable and eventual consequences of an attack are greater, as several supply lines may become paralysed. Furthermore, if personnel movement control procedures perform correctly, risk level is more contained.

Seal integrity should be checked on packaged merchandise. Every supply should be controlled. Even goods carried by crew members on eventual exits should be inspected. Any personnel entry or exit to or from the ship should be addressed with the same keenness throughout her stay, whatever its duration.

Safety procedures and provisioning contractor approvals should be audited periodically.

Unsolicited merchandise should not be admitted on the ship.

The possibility should be considered of ship supplies being requested by the crew to the Port Authority through official channels, who would handle the supply. The Authority, after checking proper system performance, could delegate to the shipping company. This is the more important when creating authorised company registers. In this way, responsibilities may be defined for supply delivery control. Supplier vehicles, even when belonging to authorised suppliers, should be inspected on arrival and departure to or from the facility.

Stevedoring

The following are considered to be integral activities of this public service:

Merchandise loading, unloading, stowage, unstowage and transshipment tasks within port areas, as a part of ship maritime traffic.

Loading and stowage comprise: merchandise collection from roofed or unroofed port areas; horizontal transport to ship side; application of hook, scoop grab, spreader or any other device permitting to hoist the merchandise directly from a transport vehicle, either internal or external to the port, or from the dock, having been previously laid thereon or stacked at the operations area by the ship side; merchandise hoisting and placement in the hold or aboard the ship or, alternatively, Ro-Ro cargo boarding and stowage in the hold or aboard the ship.

Unstowage and unloading comprise: ship hold merchandise unstowage, including all necessary operations for cargo division and location within hoisting equipment range; application of hook, scoop grab, spreader, or any other device permitting to hoist the merchandise; merchandise hoisting and location by ship side, hanging over the dock or, alternatively, a load vehicle; merchandise unloading, directly on land transport vehicles, either internal or external to the port, or on the dock for collection by vehicles or horizontal transport means and direct transfer outside the port or to a depot or storage area inside the port; merchandise placement and stacking in roofed or unroofed port areas.

Transshipment comprises unstowage on the first ship, direct merchandise transfer from one ship to the other, and stowage on the second ship.

On risk ships, even when an inspection has been carried out prior to entry to the port, every unloading operation should be supervised by the Port Authority inspector.

Containers showing signs of tampering may not be unloaded without being examined.

Unloading should be scheduled so that frequencies allow for detailed inspections, unloading operations not being permitted to continue until the inspected segment complies with the established safety criteria, i.e., partial merchandise certification will take place. Ship departure will not be authorised until the cargo is certified to be non hazardous. Minimum security level for such cases is 2, as previously defined by the Ministry of the Interior, since if may not be established on a routine basis for a given operation.

During unloading, the complete crew should stay on the ship; no landing will be permitted until the whole cargo is verified.

Ro-Ro operations and vehicle loading and unloading on passenger ships will be considered as of maximum risk. This is foremost in cases in which vehicles are driven by passengers themselves.

No transshipment operations will be allowed without a safety inspector present, and unless cargo inspection, as a minimum, is facilitated. Procedures should be studied for the eventual need of breaking container seals, so that they may keep the same IMO number, but marked in a manner to show that they have been opened. If such mark is present, but without the accompanying documentation (the inspection certificate), it will be considered that the container has been opened without authorisation during the voyage, the previous port call or at the current port in the area previous to stowage, or during railway or road transportation.

4.11 Loading and departure of road transport vehicles

Departure will always be subject to departure authorisation by the Port Authority.

Merchandise routine checks should be in place.

Always, in every case, vehicle and occupant departure should be recorded, so that IT based verifications of vehicle and personnel balances (entries and exits) may be made. The IT system should enable these verifications to be made at will and hourly.

Random checks of personnel staying within the Port Authority should be carried out, to verify physical presence. If deviations are detected, the system should be checked, and the PSO should be notified.

Railway

Procedures for railway traffic will be aimed mainly at detection at the origin (when merchandises are coming from a railway station). To that end, the adoption of similar inspection systems at railway stations is recommended.

Regarding the departure of merchandise received from the water side at the Port Authority, similar procedures to those for road transport should be followed. Since merchandise is not accompanied, suspect recognition systems are not necessary to the same extent.

At Port Authority railway infrastructures, transport safety should be enhanced by improving rolling surfaces: concrete is safer than ballast, as strange elements may not be concealed therein. Similarly, it should be known whether the railway is electrified or not, both for safety purposes and to allow various types of tractor units.

Chapter 5. Identification technology

5.1 Fundamentals of biometric authentication

Biometric authentication (BA) is the verification of an individual's identity using as identification parameters certain human morphological traits that have a minimum probability of repetition from one individual to another, so that it may be virtually considered that they will only appear in such form on that one individual.

It is intended through BA to collect information on a distinctive trait of a person (voice, fingerprint, iris, retina, scent...) for subsequent comparison of this register entered into a database with another one taken on the moment of identification, thus verifying whether it is the same individual. In a similar manner, animals recognise other animals and human beings by biometric features such as scent or voice.

BA difficulties lie with developing technologies that may carry out such identifications in a speedy, error free manner. As with other human capabilities, such as speech, enabling a machine to effectively carrying out BA has proven a highly complex task.

BA operation

The determining parameter is choosing the distinctive traits that will unmistakably identify each individual. Even though user identification through biometric methods is possible by using any unique, measurable individual characteristic (this includes from the way of typing on a computer, through corporal scent, to the patterns of certain veins), it has been commonly accepted over decades that traits such as fingerprints, iris or voice are unique to each person and fully valid for BA automation.

Other less commonly known traits, or which involve greater difficulty for machines, are the retina venous system, facial features or hand shape.

The optimum for a BA system would be to focus on those traits that, besides being distinct for each person, do not vary over time due to natural ageing processes or body mass changes. Thus, the former three features (fingerprint, iris and voice) are those engaging the majority of the current research efforts.

Once the trait to be used for the BA authentication process has been decided, for which purpose it is important to consider the destination activity or industry for the system concerned, it is then necessary to find the parameters that may be quantified and/or characterised. For example, it is known that human fingerprints have a number of points (intersections, line ends, etc.) that are unequally distributed for each person; therefore, when comparing two fingerprints, the complete print is not compared, but rather the location of those points and their relative positions.

The analysis of the patterns that these points create constitutes in itself the biometric authentication process.

Along this line, BA commercial applications are available in the form of fingerprint readers built into laptops, which replace or enhance the traditional password protection. Fingerprint and iris controls are also being used in facility access control systems. Fingerprint readers or voice recognition devices may, in the medium term, replace mobile phone PIN numbers or car keys.

Nevertheless, BA alone may not cover all safety and authentication requirements, but it should rather be considered as yet another tool in the set; in the specific case of access control for merchandise arriving to port on road transport, the ideal combination would be with suspect detection techniques. BA systems may be the perfect backup for putting pressure on an individual and to increase the safety of port personnel individual identification credentials. In fact, it would be useful not only within the merchandise access control scope; towards enhancing data protection in office equipment, a fingerprint recognition system could replace the traditional card readers, both for clocking in and at the various company IT equipment, which could also be fitted with fingerprint readers so that only authorised users might access each set.

In the same manner, such systems installed on laptops may prevent unauthorised access to sensitive company data, or that may be stolen or misplaced. Thus, the company may be certain that only their personnel is accessing their facilities, handling their information and, furthermore, that clocking in is done correctly.

If the company has a Public Key Infrastructure (PKI) to ensure confidentiality of their communications, the BA may play a significant role towards increasing confidence levels for two of the most important PKI features: irrefutability and confidentiality. I.e., when an employee intends to send an electronically signed and encrypted message, he/she will use the fingerprint reader in order to authorise the message signature.

When the addressee receives the message and attempts to decipher it, he/she will have also to provide authentication through the BA system. Thus, both may be sure that the message has been issued by the alleged issuer, and only the intended addressee may read it. If the digital signature is the employee's IMO code, the creation of which is hereby recommended, in addition to the IMO emergency code that may be used in case of kidnapping, the code would be authenticated with one or two biometric parameters.

These BA based operations replace two items that hitherto have been key to all IT based safety systems: passwords and cards.

Thus, BA roots off all issues deriving from identification card misplacement or theft, or from the use of passwords that are simple or easy to find out, steal or forget. It has the advantage that patterns may not be misplaced or stolen; neither may they be used by other individuals even if they may access personal cards or PINs.

In contrast to older methods, in which something had to be carried, with biometric systems, the identification parameters are "incorporated" in the individual. In this manner, company IT safety is increased to very a high level, while many daily operations are simplified.

These systems may increase control access transit rate.

In the same manner as preliminary studies are on their way for developing a BA based digital National ID, it is deemed that its use for creating the aforementioned authorised company worker identification credential would be optimum.

In fact, a large scale project is currently on its completion phase in Switzerland for issuing yearly close to 100 000 biometric passports, from 2005 to 2010. To enter the USA without a visa, from the 26th of October 2005, individuals will be required to hold an optically readable passport (2003); i.e., a new passport with biometric data.

North Americans have furthermore set another requirement. In order to take advantage of the Visa Waiver Program, countries undersigning the convention are required to seriously work at least on preparing a passport containing such biometric data. It is estimated that such requirement will most likely be imposed at an international scale, particularly in the European Union. The new passport, the same as with the proposed credential, will incorporate an electronic chip containing biometric data. It should be mentioned that the current passport (2003), which may be optically controlled, will still be issued, although biometric data registrations will begin in some of the offices throughout the country (see Table 5.1).

Credential or passport validity will likewise have to be reduced from 10 to 5 years, due to technical reasons related to the electronic chip lifetime.

Biometric devices have three main parts: there is an automatic mechanism reading and capturing a digital or analogue image of the feature to be analysed; there are unit handling aspects such as data compression, storage and comparison against those in a database (which are considered as valid); and there is an interface for user applications.

The general authentication process follows some common steps to all biometric authentication models: *capture* or reading of data presented by the user to be validated; *extraction* of certain features from the sample (for example, fingerprint minutiae); *comparison* of such features with those stored in a database; and a *decision* on whether the user is validated or not. It is mainly in this decision where the two basic reliability characteristics of every biometric system (in general, of every authentication system) play their role: False Rejection and False Acceptance Rates.

False Rejection Rate (FRR) is the probability of an authentication system rejecting a legitimate user because it is incapable of correctly identifying the user; *False Acceptance Rate* (FAR) is the probability of the system verifying an illegitimate user (impostor).

Biometrical method comparison.						
	Eye – Iris	Eye - Retina	Fingerprints	Hand geometry	Writing - Signature	Voice
Reliability	Very high	Very high	High	High	High	High
Ease of use	Medium	Low	High	High	High	High
Attack prevention	Very high	Very high	High	High	Medium	Medium
Acceptance	Medium	Medium	Medium	High	Very high	High
Stability	High	High	High	Medium	Medium	Medium
Identification and Authentication	Both	Both	Both	Authentication	Both	Authentication
Standards	-	-	ANSI/NIST, FBI	-	-	SVAPI
Interferences	Glasses	Congestion	Dirt, wounds, hard skin...	Arthritis, rheumatism ...	Simple or changing signatures	Noise, colds...
Application	Nuclear facilities, medical services, prisons	Nuclear facilities, medical services, prisons	Police, industrial	General	Industrial	Databases or bank remote access

Table 5.1

Obviously, a high FRR will create dissatisfaction amongst system users, but a high FAR will create a serious safety issue: access to a resource is being provided for unauthorised personnel. Therefore, as previously underlined, it is an ideal system for combining with other methods.

For an appropriate classification of each technology, the Average Error Rate (AER) is used (see Table 5.2).

Vulnerability to simulation attacks is a falsehood. In fiction, biometric authenticators are always "tricked" with such attacks in order to gain access to certain facilities: the relevant body part to be analysed is simulated with some model or even using limbs severed from a corpse or from the real user (amputations, etc.) to force the system to permit access.

5. Identification technology

Fingerprint biometrics ~ Performance				
Level	False Acceptance	False Rejection	Other errors	AER
1	0.01 %	1.00 %	0.01 %	0.51 %
2	0.10 %	2.00 %	0.02 %	1.07 %
3	0.50 %	3.00 %	0.05 %	1.80 %
4	1.00 %	5.00 %	0.10 %	3.10 %
5	2.00 %	7.00 %	0.15 %	4.65 %
Fingerprint biometrics ~ Ambient Conditions				
Level	Minimum Temperature	Maximum Temperature	Relative Humidity	
1	−10	60	100	
2	−5	55	95	
3	0	50	90	
4	5	45	75	
5	10	40	60	

Facial Recognition ~ Performance				
Level	False Acceptance	False Rejection	Other errors	AER
1	0.50 %	5.00 %	0.01 %	2.76 %
2	1.00 %	8.00 %	0.02 %	4.52 %
3	3.00 %	12.00 %	0.05 %	7.55 %
4	6.00 %	18.00 %	0.10 %	12.10 %
5	10.00 %	25.00 %	0.15 %	17.65 %
Facial Recognition ~ Ambient Conditions				
Level	Minimum Temperature	Maximum Temperature	Relative Humidity	
1	−10	60	100	
2	−5	55	95	
3	0	50	90	
4	5	45	75	
5	10	40	60	

Iris Recognition ~ Performance				
Level	False Acceptance	False Rejection	Other errors	AER
1	0.00 %	0.50 %	0.01 %	0.26 %
2	0.00001 %	0.75 %	0.02 %	0.39 %
3	0.0001 %	1.00 %	0.05 %	0.55 %
4	0.001%	2.00 %	0.10 %	1.10 %
5	0.005 %	3.00 %	0.15 %	1.65 %
Iris Recognition ~ Ambient Conditions				
Level	Minimum Temperature	Maximum Temperature	Relative Humidity	
1	−10	60	100	
2	−5	55	95	
3	0	50	90	
4	5	45	75	
5	10	40	60	

Tables 5.2

By appropriately analysing systems and their reliability, as well as their technological evolution, it may be stated that this happens only in fiction; nowadays, any biometric system —with maybe the exception of some voice based models that will be addressed later on— is highly immune to such attacks. Retina, iris, fingerprint and hand geometry analysers are capable, besides deciding whether the limb belongs to the legitimate user, of determining whether the user is alive or is a corpse.

Bearing in mind the fundamental features of the various biometric measurement parameters, a study may be carried on in terms of precision (P), cost (C), user acceptance (A) and degree of intrusiveness (I). Evidently, the ideal technology would exhibit maximum precision and acceptance, and minimum cost and intrusiveness (P++++, C+, A++++, I+).

Thus:

- Fingerprint recognition: the user needs only to place the finger tip (normally the index) on a print scanner. Evaluation: P++++, C++, A+++, I++.
- Facial recognition: the system includes a camera that takes a user image and analyses the individual's face. Evaluation: P++, C+++, A++, I+.
- Voice recognition: the individual pronounces a previously established access code (name and/or surnames, ID number, telephone number, PIN, etc.) or a different phrase each time following a system prompt ("Please say..."), and is recognised by the system based on the features of the voice recorded when accessing. Evaluation: P+++, C+, A++, I+.
- Hand shape recognition: the individual places an open hand on a dedicated scanner, and is recognised based on hand shape and geometry. Evaluation: P++, C+++, A++, I++.
- Iris recognition: the system obtains a precise image of the individual's iris pattern and compares it with the previously stored user's pattern. Evaluation: P++++, C+++++, A+++, I+++.
- Signature recognition: the individual signs on a dedicated surface and the signature is verified against a previously obtained pattern from the same individual.

However, whatever the selected technology is for a given application, limitations and peculiarities of each technology should be considered on a case by case basis, together with the characteristics of the facility to be protected, in the face of the added safety level, previously not available, that may be achieved.

Characteristics to be considered are basically given in the following items:

- Need for a specific acquisition device (fingerprint reader, microphone, camera, etc.) where the user may be.
- Possible variability over time of the pattern to be identified (voice congestion or loss, use of glasses, moustache, beard, etc.).
- Individual error probability of each of the technologies (ranging from one percent to one out of several millions, depending on the selected technology).
- User acceptance of each of the technologies, depending on whether they are intrusive or not, comfortable, respectful to privacy (at least apparently), easy to use, etc.

In this manner, depending on the situation in which safe user authentication may be required, the most adequate biometric technology (or combination of technologies) should be sought, depending on the four aforementioned fundamental parameters.

It is important to bear in mind that effectiveness in safety is not attained through the sole application of technology. Human factor must be jointly used, complementing technology as a part of an overall safety system. Weaknesses in any of these components diminish system effectiveness. The safety process requires pondering the limitations of biometric technology. An example is that some individuals may not go through the access control because they are physically lacking the part of the body required for authentication.

Similarly, errors are present during evaluation operations.

Prior to a person obtaining a biometric credential, the organisation that delivers it should make sure that such person is trustworthy as to be granted the credential.

Three key considerations have been seen to be necessary prior to deciding for the design, development and implementation of a biometric system within a safety system.

1. Decision should be based on how the technology will be used.

2. A detailed study should be carried out comparing cost with benefits, so that the latter exceed the cost.

3. A balance analysis should be carried out between the safety enhancements that biometric technology implementation may provide and the impact it may cause on areas such as privacy and convenience.

Safety aspects should be compared to costs and operational practices, in addition to political, economical and strategic interests.

In order to develop safety systems with integrated biometric technology, the highest level objectives should be defined as well as the operating procedure concepts that processes, safety personnel and technology may require for achieving such objectives. Once these questions are settled, the optimum scope of biometry for port safety may be determined.

Depending on the application, biometric systems may be used in two modes: verification and identification.

Verification, or authentication: used for verifying a person's identity, i.e., to ensure that an individual is who he/she reports to be.

Identification is used for establishing a person's identity, i.e., to determine who that person is.

Although biometric technologies measure various features be very different methods, all biometric systems begin by an enrolment followed by a validation that may be used for verification or identification.

In the course of enrolment, the system is taught to recognise a person. Firstly, the person provides an identification document, for example, the National ID. Biometrics will be combined with the other system used for ensuring the individual's identity.

Subsequently, the individual submits the biometric parameter (fingerprint, hand, iris, etc.) through a detector for feature acquisition. Distinctive parameters are identified, extracted, codified and stored for the purpose of performing comparisons in the future.

Depending on the technology used, biometric data will be stored as an image, a sound or as a measurement.

The manner of performing this identification, extraction, codification and storage depends on the algorithms used by the system manufacturer.

Templates may be stored remotely in a central database or in the memory of the biometric receiver-reader itself. In fact, their small size enables data to be stored in smart cards or as files.

Minor position changes, distance, pressure, ambient conditions and other factors have a large impact on template generation. Consequently, every time an individual's biometric data are captured, the resulting template becomes unique.

Depending on the biometric system, a person may need to be "read" several times for enrolment. Subsequently, the reference template may be a combination of all the data captured, or several templates may be stored. Template quality is critical to appropriate performance of the biometric application.

Given the fact that biometric features are subject to changes, individuals' parameters may need to be enrolled again for template update. Some systems can even update templates while performing recognitions.

Enrolment process further depends on the reliability of the ID provided by the individual.

The reference template is linked to the documented identity; therefore, if that does not reflect the individual's true identity, the reference template will be associated with a false identity.

On verification systems, the next step to enrolment is verifying that the individual is who he/she reports to be; furthermore that he/she is the enrolled individual. This may be done by information and intelligence techniques. Once the individual provides the ID, biometric data are taken, thereby creating a check template based on the manufacturer's algorithm.

The system compares the newly received template, produced by the individual arriving at the control access, to the reference template for that individual, and determines the match between the reference and the real time template.

Often verification is applied through 1:1 matching systems. Verification systems may contain databases with dozens of millions of templates; however, the arriving individual is not compared against all of them, but only with the template of the person that he/she reports to be.

On more advanced systems, all verification systems may perform the matching detection process in less than a second. A system aimed at identifying employees prior to them accessing a building or a computer is a verification system.

On identification systems, the subsequent step to enrolment is individual identification. Conversely to verification systems, no ID or proof of identity is produced here. For matching, instead of locating and comparing the reference template with real time acquired data, the latter are compared with all reference templates found in the database.

Therefore, identification systems are referred to 1:N matching.

Two identification systems exist: positive and negative.

Positive identification systems are designed to ensure that an individual is enrolled in the database. The expected result is a match.

This is a fast system for employee identification; employee identity is irrelevant, but it is relevant to know that he/she is an employee.

Negative identification systems are designed to ensure that an individual's biometric information is not in the database. The expected result is a no match.

An example would be those systems that scan databases in order to check that a person who is requesting a grant has not had it already awarded.

Individuals with biometric data enrolled in databases may not have provided them willingly. In fact, biometric data from individuals' faces may be acquired through cameras placed in public locations.

A no match is always a good result, both for identification and for verification, since every time biometric information is captured, the template is unique. Therefore, biometric systems may be configured to make a match or no match decision based on a predefined probability number, the threshold, which is the acceptable degree of similarity between the real time template and the reference template.

After comparison, a result is generated that represents the degree of similarity; this result is compared to the threshold to produce the match verdict.

Depending on the identification system threshold, sometimes several reference templates may match the real time template.

5.2 Various biometric technologies

The amount of biometric technologies has grown over recent years. Only in the past five years those that had a wider application have been replaced by alternative technologies.

Some technologies adapt better to certain processes than others; the same may be said for the various user types.

The seven most significant biometric technologies are listed below:

- Facial recognition
- Fingerprint recognition
- Hand geometry
- Iris recognition
- Retina recognition
- Written signature recognition
- Voice recognition

5.2.1 Facial recognition technology

Facial recognition technology allows identifying individuals by analysing face features that may not be easily altered (superciliary arches, cheek bone surrounding areas or mouth sides).

This technology is normally used for comparing real time facial data acquired even in motion with stored templates, but may also be used for comparing static images like those on passports.

Facial recognition is used both for verification and identification. Furthermore, since face images may be easily taken from video cameras, facial recognition is the only biometric system that may be used in surveillance.

It is therefore a controversial technique. From the user's standpoint it is an attractive method, but it presents many practical difficulties, such as recognising a face amongst a group of people, which is different to comparing two images.

Once technical limitations are resolved, it evidently becomes a technology with a promising future.

5.2.2 Fingerprint recognition

Fingerprint recognition is one of the most developed and more widely used biometric systems.

Automated systems have been commercially available from the early seventies, and currently up to 75 companies can be found developing and enhancing fingerprint recognition systems.

Until recently, they were basically used by State Security Forces.

This technology extracts features from fingerprints; data acquisition may be done by flat or peripheral acquisition devices. A flat print captures only one area between the beginning and the end of the first phalanx, while a peripheral capture includes sides and even the top side of the phalanx.

The fingerprint image is captured with a scanner, divided and converted into a template. Scanners may be optical, silicone or ultrasound.

Ultrasonic technology, though the most precise, is not however the most extended; optical technology is the most used.

During analysis, the "noise" originated by dirt, cuts, grazes, wrinkles, dryness or humidity, wear, etc., is reduced, and ridge definition is amplified.

Approximately 80% of the manufacturers base their algorithms on the extraction of "minutiae" that mark ridge ends.

Along this line, some techniques attempt to detect when the fingerprint corresponds to a "live" finger. These techniques exhibit a high precision, except when inappropriately used. Verification through fingerprint may be recommended for daily use systems, where users may be appropriately trained, and also because of its low cost and small detector sizes, which may be integrated, for example, on computer keyboards.

An individual's fingerprint has traditionally been an appropriate pattern for unequivocally determining identity, since it is accepted that two fingers will never exhibit similar fingerprints, not even in the case of twins or with fingers from the same individual.

Therefore, it seemed evident that fingerprints would become, sooner or later, a biometric authentication model: from the past century to our time, systematic fingerprint classifications have been carried out successfully in police environments; for this reason, the use of such patterns was one of the first to become established as a biometric authentication model (see Figure 5.1).

Fingerprint with extracted minutiae

Figure 5.1

When a user wishes to be identified by the system, he/she places the finger onto a defined area (the reading area; an ink imprint is never required). An image is there taken, which will subsequently be normalised through a system of fine mirrors for angle correction; it is from this normalised image that minutiae are extracted (certain arches, loops and whorls in the fingerprint) to be compared with those in the database; it is worth highlighting that what the system is capable of analysing is not the fingerprint itself, but rather the minutiae, particularly the relative position of each one. It has been proved that two fingers can never possess more than eight common minutiae and that each has 30 or 40 as a minimum. If the comparison between the relative positions read and those stored in the database is correct, the user is permitted access, and obviously denied in the opposite case.

Fingerprint recognition based systems are relatively economical (as compared to other biometric systems, such as retina pattern based systems); however, against them stands the temporary incapability of authenticating users that may have a wound on their finger (a small graze or burn affecting several minutiae that may render the system useless). Other elements such as finger dirt, pressure exerted onto the reader or skin condition also may cause erroneous readings.

Another factor to take very much into account against these systems is not technical but psychological: it has been said in the introduction that a user authentication system should be acceptable to the users, and generally fingerprint recognition is associated with criminals, for which reason many users have misgivings about the recogniser and its use.

5.2.3 Hand geometry recognition

Hand geometry recognition based biometric systems have been used for about 30 years in access control at nuclear and other facilities. This method is based on taking 96 hand metrics parameters, including finger widths, heights and lengths, distances between fingers and knuckle shapes.

For data acquisition, an optical camera and LED light is used, together with mirrors and reflectors that capture two 2D orthogonal images of hand dorsum and sides.

Although the basic hand shape of an individual will remain relatively unaltered throughout life, natural and environmental factors may involve slight changes. Shapes and dimensions of our hands are reasonably varied, but not highly distinctive; therefore, this system is not used for identification purposes.

These systems are adequate for bases of many users with infrequent access and less predisposition and discipline towards being detected. Precision may be adjusted to a high level; furthermore, this technique is very scenario adaptable.

5.2.4 Iris recognition

Iris recognition biometric technology is based on the distinctiveness of the colour rings surrounding the eye pupil. Made of an elastic connective tissue, the iris constitutes the source of a large amount of biometric data, containing about 266 distinctive features, amongst which the trabecular meshwork, a tissue providing an apparent radial division of the iris including furrows, rings, a corona, wrinkles and freckles.

Iris recognition technology uses normally up to 173 of the 266 distinctive features.

These features, which are formed during the eight month of pregnancy, remain very stable throughout the individual's life, unless eye injury occurs.

Iris recognition may be used both for verification and identification.

These systems use small, very high resolution cameras to take a black and white image of the eye. During information processing, iris limits are defined, a coordinate system is set on the iris and areas to be analysed are defined and located with reference to the coordinate system.

Infrared analysis makes the use by an attacker with replicate or simulated organs attempting to obtain a false admission virtually impossible, since it is capable of detecting with a high probability whether the iris is natural or not.

Iris scanning is doubtlessly the least intrusive technology, since it uses a conventional CCD camera and does not require intimate contact between the recording system and the individual. Its precision is good, and registration of individuals wearing glasses or contact lenses poses no problems. It has been tested on various ethnic groups.

The present study shows two iris based systems developed by the authors.

The first system is based on iris phase information obtained by the application of a Gabor filter bank.

The second system uses the zero crossing representation of the wavelet transform of a 1D signal, formed from a virtual circular corona of the iris image, producing what is known as the *iris signature code*.

A full assessment was carried out of each of the systems, as well as a comprehensive comparative analysis between the two. From the tests performed, it is important to highlight the 100% classification success obtained for the system based on multiscale zero crossing representation using the binary Hamming distance.

Regarding verification results, a 0.12% Equal Error Rate (EER) was attained on the same system, with the possibility of achieving nil False Acceptance Rates (FAR) for very low False Rejection Rates (FRR), which makes it an optimum system for high security environments.

Amongst all existing techniques, bearing in mind the results obtained to date, the eye iris recognition system is the most adequate for high security environments. It is a non invasive technique, since only a photograph of the eye is required, and it is highly distinguishing of each individual. Indeed, various studies assert that while the general structure of the iris is genetically determined, particulars of its minutiae depend critically on initial conditions in which the embryonic phase develops; therefore, iris features are phenotypic, not genotypic, which confers this technique the same uniqueness as the fingerprint based technique, since even between univiteline twins, irises are found to be different.

As previously discussed when presenting biometrics fundamentals, the issues with biometric identification may be classified in two fundamentally diverse types of situations, with different complexities: recognition (or identification) and verification (or authentication).

Recognition refers to the issue of establishing an individual's identity by identifying the individual from amongst all system users. Therefore, the features of the individual being identified have to be compared with all users' patterns enrolled by the system. This problem requires a pattern database, with the relevant storage capacity and safety requirements, and a communications network in place, always online, linking identification stations with database.

The verification issue attempts to answer, either in the affirmative or the negative, whether the individual's identity is true. In this case, user features are compared only with the previously stored pattern of that individual the user reports to be. Pattern storage may be in this instance on a portable information system; therefore databases or communications networks are unnecessary.

Only two iris recognition system prototypes exist currently, the first developed by Daugman, the feature extraction algorithm of which may be found described with a certain level of detail, as well as a descriptive study of the statistical and singularity properties of iris patterns based in several million comparison tests, and that developed by Wildes. However, this biometric technique still presents various open issues. Thus, more recent works may be found in this direction, amongst which it is worth mentioning those based on texture analysis, which use the iris analytical image built from the original image and its Hilbert transform, based on the wavelet transform, applying Gabor filters and based on the multiscale zero crossing representation.

In this work a comparative study is presented between two iris pattern based recognition systems developed by the authors, the first using iris phase information obtained by the application of a Gabor filter bank and the Hamming distance in the comparison phase, and the second based on the multiscale zero crossing analysis of the discrete dyadic wavelet transform of the *iris signature.*

As an extension to the above, and to be able to explain appropriately the operation of iris systems, a biometric recognition system comprises specifically four stages:

    1) *Capture* of biological (or behavioural) data
    2) *Preprocessing* of captured data
    3) *Extraction of features*, particular to the user
    4) *Comparison* of extracted features with the previously stored pattern

Specifically, as previously discussed, the last stage in a biometric system may be configured in two ways:

– *Classifier* (biometric recognition), where extracted features are compared with the patterns of all users in order to determine the user's identity.

– *Verifier* (biometric verification), where the sample is compared only with the pattern of the user that the individual reports to be, in order to authenticate the user's identity.

The various blocks composing the iris pattern based biometric system design are detailed below, in addition to the results obtained both from classification and from verification.

5.2.4.1 Image capture and preprocessing

Iris image capture is performed with a high resolution photo camera. However, for future work the possibility of using a video camera is considered. In order to avoid user refusal, the necessary optics have been used to enlarge (zoom) the eye image. Figure 5.2(a) shows a sample of the image obtained.

Thus, the first preprocessing step, taking into account the characteristics of the captured images, is a conversion to black and white, followed by a histogram expansion. Once this operation is performed, iris border detection will take place. Beginning from a selected point (x0,y0), this is taken as the centre, and starting thereof the image is sampled, taking the corresponding points from radius and angle increments.

Once the external iris border is detected (see Figure 5.2(b)), all points outside the circumference encircling the iris are deleted; the same process is repeated for internal border detection, i.e., the border between iris and pupil (see Figure 5.2(c)). Finally, points inside the detected internal border are deleted, and the image of Figure 5.2(d) is obtained.

Figure 5.2, (a): Original image; (b): External border detection; (c): Internal border detection; (d): Resulting isolated iris.

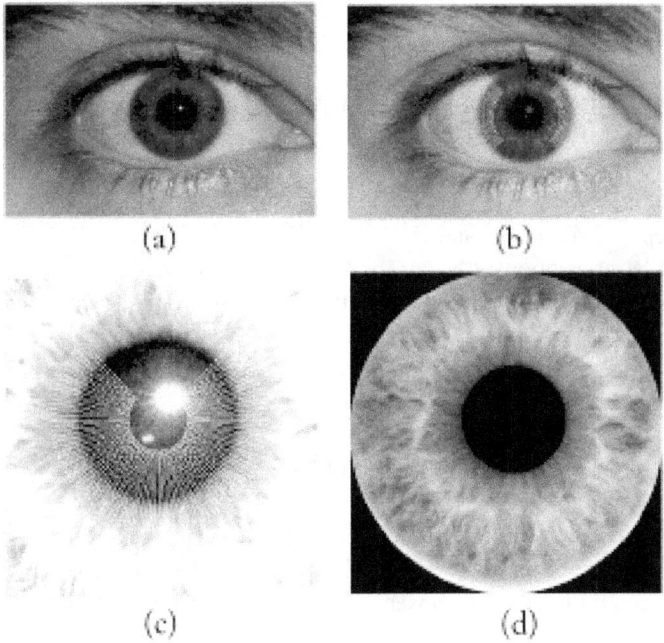

Figure 5.2

5.2.4.2 Feature extraction

This section describes the various algorithms used on the feature extraction stage for both systems here considered. Firstly, the scheme is described that is followed for the system using phase information with the application of a Gabor filter bank to certain sections of the iris image.

Subsequently, the technique used for the second system is explained: the multiscale zero crossing representation of the iris signature, obtained from a circular corona of the iris image, to the determination of the so called *iris signature code*, which will be used in the comparison phase.

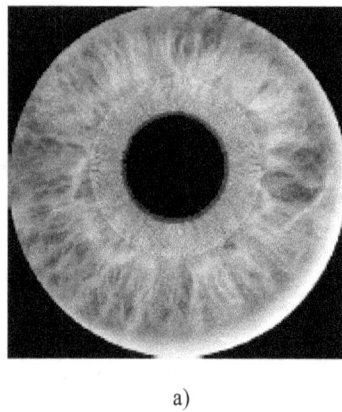
a)
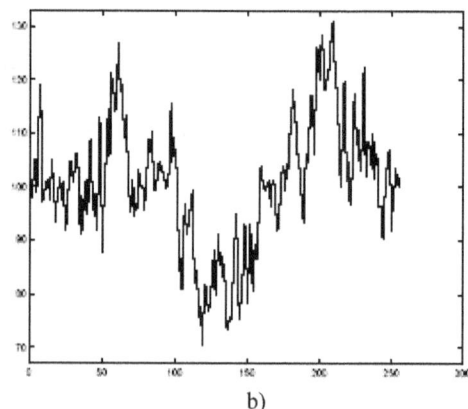
b)

Figure 5.3

Gabor filter bank

The first step in the feature extraction block of the phase information based system is an image transformation. In this transformation, upper and lower iris cones are deleted, and a log polar image sampling is performed.

Subsequently, the preprocessed iris image is multiplied by the imaginary part of a Gabor filter bank obtained from using 4 orientations (0; ¼=4; ¼=2 y 3¼=4). With this, a sequence of Gabor coefficients is obtained, corresponding to each of the square sections in which the preprocessed iris image is divided previously.

The number of selected sections will define feature vector size.

Multiscale zero crossing representation. Iris signature

On the second human iris pattern based biometric system, the first step in the feature extraction block is obtaining a data set from each isolated iris image that may allow an appropriate feature extraction. The pupil centroid has been chosen, detected as a reference point, in order to obtain the data set.

Thus, a new *iris signature* definition is proposed as an alternative to that proposed above; its elaboration is as follows: grey level values, gr, are extracted from each contour of a virtual circle centred over the pupil centroid with radius ½, such that $\rho i \leq \rho \leq \rho e$, where ρi and ρe are two previously considered radii (internal and external) (see Figure 5.3(a)), and taking angular increments of $2\pi = Ls$, where $Ls = 256$, the sequence length (previously fixed) resulting from sampling the data of each virtual circle.

Finally, the data set known as *iris signature* (*IS*):

$$IS = \frac{1}{r_e - r_i + 1} \sum_{r=r_i}^{r_e} g_r$$

Figure 5.3(b) shows and example of *iris signature*, corresponding to the isolated iris shown in Figure 5.2(d).

Figure 5.3(a): Annular region (corresponding to the iris on Figure 5.2(d)) as taken for obtaining the iris signature shown on (b).

Discrete dyadic wavelet transform

When attempting to use iris patterns for biometric identification, it is important to define a representation capable of extracting iris information from its signature. To that end, multiscale zero crossing representation of the iris signature discrete dyadic wavelet transform will be used, as described below:

Being $\psi_\tau(\chi)$ the expanded version of a function ψ by a scale factor τ:

$$\psi\tau = 1/\tau(\chi/\tau)$$

The continuous wavelet transform of a function $f(x)$ on the scale τ may be written as the following convolution:

$$W\tau f(\chi) = f * \psi\tau(\chi)$$

A wavelet is any function of $L2(R)$ satisfying the admissibility condition.

It may be observed that wavelet $\tilde{A}(x)$ may be interpreted as the impulse response of a bandpass filter. The transform of a function f, therefore, may be seen as the result of applying a family of expanded bandpass filters to function f.

Iris signature zero crossing representation

When the most significant information of a signal is contained on various scales, it is convenient to reorganise signal information in a "detail components" set, through the so called multiscale analysis. It is known that the position of points corresponding to rapid signal variations may be obtained from the zero crossings of the multiscale analysis of the signal convoluted with the Laplacian of a Gaussian.

This procedure has been successfully used in numerous applications related with patter recognition. Clearly, one of the main objectives is checking whether zero crossings define a full, stable representation of the original signal. Furthermore, it is necessary to bear in mind, particularly for those applications related with pattern recognition, that some significant components are deleted from the signal when represented by its multiscale zero crossings.

Therefore, in order to obtain a full, stable representation of the information contained in the *iris signature*, the zero crossings of the discrete dyadic wavelet transform of the *iris signature* (IS) are considered, i.e., instead of considering the zero crossings of the discrete dyadic wavelet transform on continuous scales, a restriction to dyadic scales is made, and the transform value is calculated between two consecutive zero crossings.

In practice, input signal, *iris signature* in this case, has been measured with a finite resolution, which imposes the finest scale for calculating the dyadic wavelet transform; on the other hand, it would not be possible to calculate the transform for all scales $2j$ for:

$$-\infty < j < +\infty$$

Indeed, the finest and the largest scales set the limits, which are assumed to be, for the sake of normalisation, 1 and $2j$ respectively. Thus, the discrete dyadic wavelet transform of the *iris signature* (IS) is obtained.

In the present study, coarsest and finest levels have been excluded in order to obtain a robust representation in a noisy environment and, at the same time, to decrease computational load. As it is known, the information contained in the finer resolution levels is strongly contaminated by noise affecting the system, as well as by quantification errors. Therefore, in order to reduce such effects on zero crossing representation, only intermediate resolution levels are considered. Specifically, three levels have been considered in the present study, corresponding to $3 \leq j \leq 5$.

Iris signature code

In order to apply the Hamming binary distance to the feature vector obtained by using the zero crossing representation, the *iris signature code* is defined as a binary sequence obtained in the following manner: for each scale, it is considered that the value of that binary sequence is 1 when the value of the zero crossing representation of the iris signature on that scale is positive or nil, and 0 otherwise.

These ocular methods are usually considered as the most effective: over a population of 200 million potential users, the coincidence probability is close to 0; furthermore, once an individual dies, eye tissues degrade rapidly, this hindering false acceptance of attackers that might steal the organ from a corpse.

The main disadvantage with ocular pattern analysis based methods is their scarce acceptance; the fact of having to look through a binocular (or monocular), which is required for both models, is not comfortable for users, neither acceptable for many of them: on the one hand, users *do not trust* a light beam analysing their eye, and on the other hand, an examination of this organ may reveal diseases or medical features that many persons may wish to conceal, such as alcohol or drug consumption.

Although manufacturers of reading devices assure that the eye is analysed only to obtain authentication related patterns and in no case user privacy is violated, many persons do not accept this official positioning (besides the fact that information is software processed, which enables the introduction of modifications on what is being advertised so that a reader may perform other tasks under cover).

Furthermore, systems are too expensive for most organisations, and the authentication process is not as speedy as it should be for large user populations. Thus, its use becomes restricted almost to only the identification in high security systems, such as military facility access control or in Port Authority sensitive areas.

Probability of false acceptance is the lowest of all biometric models.

5.2.4.3 Retina recognition

Retina recognition technology captures and analyses vascular network patterns in the very fine nerve located at the rear of the ocular globe, by introducing light through the pupil.

Retinal patterns constitute highly distinctive parameters.

Each eye possesses its own, unique vascular pattern; even eyes of identical univiteline twins are different. Although each pattern remains normally stable throughout a person's life, it may be affected by diseases such as glaucoma, diabetes, hypertension, and even AIDS.

Since the retina is small, interior and difficult to measure, capturing its image, and therefore its specific features, is the most involved of all biometric technologies.

The individual should place the eye very close to the retina scanner lens, staring straight into the lens and remaining totally motionless; an infrared light beam focuses on and follows a spiral path while a camera scans the retina through the pupil. Any movement may interfere with the process, causing it to reinitiate. This recording may easily take over a minute.

This is a drawback if the individual wears glasses or is reluctant to placing the eye on the receiver.

5.2.5 Writing (signature) recognition

Writing recognition authenticates identity through the measurement of handwriting.

The text or signature contains the tracks of a series of motions that include unique biometric data, such as writing rhythm, acceleration and pressure flow.

Conversely to electronic writing capture, which handles writing as an image, writing recognition technology measures how it is done.

In a writing recognition system, an individual writes his/her name on a digital tablet or on a device designed for the purpose. The system analyses the dynamic writing parameters, such as velocity, relative velocity, order of strokes, number of strokes and pressure flow. This technology is even capable of tracking and recording the natural writing fluctuations of a person along time. The information on dynamic writing parameters is encrypted and compressed into a template.

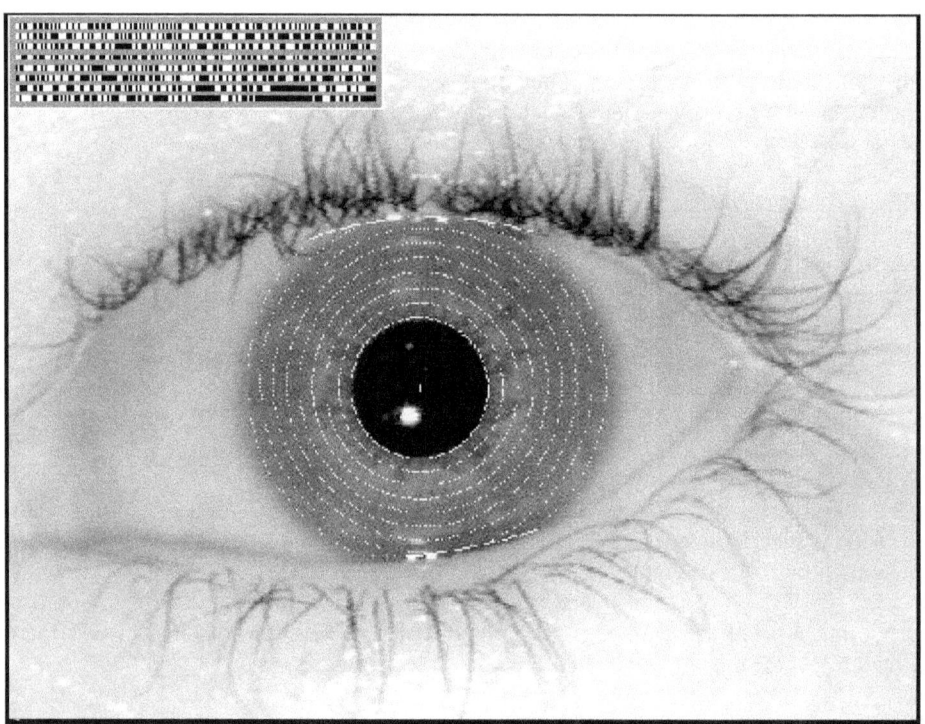

Figure 5.4

Signature verification is more accepted than other technologies. It is sufficiently precise, and its use is particularly adequate to applications where signature is an accepted identifier. Strangely enough, it has not seen the development it should.

Although writing (generally the signature) is not a strictly biometric feature, it is usually grouped within that category; as the case is with voice verification, the objective here is not interpreting or comprehending what the user is writing on the reader, but rather authenticating the individual, based on certain traits found both in the signature and in the flourish.

Verification through signature is an everyday method used and accepted by all for documents or checks; however, a fundamental difference exists between the everyday use of signatures and biometric systems; while signature verification usually consists of a mere visual analysis of a static imprint on paper, it is not possible to authenticate users with automatic systems based on the representation of signature strokes. Biometric models make use also of the manner of signing, the dynamic characteristics (hence they are normally referred to as *Dynamic Signature Verification*, DSV): time used on the flourish, the times the pen loses contact with the paper, the angle at which each stroke is made.

In order to use a signature based authentication system, firstly future users are requested a given number of example signatures, from which the system extracts and stores certain features; this stage is known as *learning*, and the main obstacle to its correct execution are those users who do not tend to sign uniformly. Against this problem, the only solution (besides user education) is relaxing system restrictions when *learning* signatures, which decreases safety.

Once the system knows the users' signatures, when they intend accessing they will be requested to sign, with a limited number of attempts (generally more than with password based authentication systems, since an individual's signature may vary due to multiple factors).

The signature is captured by an optical pen or a sensitive reader (or both), and access is granted once the user has provided a signature that the verifier is capable of distinguishing as authentic.

5.2.6 Voice recognition

Differences between voices of various persons are produced by physiological variations of vocal cord shape and acquired speech and pronunciation habits.

Voice recognition technology uses these differences in order to discriminate between various speakers.

During recording, voice recognition systems capture characteristic points in the individual's monologue while repeating a text for a predetermined number of times.

This information, known as "key phrase", may be the name, month of birth, birthplace, favourite colour or a number sequence.

Text independent systems also allow individual recognition, without using a predefined phrase. Such phrases are converted from analogue to digital format, and distinctive vocal features are extracted such as tone, cadence, timbre, so that a diction model is created, whereupon a register is generated and stored for future comparisons.

Voice recognition may be used for identity authentication or for individual identification. It is often used when voice is the only biometric parameter available, like on telephone recordings.

Unlike what many may think, voice recognition systems do not attempt to comprehend what the user is saying, but rather to identify a series of sounds and their features for deciding whether the user is who he/she reports to be.

Voice recognition based user authentication requires certain conditions for data recording, such as absence of noise, reverberations or echo; ideally, such conditions should be the same every time authentication is required.

Text dependent systems provide a low security level in comparison with text independent systems.

As the user speaks, the system records all useful information; when the phrase if finished, it should be able to either grant or deny access, depending on the information it has analysed and compared against the database.

The main issue with voice recognition is immunity to *replay attacks*, a simulation attack model in which the attacker reproduces (from a magnetic tape recorder, for example) phrases or words pronounced by the legitimate user when accessing the system. This problem becomes particularly serious on systems based on preestablished texts: going back to the former example, with the user name, an attacker would only need to record a person pronouncing his/her name in front of the authenticator and then replay the sound for gaining access; practically, the only solution is to use another authentication system together with voice recognition, and even the pressure exerted by an access control inspector.

Conversely, on text independent models, which are more interactive, this attack is not so simple because authentication is really performed through a kind of challenge-response interaction between the user and the machine, so that the quantity of recorded text would need to be much larger, and the speed to locate the text section prompted by the machine would have to be high.

Another serious problem with voice recognition based systems is the time used by the user speaking in front of the analyser, to which the time required for information extraction and comparison with the database should be added; even though nowadays most systems require only one phrase, it is normal that the user is prompted to repeat it because the system denies access (a simple congestion modifies the tone of voice, slightly as it may be, and the system is incapable of deciding whether to authorise access or not; even a person's state of mind causes the timbre to change...).

As a pro, voice recognition has the quality of being very well accepted by users, as long as it operates correctly and they are not prompted to repeat over and over the same thing, or they are denied access because of not being appropriately recognised.

There are many advantages attached to voice recognition, such as:

- It is considered to be a "natural" biometric technology
- Leaves eyes and hands free
- Reliability
- Flexibility
- Time savings on information entry
- Eliminates pronunciation errors

The main concern on voice identification systems is how to recognise voice variations every time someone speaks. In order to eliminate such type of variations, the Hidden Markov comprehension process is applied.

The basis for this software system is that it utilizes language models to determine how many different words resemble one specifically. The advantage is that word groups (matching word pools) that sound similar are dramatically reduced. Error indices in this language type range from 1% to 15%.

Apart from the two described systems, text dependent and text independent, other voice identification technologies exist, currently available or under development:

Discrete Speech Input

Based on the fact that when the person speaks, small pauses take place, of about 1/10 of a second, between words. This enables the system to recognise the beginning and the end of a word.

Continuous Speech Input

Users may speak continuously, but the identification system may recognise a limited amount of words and phrases. Only applicable to predetermined word recognition.

Natural Speech Input

This is the desirable system, which recognises natural speech, but it is still undergoing development.

There are two application methodologies associated with the use of voice identification: dedicated hardware or software.

5.2.7 Other biometric recognition systems

Researches indicate that human ear analysis may be used as an identification method.

Currently, experts at Leicester University (United Kingdom) are developing this technology, based on photographs taken from this organ for subsequent software based analysis and comparison against an existing database.

The advantage with this system is its much lower aggressiveness with respect to others such as retina or fingerprint scanning, since no physical contact is required.

Furthermore, the study looks into the maximum distance from which photographs could be taken in order to perform a reliable identification.

Figure 5.5 shows an image of an ear and the software based definition of the most significant data for comparison.

The big disadvantage of this system is the simplicity, given the advances in makeup and plastic surgery, to deceive the system with false elements since, as discussed, only ear shape is analysed, and no other parameter.

As for many of the systems described, information generated by this analysis may be stored in smart cards, so that databases are no longer required; the system itself may perform the identification and compare against the information stored in the card. In this manner, the user may hold a personal card with biometric data that may be used as an unequivocal identity recognition method.

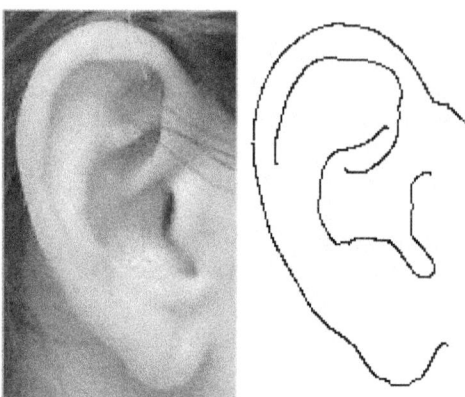

Figure 5.5

Biometrics is an ever expanding field, expected to be in the future the standard for authentication systems; meanwhile, researchers will continue enhancing their products, attempting to solve one of the major problems faced by biometric safety, namely false positives and false negatives; although they have been reduced to a large extent, it is essential to reduce them to 0%.

Chapter 6. Control of individuals and goods

6.1 Passenger control and baggage search

A passenger list should be prepared, and ticket data should be checked against IDs or passports. Company employees will fill in the attached data for passenger baggage labelling prior to searches (see Table 6.1).

Baggage search should be carried out in a concealed area, witnessed by the passenger. Searches will be random, following the indications of the terminal common area control personnel, who, by applying the aforementioned suspect detection techniques will mark those passengers to be checked.

Given the peculiarities of maritime transport, procedures as followed in civil aviation become ineffective here, since passengers board frequently with bulky packages and a large number of suitcases that hinder automatic detection due to their size. This forces having to enable a parallel check line for manual search.

Inspection speed will depend on security personnel's skill and technical means available.

Passenger admittance questionnaire:

Nº 0000	(SHIP DATA) PASSENGER CONTROL	DATE: 00/00/00
		REMARKS
NAME		
1st SURNAME		
2nd SURNAME		
GENDER		
AGE		
NATIONALITY		
ID / PASSPORT No.		

BAGGAGE ITEM	SECURITY LABELLING	REMARKS
1st	No. XXXXXX/YYYY	Description
2nd		
3rd		
4th		
5th		

Table 6.1

6.2 Ticket control and baggage search area

Once the boarding pass is delivered, all passenger baggage will proceed to the preboarding area through the access control, following the appropriate safety protocols. Once inside the safe area, baggage will be handed back (see Figure 6.1).

Reinforcement of level 2 and 3 safety measures will focus on systematic search of all baggage; on voyages shorter than 4 hours, baggage will be handed back at destination.

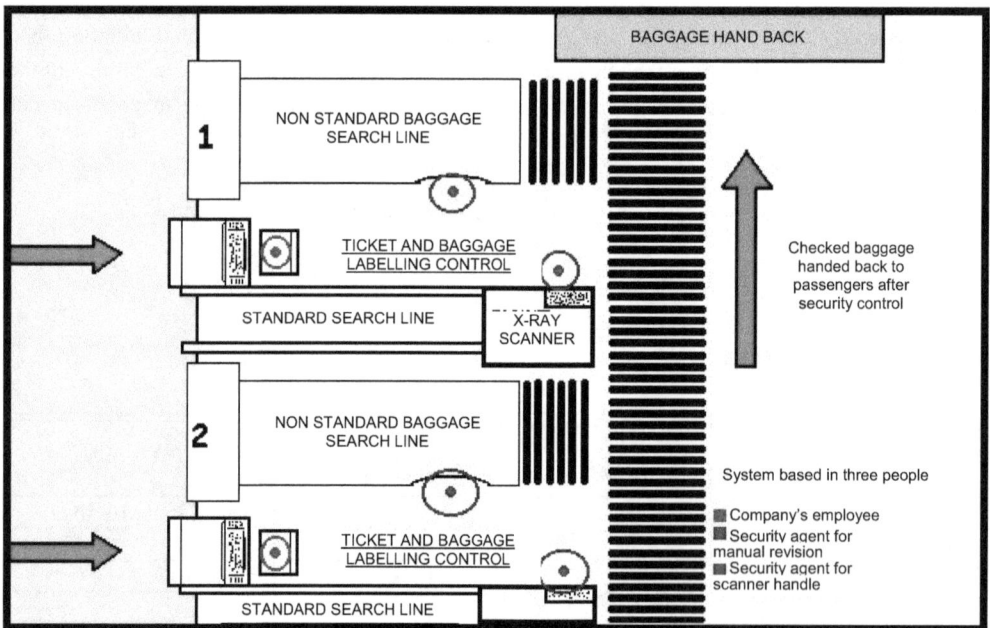

Figure 6.1

Passenger questioning by suspect detection experts and manual baggage search show to be very effective as a complement to the recommended measures for level 1. In any case, general risk level should be evaluated, as well as specific risk for particular ship types, which may vary.

6.3 Access control

Access controls should be categorised based on filtering level. Level evaluation, scoring from 0 to 5, should consider the number of barriers to be crossed by the aggressor, accessed area safety level, access control risk level as an objective, and allocated means to assist the task of the human factor performing control (see Table 6.2).

LEVEL	ACCESSED AREA:	RISK LEVEL	Remarks
0	Free transit	1	Normally exits and no strategic interest areas
1	Free transit with suspect detection	2	No strategic interest areas, close to sensitive areas
2	Restricted	3	General services, Pilot's Office, port medical services
3	High risk restricted	4	Preboarding areas and public concentration areas
4	Prohibited	4	Damage on infrastructures and emergency control centres
5	High risk prohibited	5	Damage on infrastructures and great loss of human lives

Table 6.2

Area and access control examples:

- **Level 0**   Port boundary area, away from any sensitive area
- **Level 1**   No strategic interest port areas, such as sheds and warehouses
- **Level 2**   Port general services areas, such as pilot offices
- **Level 3**   Preboarding areas, ship access gangways
- **Level 4**   Maritime control and emergency centres
- **Level 5**   Chemical and radiological product storage areas

All these levels may vary depending on port characteristics, both constructive and operational. Neglecting this and setting standard parameters will lead to a sensitive degradation of port performance without a clear benefit to safety.

Review of control measure adaption and application of operating schemes should compensate for alert levels with the risk and vulnerability levels of the areas separating access controls.

Bidirectional access controls should always cross data by real time information processing. The support provided by the means as described in the project are a support to human factor, but they never guarantee access tightness. The only guarantee for performance is security personnel training.

6.4 Passenger access control structure

This access allows entering a high risk restricted area; the free transit area with suspect detection is in turn a significant risk area, due to the concentration of public.

Regretfully, access control may not be set up for accessing this area. The control system should be a mixed system, one part being visible, including security agents in uniform, another part not being apparent, with security agents mixing amongst customers for suspect detection.

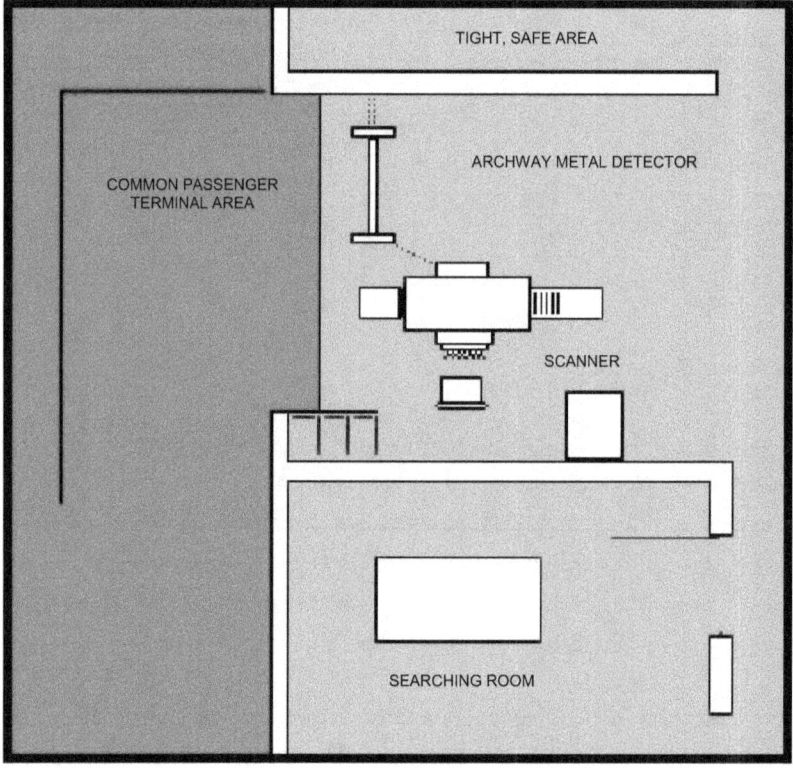

Figure 6.2

6.5 Non admitted or restricted goods at the access

The port represents the first control filter for persons and materials before reaching the ship. The presence of goods with restricted use in port areas, which may be identified by any crew member of a ship, represents a possible safety violation, and should be taken into account if other indications appear leading to a risk criterion.

The items listed below may not be carried when going through access control. If such were the case, the bearer might be committing an offence against the regulations in force, and may be forced to deposit or deliver the suspicious item.

The access control inspector should apply his/her judgement to perform such characterisation, depending on the item and the circumstances, since carrying an object subject to seizure into an access control is considered to be illegal, even if done by mistake.

The item should be examined; its potential use as an attacking object or its risk to cause an accident should be assessed. If the option should be considered, the possibility may be consulted of carrying the item in the checked in baggage, by leaving the access control after registering in a special log, or relinquishing the item.

The list below shows permitted and prohibited items, both for hand baggage or personal belongings and for checked in baggage in the case of travellers, or that may or may not be carried inside a vehicle when accessing the Port Authority facilities.

Particular attention should be paid to the footnotes of each table, which include valuable information relevant to restrictions. The inspector will always have the authority to declare an item as hazardous, even though it may appear as authorised in the list.

Tables should not be considered as final; they may include new items:

- Materials that may be hazardous because during inspection they may be considered as harmful or as weapons (the so called double purpose items).
- Heat sources. Explosive or incendiary items and artefacts.
- Chemical, biological or radiological/nuclear agents or sources.
- Illegal or illegally borne weapons.
- Acetylene tanks not appropriately traced at each Port Authority.

The following tables show a checklist procedure that provides inspection consistency, whatever the inspector's expertise; it provides for time saving and successful follow on management.

List

Permitted through access control?	Hand carried	Checked in
Personal belongings.		
Cigar cutters.	Yes	Yes
Cork screw.	No	Yes
Nail clipper and files.	No	Yes
Spectacle repair tools (including screwdrivers).	No	Yes
Eyelash curlers.	No	Yes
Knitting needles or crochet hooks.	No	Yes
Round tip (butter spreaders) or plastic knives.	No	Yes
Lighters.	Yes*	No
Personal care or beauty products including aerosols to a limited amount (hair lacquer or deodorants).	No	Si
Safety razor blades (including disposables).	No	Yes
Rounded tip metal or plastic scissors.	No	Yes
Pointed tip metal or plastic scissors.	No	Yes
Toy transformers robots.	Yes	Yes
Toy weapons (not replicas).	Yes	Yes
Depilation tweezers.	Yes	Yes
Umbrellas and parasols (permitted with hand baggage once inspected for concealed hazardous items).	Yes	Yes
Crutches and sticks (permitted with hand baggage once inspected for concealed hazardous items).	Yes	Yes
* Up to 2 lighters or 4 matchboxes are permitted in hand baggage, NOT IN CHECKED IN BAGGAGE. Disposable lighters are permitted. Petrol lighters or similar are NOT permitted. All-weather matches are NOT permitted. Some personal care items containing aerosols will be considered as hazardous materials.		

Medicines and special care items.		
Braille writing capture devices, blackboards and chalk (composition of which should be checked), magnifying lenses.	Yes	Yes
Items for diabetics including: insulin and insulin preloaded syringes; medicine flasks or boxes; pens and markers; needles; glucometers; glucometer strips; insulin pumps; insulin pump accessories. Insulin in any form should be appropriately marked with a printed label by a registered practitioner or a laboratory identifying the substance and manufacturer. These items should be inspected for concealed hazardous items.	Yes	Yes
Nitroglycerine pills or sprays for medical purposes (if appropriately marked with a printed label by a registered practitioner or laboratory identifying the substance and manufacturer).	Yes	Yes

Prosthetic tools or utensils, including drills, hex key wrenches, straps for securing or removing prostheses if accompanying the prostheses (once inspected for concealed hazardous items).	Yes	Yes

Electronic devices		
Cameras (once inspected for concealed hazardous items).	Yes	Yes
Camera accessories. Some baggage checking devices may damage unused film; it is recommended that unused films should be carried separately in the hand baggage for inspection.	Yes	Yes
Laptops (once inspected for concealed hazardous items).	Yes	Yes
Mobile telephones (once inspected for concealed hazardous items).	Yes	Yes
Agendas (once inspected for concealed hazardous items).	Yes	Yes
Note: Permission should be requested to use during voyage or within Port Authority facilities.		

Sharp items		
Cutters.	No	Yes
Ice picks.	No	Yes
Knives of any length.	No	Yes
Carving knives.	No	Yes
Blades of any types, including those in multipurpose tools.	No	Yes
Swords.	No	Yes
Note: Any sharp items in checked in baggage should be appropriately packed in order to avoid injuries during baggage handling.		

Sports goods		
Baseball bats	No	Yes
Bows and arrows	No	Yes
Cricket bats	No	Yes
Golf clubs	No	Yes
Hockey sticks	No	Yes
Tennis rackets	No	Yes
Polo sticks	No	Yes
Ski sticks	No	Yes
Harpoons	No	Yes

Weapons		
For each case, an ammunition transfer study should be performed. If admitted, carried goods should be declared. Wood, fibre, metal or specifically designed containers should be used for carriage. Quantity and type limitations should be established.	No	Yes
Airsoft weapons.	No	Yes
Airguns.	No	Yes
Firearms.	No	Yes
Flares.	No	No
Lighters and flamethrowers.	No	No
Gunpowder.	No	No
Weapon components and parts.	No	Yes
Firearm replicas.	No	Yes
Note: A procedure should be in place for firearm carriage during voyage or within facilities. As a general rule, no weapons may be carried whatsoever. Those carried in the baggage (as long as they are not weapons requiring to be deposited) should be carried in cases with code locks, unloaded, without ammunition and with clips separate from the weapon. Only the owner should know the lock code or hold the key.		

Tools		
Axes.	No	Yes
Branding irons.	No	Yes
Levers.	No	Yes
Hammers.	No	Yes
Drills (including battery powered).	No	Yes
Saws (including battery powered).	No	Yes
Screwdrivers (including battery powered).	No	Yes
Tools (including spanners, pliers and pincers).	No	Yes

Martial arts or self defence items		
Billy clubs.	No	Yes
Blackjacks.	No	Yes
Brass knuckles.	No	Yes
Protections.	No	Yes
Tear gas sprays.	No	Yes
Martial arts weapons.	No	Yes
Cyalume light sticks.	No	Yes
Electric pistols.	No	Yes
Shurikens.	No	Yes
Nunchakus.	No	Yes

Explosive materials		
Detonators.	No	No
Dynamite.	No	No
Fire crackers.	No	No
Flares.	No	No
Grenades.	No	No
Plastic explosives and detonator cord.	No	No
Replicas of artefacts.	No	No

Flammable items		
Aerosols (all except for personal care sprays in limited quantities).	No	No
Fuels (including those for cookers and any flammable liquid).	No	No
Petrol.	No	No
Gas cartridges.	No	No
Lighter recharges.	No	No
All weather matches.	No	No
Turpentine, paint strippers.	No	No
Replicas of artefacts.	No	No

Chemicals and other hazardous products		
Chlorine for pools and spas.	No	No
Pressurised gas cartridges or bottles, including fire extinguishers.	No	No
Liquid bleach.	No	No
Batteries (except those on wheelchairs).	No	No
Spray paint.	No	No
Tear gas.	No	No

6.6 Suspect identification through body language

The need for detecting suspects appears from the moment in which, having analysed those events that may pose threats to the safety of maritime operations and transport in general, it has been proven that such risks are associated with individuals to a major extent. It may be said that as long as current safety systems are appropriately applied and while there be no failures in this sense, possibilities of unaccompanied goods becoming a risk to the maritime industry are dramatically reduced.

The object of the application of body language techniques to suspect detection is focussed on capturing intentions and detecting states of mind.

When an individual decides to perform an action that in one way or another may constitute a threat to some goods or a person, the individual's internal tension undergoes a number of changes that may make intentions apparent. Even on individuals with a good level of training on body language concealment, certain indications may surface. Their magnitude will be the larger, the bigger the risk that the individual may be incurring is.

Anticipating the action involves breaching the attacker's initiative at the time of committing an action. This anticipation, besides providing and added tool for defence, represents a setback for the attacker so that the individual's internal tension based indications are magnified, thus making it easier to identify a suspect.

Taken as a defence tool, it allows responding with a more effective capacity by breaching the attacker's initiative, even if the detected suspect is made unaware of the fact that information is being drawn from him/her.

In situations of tension, all the involved elements are under tension, so that it may be possible also for the suspect to identify the defender's condition; particular attention should be paid to this aspect when managing the decision making process for a given intervention.

Within the scope of the present case, elements placing pressure on the suspect in the face of an eventual detection are physical injuries, if the aggression is suppressed, and legal consequences of the action. This aspect should be carefully examined for cases of integrist terrorism, since tension parameters based on legal consequences do not generally have a bearing on actions by such individuals.

Implementation of body language techniques in the procedures should begin by training security personnel.

The process begins by enhancing observation processes (sight provides only for data collection, but observation leads sight to those indications that are relevant to collect) of gesticulatory indications (particularly of contradictions) and memorisation of physiological, physiognomic and psychological features of the individual under examination. Subsequently, knowledge of gesticulatory indications would be added.

Questioning techniques are added on a third level, so that the inspector performing the control may have the necessary tools available in order to place the individual under a directed pressure, with the purpose of checking possible actions aimed at finding behavioural breaches in the individual.

Basic states of mind to be detected are:

- Barriers – Defences
- Insecurity
- Tension
- Nervousness
- Lies.

And, encompassing the above, the appearance of contradictions, both gesticulatory and verbal.

Such contradictions will constitute the clearest indication on which to base suspicions.

The detection process begins by observing the appearance, magnitude and changes of the indications. The three reference points for developing the process are: observing the adoption of defensive positions in contradiction to the role of the potential suspect; the magnitude or magnitude variation of the individual's actions; and, the appearance of signs of retreat.

Throughout the process, pressure placed on the individual should be administered in order to keep the situation under control.

6.7 Observable indications

DEFENCE & BARRIERS

Arms crossed over.
Lowered head, looking aside.
Crossed legs.
Concealed hands.
Concealed body areas.

TENSION

Tense or stiff limbs or features.
Contained or superficial breathing.
Itching.

INSECURITY

Search for furniture support.
Doubtful motions.
Lassitude.

NERVOUSNESS

Coughing and throat clearing.
Sighing.
Half spent cigarettes or chain smoking.
Uncontrolled limb motion.
Involuntary, unaware fiddling.

CONTRADICTIONS

Lack of natural acting.
Forced smiling.
Becoming withdrawn.

PHYSIOLOGICAL PARAMETERS

Perspiration.
Breathing.

6.8 Light weapons, incendiary and explosive items

6.8.1 Introduction

Recent terrorist acts have shown that light weapons and explosive and incendiary items have caused a more significant impact than non conventional or mass destruction weapons. On 1996 the World Health Organisation (WHO) set a priority on the prevention of violence and related damages, as it is estimated that this will be, together with wars, one of the main death causes by 2020. From a public health standpoint, such damages have a common factor: they are caused by an inappropriate energy discharge from a light weapon, a bomb explosion or an incendiary device, such as an AK-47, a Molotov cocktail or a fuel laden commercial aeroplane.

Many damages are caused by an abnormal energy transfer or interference: mechanical energy; kinetic energy, causing three quarters of the total damages (missiles, bullets, shrapnel, rubble, car collisions); thermal energy (Molotov cocktail); chemical energy (chemical explosion); radioactive energy (dirty bombs); or the absence of essential elements such as oxygen due to carbon monoxide poisoning after an explosion. Damage prevention strategies lie on the understanding of causal factors, fortuitous connections and intervention procedures.

6.8.2 Light weapons

It is estimated that over 500 000 people die yearly because of light weapon attacks, and for each death, several others are injured or traumatised. Mortality associated with this type of weapons varies depending on the context. Suicide attempts with firearms are mostly fatal (in 92% of the cases); conversely, assaults are often less fatal. War injury indices double war time casualty indices, sometimes becoming 13 times higher. However, when military weapons are used against civilians in confined spaces, like during terrorist strikes or mass killings, injury to death ratios decrease to values below 1:1.

On a worldwide basis, the percentage of deaths caused by light weapons considered to be terrorist acts is low. However, light weapons are very much used by terrorist organisations worldwide to support a large number of activities: robbery, hijacking, armed conflicts and massacres. Terrorist violence does not only cause death, injuries and psychological stress, but also hinder economical development and essential services supply. Light weapons are the terrorists' main tools. For example, in Colombia, where fight between factions is considered as terrorism, has produced the highest manslaughter index in the world, 80% of the deaths having been caused by light weapons. In Afghanistan, Al Qaeda activists have been well kitted with military sourced specific light weapons. The Irish Republican Army (IRA) deactivation seems to be a big step towards peace. An analysis of 400 terrorist events between 1997 and 2001 reveal that light weapons were clearly used on 119 (30%) of them, and probably used on 40 kidnappings and hijackings.

Many terrorist acts occur within a political conflict context, but acts of violence considered as terrorist acts are generally those aiming at civilians. In the past 30 years, light weapons have been widely used for massive attacks on civilians. One of the first renowned attacks took place on the 5th of September 1972 at the Olympic stadium in Munich, when eight members of Black September, Palestine Liberation Organisation (PLO), killed two Israeli athletes and held hostage another nine who were murdered.

Other terrorist strikes on civilians:

February 1994: A Kach militant and the Jewish extremist Dr. Baruch Goldstein killed 39 worshippers at a mosque in the Cave of the Patriarchs on the West Bank in Hebron; they were acclaimed as heroes by their sympathisers.

November 1997: In Luxor, Egypt, 62 were murdered and 26 injured with light weapons; nobody claimed responsibility for the action; Al-Gama'a Al-Islamiyya is considered to be the possible responsible group.

August 2000: Right wing paramilitary forces, armed with small weapons, attacked two towns in Colombia, killing 22.

Research shows that indices of deaths and injuries caused by light weapons are related to easy acquisition. In industrialised countries, death indices are strongly related to owned firearms. In post conflict situations, presence of small weapons in society leads to violence even when the formal conflict is over. A study comparing injuries within a region during a conflict and in peacetime reveals that weapon caused injuries decrease only between 20% and 40% after peace is restored. Another study compares two areas within a country, one in peace and the other with an armed conflict between factions; a high injury index was identified for non combat produced injuries even in the pacified area, and 80 deaths for every 100 000 people, half of which were caused by light weapons. All this points at the risk of terrorism increase in places where light weapons may be easily acquired.

6.8.3 Types of light weapons

Light weapons are low weight and portable; they include revolvers, pistols, rifles, carbines, submachine guns and assault rifles (like the AK-47). Hand grenades, landmines and small mortars may be included. Military assault weapons, which include large capacity clips and automatic or semiautomatic shooting, are very efficient, but require some skill and training. A single armed person may kill dozens within a short period of time.

6.8.4 Light weapons, bullets and penetrating traumas

High velocity bullets create a permanent cavity, cause haemorrhage and produce a temporary cavity which expands and contracts between three and four times after the bullet has penetrated. This cavity may be 30 to 40 times longer than the bullet; tissues and structures far from the initial impact become damaged. A knife injury may or may not cause a small cavity. When a light weapon is used during an assault, it becomes 12 times more lethal than a knife.

Bullets are designed to effectively kill and wound, and some are specially designed to increase tissue damage. For example, hollow point bullets are designed to present a large front area; they expand and stop once they have impacted, passing all the impacting energy on to the tissues. The USA rifle M-16 carries bullets that decrease their velocity upon impacting the tissues and tumble within, increasing disruption. Other bullets are designed to disperse after impact; such bullets lose effectiveness at long distances.

Main suppliers of military light weapons include Russia (assault rifle AK-47, from which the AK-74 derived), China (Norinko AK-47), Belgium (assault rifle FAL), Germany (rifle G-3), the USA (rifle M-16), Israel (sub machine gun Uzi) and France (assault rifle FAMAS). The USA, Austria and Germany lead the production of handheld weapons.

The USA sold or transferred 463 million dollars in small weapons and ammunition to 124 countries in 1998. From these countries, some 30 were at war or suffered continued civil violence in 1998. In at least five of these countries, UN or USA troops in peace enforcement missions have been shot at or threatened with North American weapons; this is known as the "boomerang effect". Weapons have been supplied even through secret military operations, which are currently being used against many countries that initially supplied them. For example, during the 80s, in order to overthrow the Soviet invasion of Afghanistan, the USA government supplied at least 2 million dollars in weapons and training to Islamic rebel groups (the mujahidin). The North American Congress approved in 1985 the transfer of a limited amount of Stingers; about 1000 were transferred, of which a few hundred are still there. The Central Intelligence Agency (CIA) introduced weapons and money through Pakistan's army intelligence service. The Taliban armed themselves with weapons left by the Soviets, American leftover weapons used during the construction of an oil pipeline in the 80s, and they purchased more material in the black market. The CIA allocated 55 million dollars to buy back the Stingers in the black market, but they were not completely successful.

There are also many documented cases of military and police weapons, and weapons seized after a crime, which go into an illegal market.

All over the world there are many light weapons in the hands of citizens as well as in the hands of States. A large amount of these weapons have been illegally supplied. In many countries, many of the weapons seized after crimes were originally legal, purchased by an individual or a State. In countries where it is legal to possess a small weapon, the illegal market increases. In the USA alone, with a 260 million population, there are an estimated 200 million firearms, of which about 500 000 are stolen yearly to be introduced into the illegal market. Inadequate control of weapon sales also increases illegal markets. Approximately 50% of the illegal handheld weapons in Canada, 80% of the small weapons in Mexico, and many of the small weapons of the Irish Republican Army (IRA) come from the USA. Weapons illegally sold in the USA are not terrorist related. Some ways by which legal weapons have been distributed to terrorists are presented below.

A Danish citizen and a British arms dealer purchased a Russian cargo aeroplane in Latvia and flew to Bulgaria, where it was loaded with 77 crates containing weapons, including 300 assault rifles, ammunition, pistols, hand grenades and missile launchers. Subsequently, the aeroplane flew to India, where the weapons were parachuted into the township of Purulia. The weapons were addressed to a violent religious sect.

Supposedly, IRA members organised weapon transfers with bribed officials in South Africa. Subsequently the IRA members were arrested on a charge of boarding AK-47s from Mozambique.

Four Irish citizens were arrested on a charge of having purchased over 50 weapons and hundreds of ammunition and having sent it to IRA sympathisers. An arms dealer admitted having supplied them from Boynton Beach, Florida, with dozens of weapons, and for an extra 50 dollars every weapon, they were not registering them officially.

A Canadian dealer was charged on smuggling over 40 000 military light weapons into the USA, while their destination was the Middle East.

All illegal small weapons begin as legal small weapons. Weapons diversity both in "lawful" and in "unlawful" markets has been the greatest concern, since arms dealers do not distinguish between small offenders, organised crime members, insurgents, freedom fighters or terrorists. They are purely after the money. Consequently, efforts for preventing terrorist acts involving small weapons are part of a much larger effort, namely preventing their use. While arms dealing is associated with drug trafficking, it is still quite different. Most drugs are illegal, from production to consumption, whereas many weapons begin by being legal products, becoming in the end used illegally in many different forms. Lawful small weapons are diverted to unlawful distribution networks or illegal purposes, or to State transfers, State funds deviation, thefts, losses, robberies, document forgery, cloning and other illegal transactions by dealers. Reactivation of deactivated or disabled weapons, and reassembled weapons from components, sometimes obtained by mail, are also a problem.

Consequently, efforts towards reducing small weapon illegal traffic are based on an increased control on the legal movements of such weapons.

6.8.5 Countermeasures

It has been proven that a large link exists between mortality and disease, and the proliferation of small weapons. Measures aimed at increasing control on small weapons should be potentiated; thus, the risk of inappropriate use will be reduced. Likewise, more research is required in order to gain greater understanding of the contextual factors and to evaluate the effectiveness of specific intervention formulae. For example, measures allocated to governments and NGOs are not necessarily associated with an empirical evidence of their relative effectiveness. Rather, political convenience and symbolic significance are often dominant factors in national and international policies.

A number of international agreements are in place, linked to reducing unlawful small weapons dealing and therefore reduce the number of conflicts and crimes. Amongst them:

- The United Nations Convention against Transnational Organized Crime, which establishes regulations for importing, exporting, transferring and marking weapons (excluding transfers within a State).

A resolution established in 1997 by the United Nations Commission on Crime Prevention and Criminal Justice recommended that countries should ensure a minimum of domestic regulations, including requirements for obtaining firearms possession licences, for registration of firearms acquisition and possession and for a safe storage.

- The Programme of Action established by the United Nations Conference on the Illicit Trade in Small Arms and Light Weapons in All Its Aspects.

Regional agreements include:

- The Economic Community of West African States (ECOWAS), Moratorium on the Importation, Exportation and Manufacture of Small Arms and Light Weapons.

- The European Union Code of Conduct on Arms Exports establishes criteria for small weapon exports and a registry aimed at preventing sales in conflict areas and to human rights violating States.

- The Convention of the Organisation of American States, defining regulations to control export, import and transit in weapon trade, and also weapon marking.

Many States and most nongovernmental organisations (NGOs), including the International Action Network on Small Arms (IANSA), have insisted on doing much more in order to prevent small weapon proliferation and misuse. Furthermore, in order to make States aware and to ratify existing international agreements, a large number of various measures have been promoted.

Given the nature of the illicit market and of the misuse of such weapons, proposed measures are similar both for cases of conflicts, crime, injuries and terrorism. The measures include:

- Enforcing export and import licensing, ensuring that they are reciprocal measures, so that both the exporting and the importing country should authorise any transaction.

- Defining a global agreement on weapon marking and traceability, including appropriate weapon marking systems in manufacturing, import and export, as well as a weapon production, possession and transfer registry.

- Establishing regulations and measures in order to enforce the controls watching over weapon legal transfer, both at State and other levels, towards preventing transfer of weapons that may be used for suppression or aggression, or that may contribute to magnifying a conflict or regional destabilisation.

Even with the continued opposition of the United States, strict domestic regulation of light weapon civil possession is critical: measures that allow legitimate light weapon civil use but reduce the risk of misuse or transfer from the legal to the illegal market. Such measures include licensing, regulations, implementation of rules for safe storage and the prohibition for civil possession of military automatic assault weapons, which are not necessary to legitimate and sport activities. Efforts by the international community in order to establish domestic regulations have been consistently blocked by the United States, largely by the influence of the National Rifle Association (NRA). The Programme of Action issued by the United Nations Conference on the Illicit Trade in Small Arms in 2001 contains in all its aspects measures encouraging countries and nations to ensure an appropriate regulation of firearm civil use and possession.

More recently, in a movement that was incredulously looked upon, the Attorney General of the United States, John Ashcroft, detained over 1000 individuals as terrorist suspects under no charge, but prohibited the Federal Bureau of Investigation (FBI) to investigate whether they had attempted to acquire firearms, because this would have been a violation of their constitutional rights. While the United States are placing pressure on countries such as Canada in order to control problems that they deem as a threat to their security, they consider themselves little responsible of being the main small weapon supplier worldwide.

Measures have also been taken towards collecting and destroying surplus weapons. International laws have been proposed for destroying surplus and confiscated small and light weapons. Post conflict area weapon collection programmes are very important for peace maintenance; however, high level violence risks still exist. Although the abolition of the IRA was part of the peace agreement for Northern Ireland, the IRA rejected to comply with such requirement, which became a great hindrance to the peace process. Value of weapon collection programmes varies in other contexts. In some cases, particularly where such programmes are mandatory and accompanied by sanctions, as in Australia or the United Kingdom, large quantities of weapons have been collected and subsequently destroyed. In other contexts, this factor appears to be widely educational and aimed at creating a peaceful culture. Increasing registration, marking, information, etc., has also been emphasised by the international community.

Local measures have been reinforced, such as strict controls on access to small weapons in public areas. Some countries, like South Africa, have regulated "free weapon areas" in order to decrease risks. Efforts have also been made towards producing "intelligent weapons", which may only be activated through a code or biometric information, as well as in developing bullet impact reduction technologies, such as Kevlar® vests.

Measures have also been developed for studying factors creating light weapon demand, in order to prevent terrorism, crime and other conflicts. From a public health perspective, damage prevention should also be supported by damage control.

Addressing appropriately and in a timely manner damages caused by light weapons may significantly reduce casualty figures. Consequently, increasing emergency and training services may be critical to a global strategy towards damage control and prevention.

An approach that would not however maintain civil safety —whether on the air or land— would be increasing access to light weapons. The recent firearm acquisitions by civilians in the United States could be, for example, the major cause for concern between health professionals. Similarly, arming pilots may not be welcome with open arms.

6.8.6 Explosive and incendiary devices

The attack on the World Trade Centre in New York on the 11th of September 2001 has the highest mortality index of any terrorist attempt. While aeroplane hijacking and bombing have been previously identified as risks, this was the first instance of an aircraft being used as both a missile and an explosive and incendiary device. This awakens the phantoms of other threats, including strikes against nuclear reactors.

Between 1980 and 1990 there were 12 216 bombings in the United States, which caused 1782 injures, 241 deaths and close to 140 million dollars in damages. Between 1990 and 1994 there were 8567 bombings and an additional 2000 bomb attempts. Many of these explosions involved pipe bombs (53% in 1990), filled with low velocity elements such as black powder packed with shrapnel, which cause severe damages.

While only a small proportion of these attacks were classified as terrorism, the explosive and incendiary devices are the chosen weapons by terrorists worldwide. An analysis on 400 documents between 1997 and 2001 reveal that over 250 involved bombs and explosive and incendiary devices.

When bombs are successfully placed on aeroplanes, there are few survivors. Canada has been, and still is, holding the worst aviation terrorist activity index in history. The Air India bombing in 1986 cost 329 lives. In 1988, a bomb placed on Pan Am flight 103 exploded over Lockerbie, Scotland, killing all 259 passengers. Plastic and volatile explosives, such as SEMTEX, are the weapons used predominantly by terrorists in aviation incidents.

In many bombings, however, there are more injured than killed. For example:

- In the 1993 bombing of the World Trade Centre, six people died, but over 1000 were injured.
- In the Oklahoma bombing, 167 people were killed and 759 injured.
- In the bombing of the USA embassy at Nairobi, in 1998, 253 were killed and some 5000 were injured (3600 required plastic surgery and 1000 required major reconstructive surgery).
- 29 people were killed and 330 injured in 1998 by a car bomb in Omagh, Ireland.
- In an oil pipeline bombing in Antioquía, Colombia, 71 people were killed and 100 injured.
- In 2000, in Rajwas, India, a grenade thrown on an open fire at a communal kitchen killed 30 and injured 47.

Bomb impact goes beyond mortality. The main target is causing psychological terror in order to generate chaos and panic. Letter bombs kill 3% of addressees; nevertheless, they create general panic. Secondary devices make an area unsafe, thus hindering rescue efforts and therefore damage control.

An explosion is defined as a pressure increase within a confined space, generally caused by an exothermal chemical reaction, by which gases are produced in a relatively large quantity. A more simple definition: a sudden energy release.

6.8.7 Injury types

Powerful explosions have the potential of causing many different types of injuries on victims; however, the type of body injury is relatively consistent irrespective of the context. In any type of explosion, be it chemical, by steam, mechanical or nuclear, four injury types are produced: primary, secondary, tertiary and various.

Explosion caused primary injuries are produced by the pressure expansion wave, a sphere of compressed gas molecules rapidly expanding away from the explosion centre at hundreds of psi. The expansion wave does not last longer than 5 milliseconds, but the massive air pressure change causes enormous damage, including myocardial contusion and heart artery severance, dislocation of small intestine and colon from their supporting structures, and eardrum rupture. The respiratory system may be seriously damaged by the expansion wave; lungs may bleed or rupture, leading to a hemothorax and/or pneumothorax; embolisms can take place due to air ingress in pulmonary circulation; and the diaphragm and the tracheobronchial tree may become extirpated.

Explosion induced secondary injuries are caused by airborne bomb fragments and rubble travelling at missile velocity, close to 1400 metres per second. Such injuries include tear, abrasion, contusions with fractures and penetrations within the body. Tertiary injuries are caused by the wind after the explosion, which may reach up to 1740 kilometres per hour, as a result of the expansion wave displacing air molecules. This may cause amputations, limb and skull fractures. Various injuries are those caused by the consequences of the explosion, such as falls, broken bones, amputations occurring because of structural collapse, or fire or chemical caused burns.

Specific injuries are associated with specific explosives. For example, the Molotov cocktail syndrome occurs when people are attacked within their cars, and suffer a massive inhalation of fumes and fire produced by the combination of petrol ignition and fumes coming from the car's synthetic materials. Furthermore, those exposed to the traumatic event, particularly when threatened with possible harm or even death, will probably show adverse psychological responses. Those that lose their loved ones or friends in a disaster or during rescue and funeral services workers are also under high risk of suffering post traumatic stress. Knowledge of the potential mechanisms causing damage and injuries, of the initial signs and symptoms, and of the natural course of such problems, will assist enormously in handling patients wounded by an explosion.

6.8.8 Explosive and incendiary device types

Simple explosive devices are frequently easily acquirable substances. Although many explosive materials, such as dynamite and nitroglycerine, are kept under control in most countries, material diversity both in legal and in illegal markets is difficult to control. Many terrorist made bombs are improvised. Required raw materials for explosives are stolen or irregularly acquired from the Army or commercial explosive supplies. Bombs may be made also from fertilisers or other easily acquirable household goods. Such "homemade" bombs are known as improvised explosive devices; they have a main charge, stuck to the fuse; the fuse is stuck to a detonator. In some types, the three parts are within a single housing. The detonator activates the fuse, which ignites the charge, thus causing the explosion, a violent explosion and shock waves. The purpose of many devices is killing or mutilating. Some of the devices, known is incendiary devices, are aimed at causing damage and destruction by fire. Pipe bombs are the most common amongst terrorists and usually consist in high velocity explosives within a narrow tube. Pipe bombs are very easy to produce using gunpowder and iron, steel, aluminium or copper pipe; sometimes they are covered with nails to further increase damage. The Molotov cocktail is a really easy to produce improvised weapon, and it may cause considerable damage. Materials such as petrol, diesel oil, kerosene, ethylene or methylene, lighter fluids and turpentine are filled in a bottle, which breaks upon impact. A piece of cotton wool serves as a fuse, which is ignited prior to throwing the bottle to the target. Fertiliser based bombs contain ammonia nitrate. Hundreds of kilograms are required to cause major damage. The IRA, the Tamil Tigers and other Middle East organisations have used these ammonia nitrate bombs.

Antipersonnel land mines are another type of explosive weapon used to cause injuries, death, and to terrorise civil population. Although used by the military against the enemy, they may be considered as terrorist weapons.

6.8.9 Countermeasures

Countermeasures should be carried out by a wide research, paying attention to explosion impact and causal factors. In particular, by understanding the wide range of injuries, post traumatic stress included, which is critical. Epidemiological studies on victims of terrorist attacks may be valuable for two effective countermeasures such as victim personal care and rehabilitation. The hostile action causal system allows determining the magnitude of an explosion and the distance between the victims and the explosion, in order to evaluate, for example, the protection gained from wearing armouring when close to the explosion.

As in the case of light weapons, explosives may serve legitimate purposes, but they are often deviated to illegal purposes such as terrorist or criminal actions. Although many explosive materials are regulated, theft is the main issue. Interventions have been proposed towards reducing risk of terrorist or criminal misuse of explosives. Such interventions include regulating commercial explosives, using technology to detect explosive materials, sharing information and supporting investigations.

An effort has been made on enforcing building control, in order to make access more difficult and reduce bombing risks. An increase of wardens and keeping alert may avoid damages.

Laws vary between jurisdictions with respect to explosive material and device regulations, but international conventions and agreements are in place aimed at establishing a minimum set of laws. The United Nations Economic and Social Council (UNESCO) issued a resolution in 1998 with the following recommendation: "Recognizing that, with the increasing dimensions and scale of international transport and the growing sophistication of transnational illicit trafficking in explosives, States which have not already done so may consider reviewing the legislation and administrative regulations concerning explosives and their component parts to make those instruments more effective in combating crime". However, studies have indicated that many of the regulations in place are poorly enforced. For example, while commercial explosives are supposed to be highly controlled in the US, there are variations among States, evidence of poor storage and inadequate inspection and enforcement powers. In the US there have been proposals for mandatory licensing of all purchase of explosives and broadening the BATF's authority to conduct inspections in an effort to reduce misuse and diversion.

More recently, there have been discussions among governments about using "taggants" (coded materials), that provide better detection, tracing and control of explosives. In the United States, as a result of the US Anti-Terrorism Act of 1996, taggants must be added to all plastic explosives "to make them visible to detection". There is also research underway to explore ways to render inert the fertilizer chemicals that have been used to manufacture explosives.

The investment in screening is often a question of cost-benefit analysis. Airport security has been increased in response to the September 11th attacks and other incidents involving airlines, and airport passengers are being screened for explosives and other weapons. Research studies are in progress to improve screening and detection, including direct imaging of explosives with a nitrogen camera to detect SEMTEX and other concealed explosives with high nitrogen concentrations. Medical computed tomography (CT) scan technologies can also be used to detect explosives. Pre-boarding "shoe checks" are being performed on some passengers after the attempt by a terrorist in December 2001 to ignite explosives hidden in his shoe during a Paris-to-Miami flight. Some airlines are considering installing closed-circuit television cameras on aircraft to monitor passengers' behaviour during flights.

In order to reduce the impact of explosions, particularly secondary explosions, efforts are also directed at developing blast resistant structures as well as various types of armour to protect those detecting and defusing threats. For example, an oatmeal-type absorbing fabric called TABRE (Technology for Attenuating Blast-Related Energy) blocks flying fragments (shrapnel) and eliminates approximately 90% of the shock wave that is released in an explosion. TABRE can be used below vehicles to protect against landmines, in trousers designed to protect the legs and genitalia of minesweepers, and in blast-proof airline baggage containers and urban garbage containers. Hardened luggage containers in airplanes, for which the US Federal Aviation Administration (FAA) has developed a standard, can neutralize explosives. Hardened containers can also be used for small bags that are difficult and expensive to scan with X-rays. This shock-absorbing and shock-deflecting technology can be utilized in blast-proof and bullet-proof cockpit doors on commercial aircraft. Finally, efforts have directed at raising awareness of some risks; for example, by encouraging the public to identify and report suspicious packages or behaviours in public places.

6.9 Selecting technical equipment and means that may be installed

The market of new technologies applied to security has seen a large increase in recent years, even before the dramatic events that have occurred internationally. Numerous makes, manufacturers and designers may be found, offering the best solutions to the type or risk for which protection is sought.

While this is well known, the issue lies with the selection criteria, since the principle to be followed is that not all serves everything, as it is usually intended in the seller-buyer relationship.

When equipment is selected, it should not only comply with predetermined objectives, but personal objectives should be particularly accepted by users, who, in fact, are those who will be using the equipment and should be convinced of its suitability.

Therefore, all objective criteria as applied in a quality process become applicable here; answers to strategic questions as depicted in Diagram 6.1 should be provided.

As an example, some security equipment technical data sheets are cited:

Integrated thermal imaging surveillance system

Description: Integrated day and night surveillance system, for visual surface detection under all weather conditions of persons, vehicles and craft. It provides thermal and visible images and overlay, plus distances and orientation by a laser telemeter. The system is weatherised for outdoor use in marine environment. The head rotates 360° and tilts from −80° to +80°; it may be vehicle mounted or fixed. Capable of detecting a person at 500 metres. Although not its specific purpose, it includes video image recording.

Operating principle: The system is based in capturing infrared energy transmitted by objects, this varying for each material depending on their specific heat; this allows establishing thermal contrasts. In order to enable identification, a TV system is added to the adjustable telemeter.

Benefits: Unaffected by visible light and shades. Enables observation in the dark, even through smoke or fog. It may analyse structures, water, electricity, steam, installations, etc., and even the previous presence of persons, engines that have been operating, etc.

Disadvantages: No facial recognition available; hinders accurate identification.

Closed Circuit Television

Description: A limited set of TV cameras and displays, its signals being distributed within a closed communications network, either by cable or radio frequency; it allows visualising and recording from a central station areas and spots considered to be critical, as a support to other systems.

Operating principle: Those of TV.

Benefits: Real time information and preservation of images for subsequent examination, legal purposes, etc.

Disadvantages: Technical limitations on range and clarity. Requires human attention, which may diminish due to tiredness, lack of interest, etc. May produce excess information.

Price: Cameras: 150.00 €; display units: 450.00 € Euro; video units: 700 €.

Fence sensors

Description: System consisting in stressed horizontal wires that may detect traction as produced by climbing and wire separation or severance.

Fundamental: Wires include terminal sensors, located at the poles, capable of detecting mechanical stress variations.

Benefits: Insensitive to wind; highly sensitive to wire severance and separation.

Disadvantages: Not capable of detecting underground or over the fence intrusions; complicated installation; highly complicated depending on ground features.

Price: 2100.00 € each 300 metres.

Electronic barrier

Description: This system includes a number of equally distanced poles on which infrared transmitters and receivers are installed; it runs along the full perimeter of the port facility and in inside areas as required, in order to detect persons or vehicles going through. It should be connected to other systems in order to avoid an excess of false alarms, and should be fitted with anti-tampering measures to prevent sabotage.

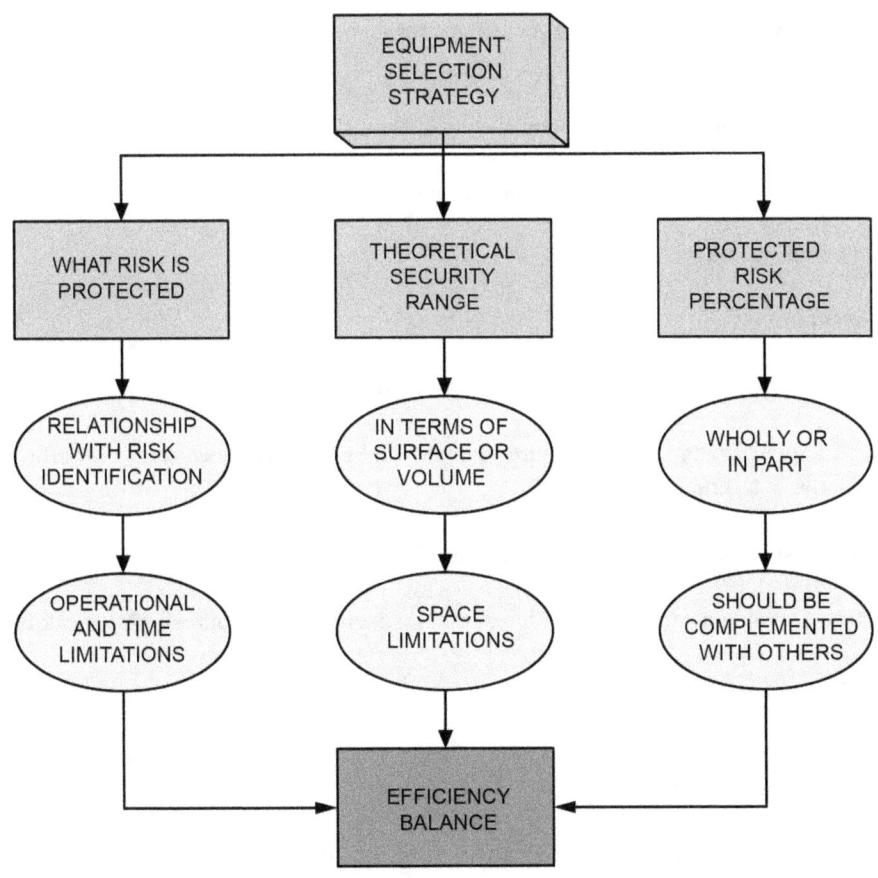

Diagram 6.1

Operating principle: Based on the disruption of an infrared beam by a person or object crossing them.

Benefits: Detection area defined; good sensitivity; difficult to neutralise.

Disadvantages: False alarms caused by fowl and small animals; difficult to adjust; requires regular ground, free of vegetation; fog sensitive.

Price: 650.00 € each 200 metres.

Ground pressure detector

Description: Around the port facility perimeter, and in combination with perimeter sensors, a buried sensor system will be installed to detect intruders crossing.

Operating principle: Ground pressure detection through analogue seismic sensors; signals are processed jointly.

Benefits: Good sensitivity; immune to weather conditions and radiation.

Disadvantages: False alarms generated by rodents and roots.

Price: 15 000.00 € each 4 800 metres.

Magnetic switches

Description: Discrete detection system for door and window opening and object removal.

Operating principle: Separation of two parts (magnet and contacts) is detected, the former normally keeping the latter in a certain position.

Benefits: Low cost; no electric supply required; low false alarm level.

Disadvantages: Possible neutralisation with external magnets; possible intrusion by breaking a door or a window.

Price: 6.00 € each unit.

Indoor volumetric detector

Description: This system allows detecting persons inside rooms and other enclosed spaces; to be installed in access ways, and in areas containing critical information, valuables and safety systems or means.

Operating principle: The motion of persons is detected by analysing ambient infrared radiation variations; it is considered as passive because it does not transmit any signal; it analyses the ambient intermittently in order to detect sudden radiation variations.

Benefits: Very easy to install.

Disadvantages: Low sensitivity; sensitive to ambient temperature; easy to shield; false alarms due to small animals.

Price: 40.00 € each unit.

Microphone detector

Description: Sensor located on windows panes, doors or even walls, in order to detect breakage.

Operating principle: Sound and vibration detection.

Price: 10.00 € each unit.

Archway metal detector

Description: This system is aimed at detecting persons walking through when carrying a metal object of a predetermined mass; its use is mandatory for access control.

6.10 Conclusions

The public health approach, in part, addresses environments that give rise to problems. In order to prevent terrorism with small arms, explosives and incendiaries, we must reduce the diversion of legal small arms and explosives to illegal markets, improve information exchange and investigations, "harden" targets, and strengthen injury control and emergency preparedness. We must also ensure that there are well-developed alarm systems as well as evacuation and emergency procedures in public buildings. The public health approach brings together professionals of various health, safety and security disciplines and their agencies and organizations. Liaisons with various communities are critical for collecting information and implementing countermeasures. Finally, the focus must be not only on managing terrorism, but also on managing anxiety and fear of terrorism, which are often disproportionate to the risk and sometimes accompanied by backlash against particular communities and hate crimes. We must also address the root causes of terrorism.

Chapter 7 Human response to security related situations

7.1 Human behaviour under pressure

Although affecting every person and all type of ships, passenger ships should be considered as a special, since they cover a very different objective to any other ship type. In a passenger ship there is a concentration of persons who wish to be taken care of, and who are mainly unaware of the medium. Furthermore, the crew becomes affected by the need of adding to the navigation related responsibilities all tasks that have to do with providing service to passengers. Behaviours of possible aggressors, of secondary task forces and of the relatives of all persons involved in an eventual crisis aboard should be considered in addition to crew and passenger behaviour.

Human behaviour should be addressed not only with regard to pressure situations, but also for routine situations.

The unleashing factor for many critical situations occurring aboard originate from a lack of prevention, by being unaware that individuals involved in such actions are subject to high stress levels. This latter condition facilitates aggressor detection and allows preventing crew behaviours that may produce negative actions.

Human behaviour complexity demands rigour when expounding its many difficulties, when addressed under the basic aspects of both individual behaviour and collective behaviour. *Behaviour* is any action by an individual that produces consequences, both for the individual and for other persons or the physical environment. The base for these actions include many psychological, environmental, social, biological, learning related, perceptive, cognitive, etc. determinants or factors; i.e., it is a unique phenomenon with multiple causalities.

7.2 Individual behaviour

By knowing the individual behaviour of persons, the mechanisms operating on the masses in crisis situations may be known. There is no such thing as spontaneous behaviour; every action has a triggering circumstance that forces the individual into responding, establishing an action-reaction chain. It is this very chain and its consequences what modifies the behaviour of persons in their relationships and with the medium. In an emergency situation case, different individuals will react differently. Such behaviours may have results that adapt to the situation or that are totally erroneous.

Experience shows that in most critical events, numerous individual reactions are produced that save the day when all designed intervention systems fail. What is common to the individuals that survived crisis situations?

In front of any situation posing a threat to an individual, who may suffer harm whatever its type, a pressure situation is faced. Such situations produce a given stress level.

Many factors contribute the result when struggling with the stress produced by a crisis situation; furthermore, it will vary considerably from one individual to another. However, there are some common parameters to all individuals.

These parameters may be plotted to evaluate critical situations and the behaviour of persons involved.

Time, running second by second, is a parameter; it may become a stress precursor, if a required task is not performed within the deadline.

In some situations, time may be an unimportant factor; in other cases, it becomes decisive.

Another factor setting a scale in relation to time is the activity level of the individual subject to the critical event. This activity level includes several areas that show the endured stress level together with normal activity level and the distress line (see Figure 7.1).

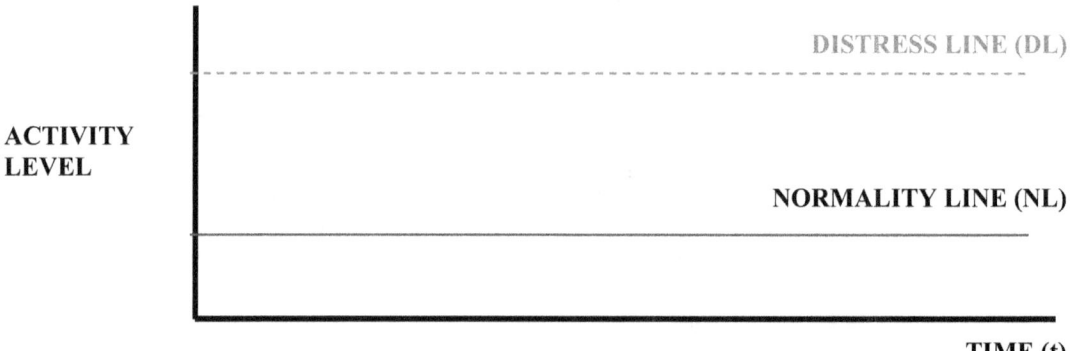

Figure 7.1

Distress levels are reached in everyday situations in all orders of life; extraordinary things happen for which a logic explanation is not available; however, a time perspective analysis provides an objective approach to the event.

Situations generating pressure vary significantly; as previously mentioned, they configure very different charts. For example:

a) Time pressure

Time sets a priority for crisis resolution. This disrupts the balance and stress levels soar depending on the requirements of the task to be performed and on the impossibility of complying with the deadline; furthermore, the greater the individual's loss, the larger the unbalance.
Many types of pressure exist, but these are the most usual:

b) Social pressure (Success - Fear of Failure)

Time has no particular bearing here on crisis resolution. Pressure level is determined by the environment and the loss of family, social, etc. support. Pressure level is cumulative, and the distress line is reached when the individual collapses, mainly due to role conflicts.

c) Internal built up pressure (Frustration)

Frustration generated stress is cumulative, and requires a more or less extended period of time to saturate the resolving capabilities of the individual and rush him/her to the distress line.

d) Fear induced pressure

Fear induced pressure creates a need for resolving the situation in the shortest possible time. Together with the fact that it is physical integrity that is at stake, this produces a very high stress peak that rushes the individual to the vicinity of the distress line, many times beyond.

7.3 Shock and panic reactions

Fear induced pressure is the most useful for public order control and subsequent learning of group and mass actions. Possible reaction is equal for all individuals. No human being fails to comply with this principle; only differences in terms of reaction magnitude exist between one and another. Under pressure, reactions range from shock to panic (see Figure 7.2).

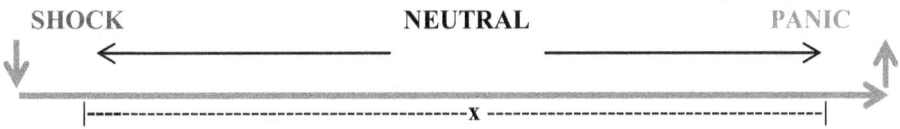

Figure 7.2

Shock is characterised by slow or nonexistent motion, cold perspiration, lividity, silence, and closed barrier like protective postures, even fetal. The output communication channel is blocked, but not the inside channel (see Figure 7.3).

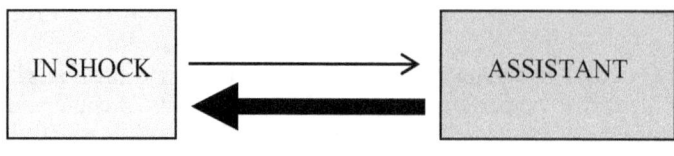

Figure 7.3

Panic is the contrary to shock; the individual experiences hyperactivity, hot perspiration, blushing, shouting or loud voice and open postures. The output communication channel is open, but saturated to the extent of blocking the input channel (see Figure 7.4).

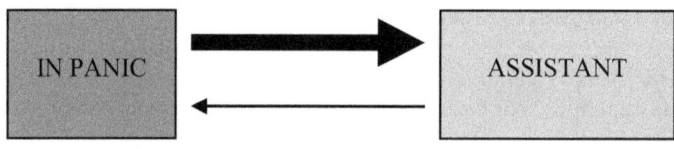

Figure 7.4

Therefore, it may be determined that everyone goes through a more or less durable period of shock, to enter then in a more or less profound phase of panic.

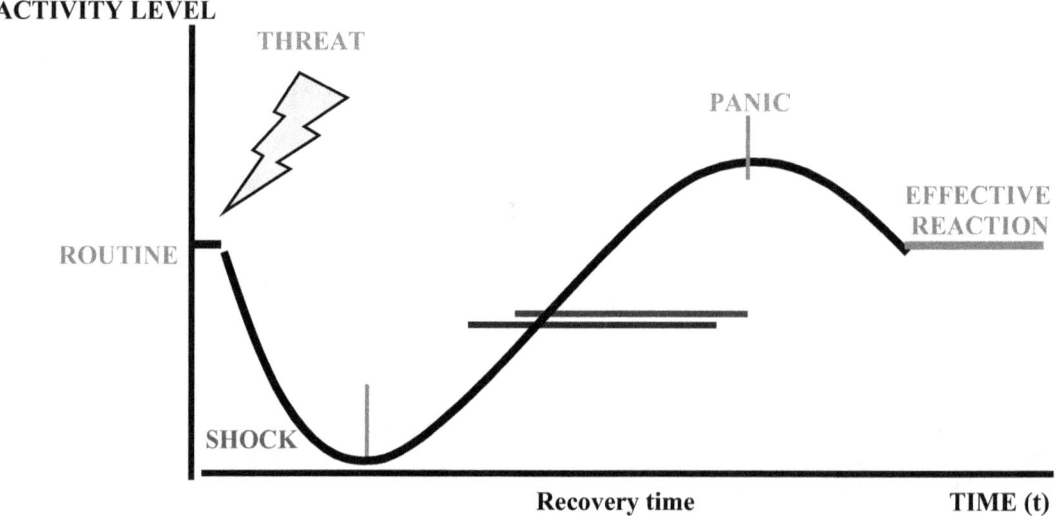

Figure 7.5

The effective reaction is reached later; this is the objective, since only this phase may give place to a crisis solving action (see Figure 7.5).

Time elapsed from threat to effective reaction is known as recovery time. This time should be reduced in order to increase possibilities for survival. Amongst the methods to achieve this goal are simulation drills, which intend to generate the required experiences and knowledge in order to overcome limit situations that are faced during a crisis.

During effective reaction, which is considered most important, actions are generated to avoid the threat and make damage scope acceptable; actions are required to be performed in the appropriate time, magnitude and location.

Every effective reaction involves a systematic decision making process; decisions will exhibit specific characteristics depending on the individuals' systems of thinking:

   a. *Conscious*: low, reflective, easily controllable responses; good decisions are adopted.
   b. *Subconscious*: swift, non reflective responses, learnt by repetition. Appropriate use of safety equipment (fire hoses, extinguishers, artificial respiration and heart massage).
   c. *Unconscious*: very rapid, non reflective, involuntary responses. Hands protecting the face, blinking.

Furthermore, the individual's state of mind with respect to interaction with *personal feelings* will contribute to a better, more appropriate response. The most evident example is when an order of priorities has to be decided for abandoning a ship: those with a higher survival probability should prevail, going down to those with lower survival levels.

Finally, an effective reaction should include a large proportion of a conservation instinct, ready to fight, altruistic and humane, as assumed by each individual according to his/her personality.

7.4 Simulation drills

During a properly directed drill, a fire drill for example, each individual develops a self protection system that will modify his/her conduct in similar real cases. This should favour the arrival of the effective reaction by shortening the recovery time. What are the benefits contributed by drills when facing a similar event?

1) The individual gains a previous fire experience, which will reduce the negative surprise factor.
2) The individual will have subsequently read or collected information on such type of situations, becoming sensitive to the matter and becoming more aware of reality.
3) The more realistic the drill is, the higher will be the perception level developed for detecting possible critical signs and indications.
4) The individual will mentally go over this type of situations, considering first time mistakes, both personal and those made by others.
5) The individual will think or will collect information on more effective actions, thus increasing the quality of option selection.
6) Psychologically, the individual's predisposition will not be the same, but much more realistic.
7) Psychological aspects are not necessarily the same, and they may be either positive or negative, the drill not affecting them decisively.

8) Reaching the effective action earlier on each critical event.

7.5 Psychological aspects of stress situations

The magnitude of changes caused by such emergency situations varies from one individual to another, and it depends on:

- The subjective perception of the threat magnitude
- Hazard nearness
- Previous experience (in similar situations)
- Personality
- Awareness of own capabilities for successfully overcoming the hazard.

Effective reaction phases

The effective reaction in the face of a threat depends on many factors that impact differently on each of the phases.

a) **Analysis phase**

There is a tendency to act without analysing, and the information that, in many cases, is provided by sight perceiving the main threat, does not include the significance of secondary threats. Analysis takes place in the brain, not the eyes. An incorrect analysis will produce an ineffective reaction to the risk.

In order to attain a correct analysis, it should be taken into account that a large amount of information is available, stored in the unconscious mind. This information will assist, although not always adequately, since the necessary knowledge may not surface with the required precision, or even reactions that are not correct may be thought to be so (see Figure 7.6).

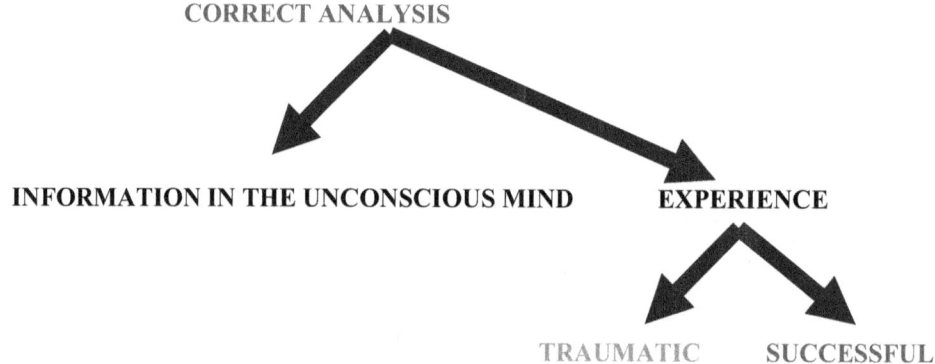

Figure 7.6

Existence of a previous experience will vary the analysis result and the recovery time. It may not be true to consider that a past action that solved a crisis may solve the current situation.

Furthermore, an untreated post traumatic shock derived from a similar situation may cause a lack of analysis (see Figure 7.7).

b)   Option consideration

Based on the analysis performed, options aimed at mitigating crisis effects should be considered. There may be two reactions:

1. To address the hazard in order to overcome it.
2. To escape the threat.

Analysis phase objectives are:

Figure 7.7

7.6 Option consideration interfering factors

Lack of control of affective messages

Annoyance, honour, fear, hate, love, etc. may produce serious interferences when analysing, even more when considering options. A lack of emotional control creates a lack of discipline, impatience and a false sense of safety.

Lack of experience or practice

- Doubting of own capabilities, even when possessing them.
- Unawareness of critical event keys, like where it is taking place or other technical aspects unknown to the individual.

Excess confidence and previous success

- They do not guarantee an appropriate outcome of the current situation.
- The situation is underestimated.

Decision

After analysis and consideration, the best option should be chosen and all attention and efforts should be concentrated in that direction. Indecision in favour of other options is to be avoided. Achieving this depends on:

- A systematic, conscious analysis and option consideration process
- Operating capabilities, previous practice
- Objective data availability
- Threat magnitude
- Available information
- Availability and condition of supporting means.

Reaction phase

Though infrequent that this phase should be reached and execution should not take place, cases of blockage exist when undertaking actions as decided during option consideration. Problems in this phase are:

- Quick or erroneous analysis
- Reacting without considering options
- Deciding without operating capabilities.

It is important to activate a reaction system that reviews results, in order to reassess quality of decision-option consideration-analysis.

All these phases evidently use precious time, unavailable in some crisis. If it is believed that under pressure judgment and reflection are altered, it becomes clear that decisions should be made in routine circumstances. This allows stating that work on simulators, preparation of intervention plans and realism during training will provide for shorter recovery times. This will in turn increase probability of overcoming on board crisis situations.

7.7 Communications and messages

Emergency resolution is the result of the level and quality of the information received during its development. Passenger control is also attained by the information transmitted and the degree of understanding and comprehension reached. It is therefore evident that communications and information contents are critical to all cases in which human factor is the main agent in the emergency scene.

Any disturbing elements that may hinder the best clarity when receiving notifications should be identified and corrected in as short a time as possible, by modifying equipment and procedures, adding new organisational aspects, etc.; i.e., by doing everything necessary to ensure that what is transmitted reaches the selected destination.

One of the main problems appears with the acoustic characteristics of the spaces in which the inside PA system delivers messages. Voice distortion, poor clarity and superimposed noise are usual.

The presence of *variable level noises* shall be considered a disturbance, such as *stable noises*, *fluctuating noises* with pressure levels above 2 dB, *intermittent noises* with level drops lasting over a second, acoustic energy *pulses* with periods below a second, and *quasi stable pulses* as series of pulses with comparable amplitudes, with periods below 0.2 seconds between individual pulses. These are all determinant for an appropriate hearing as required; total sound pressure level should be also added, which may mask the message within a noisy background.

On a ship, many of such noises are generated; sound pressure levels are quite high, PA systems are not always balanced with the background; furthermore, noise level is higher during an emergency, which further hinders communication.

In order to gain an impression of the difficulty of being heard when high noise levels are present, a list is provided with limiting distances (see Table 7.1).

In the Annex of the recommendation on methods of measuring noise levels at listening posts on ships (Resolution A.343-9), it was established that background level noises should not exceed:

a. 68 dB in the octave band centred on 250 Hz

b. 63 dB in the octave band centred on 500 Hz

CONVERSATION INTERFERENCE LEVEL (dB)	Maximum distance at which a conversation is considered to be satisfactorily intelligible using a normal tone of voice (m)	Maximum distance at which a conversation is considered to be satisfactorily intelligible using a loud voice (m)
35	7.5	15.0
40	4.2	8.4
45	2.3	4.6
50	1.3	2.6
55	0.75	1.5
60	0.42	0.85
65	0.25	0.50
70	0.13	0.26

Table 7.2

Regarding dominant frequencies, little research is done that would allow installing PA systems with markedly different tones to the frequencies at which usual dominant noises appear (in routine situations) (see Table 7.2).

In this sense, alarms should have a limited sounding time, since once they have fulfilled their role, alerting either partially or totally the crew and/or passengers, it is not desirable that they should disturb the appropriate hearing of messages delivered through the inside communication systems. The required alert time, increased by a safety margin to cover contingencies, would provide the total effective alarm time.

Once the attention of persons is obtained and outside alarms and inside bells are deactivated, it is the moment to initiate message broadcast.

Messages should be brief, concise, direct and to the point; they should not allow for inaccurate or equivocal interpretations, and should not generate more uneasiness, but rather diminish that caused by the emergency itself. In order to attain these goals, the following considerations are submitted:

DESIRABLE LEVELS IN PASSENGER SHIPS	dB(A)	DETECTED
Luxury cabins	50	> 60
Tourist cabins	55	
Rest areas on weather decks	60	
Passenger restaurant and smoking lounge	55	
Cinema, shops and infirmary	55	
Gym	60	
Officers accommodation	55	
Crew accommodation	60	
Steering hut	60	
Bridge wings	65	> 70
Galley, pantry and playrooms	65	> 70
Control chambers or centres	65	> 75
Workshops	85	
Engine room	90	> 100

Table 7.2

a. Languages in which messages should be delivered. It is evident that they should be the minimum reaching the maximum of the population; in Spanish ships it should be Spanish exclusively, since other languages in the country are not understood by all. With destination ports with passengers speaking other languages: it could be Arab in the Gibraltar Strait area, German in the Balearic Islands, and French, depending on the touristic season, and always in English after the message in Spanish.
b. Message texts should be reviewed previously, so that their contents include just the appropriate words; if possible, written by communication experts.
c. Messages may be delivered by a ship crew member, as long as the delivery point is isolated from the environment, in a manner that the PA system may not reproduce eventual noise and speech produced by eventual onlookers.

In this sense, it should be borne in mind that the person delivering the message is subject to the same feelings of doubt, uneasiness, temporary shock or panic conditions, etc., which, involuntarily, may be transmitted with the message, with all the negative bearings this would have on those listening.

Direct broadcast messages have the shortcoming that they are not always delivered by experts who maintain a regular tone, volume and voice modulation; on the one hand, this may make them more personal, but on the other hand, it may not be guaranteed that variations on these parameters may not produce opposite effects to the desired ones.

Furthermore, who may guarantee that, under the emergency conditions, the individual may remain undisturbed and permanently where an unbreathable atmosphere with fumes, etc., may be building up? It is perfectly understandable that such individual may seek his/her own safety and may abandon the task.

d. For this reason, it would be convenient to have available for broadcast a sufficient number of prerecorded messages for the various general situations, almost routine situations, and use the direct personal system only when the situation variability may make it advisable. Evidently, not everything may be prerecorded, particularly for those more advanced emergency phases, where actions should follow events and emergency evolution.
e. If the emergency disables the PA and the inside communication systems, the message should be delivered directly by each crew member with responsibilities on passenger lead and evacuation.

7.8 Seamen views prior to the ISPS

As indicated in the bibliography, the same team participating in the current research work also took part in the *Identification and Analysis of the Influence of the Maritime Environment (Ports and Ships) on the Casuistry of Organised Crime* project, which allowed, through surveys, to become aware of the views of the crew towards security related issues.

Even though at that time terrorism was not specifically considered as a type of organised crime, control was exerted on drugs (the Customs Officer appears frequently, though now such role may be replaced to a large extent by other safety organisations and officers), immigration and unlawful acts, which are also included directly within security; conclusions drawn then may be therefore mentioned now as totally valid, with the particular remark that currently seamen's opinions may have become even gloomier, until the improvements brought by the ISPS Code begin to show, together with internal organisation and unlawful act management, terrorism included.

It is true that the general response to the survey of those in charge on ships was well below the expected, at least as far as written survey records go; it may be said that since the same surveys were made in another European country with similar results to those obtained at Spanish ports, there is a warranty of reliability for the data obtained from their statistical processing.

The views are backed by the unrecorded verbal discussions, which coincide to a large extent with the best part of the recorded answers; this allows stating that there is very little knowledge on issues related with the crimes that the research study addresses.

A deep rooted feeling is manifested, due to a profound knowledge, on the compliance with everything that is usual in the maritime adventure and trade, but seamen show misgivings and misunderstanding on survey objectives; they consider that such circumstances may not arrive to them, while not ruling out that it may happen to others. There is, therefore, a false sense of safety that hinders an approach to reality, a typical situation that makes them the more vulnerable to risks.

The first question in the survey, relevant to awareness of IMO Resolution A.872(20), reveals that, while most know it exists, its contents, recommendations and items specific to the subject are not well known, since in the remainder of the questions an erratic discourse may be observed, typical of a superficial, insufficiently rigorous knowledge.

The survey summary discloses the direct relationship existing with the business philosophy as applied by the shipping company on organised crime matters. If a clear preventative approach is not in place, it may not reach those responsible aboard, and therefore a full magnitude consideration does not take place; innocent passive subjects become involved in the crime materialisation (they do not expect such a thing to happen to them).

Also in general terms, there was a large unawareness aboard of procedures for event communication to the port, as well as of which official organisations should be the addressees. Such lack of information may result in reluctance to report if events do not go too far, particularly when thinking of eventual delays on setting sail or, generally, of the paperwork they may find themselves entangled with.

While a training programme becomes insufficient for solving the lack of knowledge on ship and crew vulnerability, for the procedure on reporting to shore based authorities there is no other solution than setting up wide training measures that may provide for the first step and that may clearly show the process to be followed and its benefits, even when events are only suspected.

Internally, regarding the company-ship relationship, there is a clear lack of information on philosophy and the external image that is desired; this should include the application of preventative procedures involving the first safety measures prior to access aboard. The crew would then be involved in a dynamic company policy with a will for effectiveness and possibilities of success; at least, this would show the eventual criminal a decided, active attitude.

7.8.1 Regarding merchant ships

The final survey results, once the answers selected by blocks have been substantially grouped, show the following:

As applicable to ship responsibilities

- A 64.7% of those responsible on ships knew IMO Resolution A.872(20), which constituted the reference framework for the survey itself.
- The crew mostly accepts Customs Officers' roles, by voluntarily assisting and providing all necessary means for ship search, although they believe that Customs Officers do not have free access to all the cargo.

- The crew mostly declares knowing roles and attributions of Customs Officers; however, only 60% give a positive answer about providing information on crew members.
- Regarding knowledge of Customs contact points available at ports for reporting events, there is an about 50% uncertainty.

As applicable to company responsibilities

Being asked about company responsibilities and direct involvement regarding specific policies conforming to IMO Resolution A.872(20), the following conclusions are drawn:

- Those polled believe that the company does not hinder Customs Officers' intervention, but little relationship with the official organisation is revealed, since no assistance is required for coordinating and improving the internal security personnel, particularly in cases that raise suspicions.
- Regarding cargo container, seal condition and vulnerability management, opinions are divided by 50/50, which causes great concern about current measures and their effectiveness.
- Likewise, about 65% believe that an effective access control is not in place, both for persons and for vehicles to on shore cargo storage areas; parking and cargo areas are not properly defined; permits and their registration, etc. that provide for control effectiveness are not rigorously managed.
- Those polled do not believe that companies have electronic security systems in place, and therefore that they may not be made available to Customs Officers.
- Those polled do not know whether the company reports to Customs all suspect or unjustified package events on board, or whether safety procedures have been followed in this respect.
- Those polled are unaware of policies regarding stevedoring companies or other services (between companies), and their knowledge regarding the company recruiting policy is close to nil, with respect to drug trafficking in both cases.
- Those polled believe mostly that the shipping company does not have sufficient relationship with Customs, neither for having the personnel properly trained, neither the means for attaining this. Likewise, the ship is not made aware of the level of collaboration with Customs, neither of the adopted measures for reducing vulnerability or of the preventative action plans.
- Those polled believe mostly that, as crew members, they are not being trained on fighting drug trafficking, they are not encouraged, neither is their awareness raised regarding the issue, no instructions are provided on crime response, etc.

By analysing this block's results, it may be observed that company policies regarding drug issues are not comprehensive, they are not company priorities, nor is there a concern or interest in providing personnel (on shore and crew) with information. Conversely, the answers expose a high interest on the crew's side in receiving such specific training, which collides against the company's apathy.

Regarding on board concealment

A percentage between 65% and 85% is recorded for all concealment related aspects, as the ship is considered to be an ideal instrument for drug concealment; this exposes crew awareness on ship vulnerability.

Regarding safety measures

- 75% of the crew consider that continued training complements shift safety; 55% believes that ship drug safety would improve if risks were explained, since a more vigilant and committed attitude could be then adopted.
- The crew admits not having been trained on procedures, behaviours and methods used by drug traffickers, neither on how to search persons and baggage.
- On shore employees deem acceptable the information available to them, but crew members believe that on shore employees are not able to fight drug trafficking either.
- Crew members consider safety measures applied to the ship to be ineffective, regarding both cabin access control and cargo areas; they are aware of poor lighting in risk areas, which facilitates crime commission.
- Regarding container and seal inspection procedures, the crew do not consider them sufficient, neither lorry and driver search at entry and exit of premises is considered to be sufficient.
- Ship safety measures while at port are scarce along the hull, particularly on waterside; poor lighting or scarce use of intrusion detection equipment are main issues.
- Although a light boarding control is exerted in terms of visitor identification and access control to ship internal areas, hand carried parcels are not searched or inspected on entry or exit, neither are spares or provisions followed on. As a result, no identification and seizing procedures for suspicious packages are followed.
- There are no safety measures for accessing cabins or ship internal areas, neither is support security personnel available, neither are alarms of safety devices used.

Officers have a good knowledge of ship safety plans in relation to navigational risks (fire, abandon ship procedures, etc.) and about ship layout, while knowledge on criminal actions is insufficient.

During navigation

Generally, conspicuous vessels are suspected, more on the basis of the unneglectable obligation to eventually providing succour, rather than thinking of unlawful acts; mostly an attempt is made to identifying the vessel by reporting the event to the coastal authority.

However, besides this usual attitude in seamen, no caution or prevention is adopted towards possible assaults or in order to reduce ship side, bottom or upper works vulnerability.

Should they suspect a risk situation, the ship does not have qualified personnel available to perform selective searches below the waterline. Lack of knowledge of procedures against external actions by criminals and drug traffickers is significant.

Search procedure

- Negative answers are made in relation to crew training for performing effective searches.
- Nobody believes that any of their fellow crew members may be a drug addict.
- Everyone is convinced that there is no coordination of Customs with the Captain for performing searches.
- Search plans, on board rounds, which do not cover all options, are deemed insufficient.
- Opinion is split 50/50 with regard to available equipment for an efficient search.

- Everyone believes that passengers and their baggage should be inspected on shore, not aboard.
- Personal search in not considered to be an effective method.
- Unawareness of the commercially available technologies for on board crime indication detection, such as X-ray and surveillance cameras.
- Vehicle and driver documentation review is not deemed sufficient.
- Provision embarkment is mostly not considered to be a way of entry.
- Anywhere may be a concealment location, to a larger or lesser extent; locations such as the Captain's office, the pilot cabin and crew accommodation are regarded as less likely, as they are used by the crew.

Possible irregularity detection indicators

- Generally, suspicions are not about persons or based on external signs. A 50% acceptance level is reached regarding disordered stowage, goods out of place, open packages, lifeboat alterations and little else.
- No cause-effect relationship is established on advanced freight payment or consigned merchandise value.
- Lack of attention is very evident when looking for indications or structural alterations on containers, or they are simply not sought.
- No sufficient knowledge or information is available in order to prepare a comprehensive report in case of drug trafficking detection.

On board medicine chest control

There is awareness of its contents, control and surveillance. There are doubts about its specific documentation, but it does not appear to be a risk item, except to the import/export administrative procedure.

Essential substances for drug production

Unknown; neither is it believed that producing countries exert any control on them.

Immigration

It should be borne in mind that finding a stowaway on board is one of the biggest problems a ship Captain may have to face. The stowaway causes damages, expenses, and poses difficulties with the arrival port immigration authorities. The subject is well known in terms of the ship's own spatial boundaries.

The solution of the issue on shore is not the Captain's competence, as recognised by IMO Resolution A.872(20), which considers only aspects internal to the ship, as it is meant to be, since it is an eminently maritime regulation.

The problem acquires another human and social dimension when transferred to on shore jurisdiction, but this is not covered by the survey objectives, and is addressed elsewhere in the study.

7.8.2 Regarding the commercial ports survey

As applicable to concession holder responsibilities

Overall, those polled manifest the existence of scarce positive relationships with police institutions or for coordinating actions against crime.
Specifically, with answers equal to or above 60%:

- No counselling is sought from Customs in order to enforce own security personnel; the latter have not received sufficient training.
- There are no administrative procedures in place for providing Customs with lists of containers to be landed. 50% are aware of container integrity violations, but authorities are not notified. Seals are rarely checked.
- There is insufficient access control of vehicles and persons to cargo areas; lists with license number plates, personal IDs, parking restrictions are not available. Electronic safety systems are not available at cargo areas.
- There is little communication between concession holder personnel on preventative and control measures that may be in place; Customs counselling is not sought in order to prepare safety plans or become aware of facility vulnerabilities.

Regarding safety measures

- Personnel are not sufficiently trained for performing inspections. There is no knowledge of evasive techniques, technical aids, suspect identification and search methods in order to fight crime.
- The opinion is that there is not a good coordination with Customs, and that current safety precautions are ineffective, such as physical barriers in cargo area access ways and their controls, container and seal inspection, breakage reporting, control of commercial vehicles, spares, provisions, hand carried items or equipment landed for repair.

Search procedures

- Search plans are not prepared by the Administration.
- There is no methodology for identification of inspectors and for routes.
- Physical search is not deemed a good procedure.
- Cargo and driver documentation review is deemed insufficient.
- No clear ideas on steps to be followed during search, neither of related aspects.

Irregularity detection indicators

- There is a strong lack of knowledge of suspicious circumstances, mainly due to the lack of specific instructions.
- Individuals with apparent wealth beyond their position are not suspected; this points at a low concern and a lack of interest on particular aspects of their colleagues.
- No particular interest is applied to watching container seal condition or suspicious irregularities. If such exist, there is unawareness as to whether the authorities have been notified.

Essential substances for drug production

Answers, mostly split 50/50, show a large lack of knowledge on such substances, and are therefore irrelevant.

High Speed Craft (HSC)

- There is not an extended awareness of what such craft may represent within the crime chain.
- Neither are known the Spanish laws that regulate and tend to control them.

Chapter 8. Conclusions

8.1 Introduction

Along this work the most determinant aspects have been analysed, on a totally open subject, even counting on the ISPS Code implementation.

Operational enhancements on the ship-port interface are not totally implemented, and there is still much to be done, researched and contributed until security is no longer an issue and becomes familiar to those responsible on ships, at port facilities and at shipping companies.

Nevertheless, the issue, once again, is related to the human factor: it depends on the degree of confidence provided by international security certificates plus a 14 to 18 hour training course, delivered in accordance with the contents and development of the IMO Model Courses, or by a remote training CD, available to everyone (sometimes cadets use it); or on the feeling that the depth of the matter compels to information and training, continually and comprehensively delivered, covering knowledge gaps until it may be guaranteed that Security Officer roles may be assumed. Any of these three cases applies.

Up to the ISPS Code implementation, ships used to be the object of crime, without crew participation (assaults, piracy), and it could only be said that they had done what they could in order to avoid the event, and everything was the result of being in the wrong place at the wrong time (almost a fatality). However, as of 1st of July 2004, ships and port facilities have persons in charge from which certain conducts, ranging from level 1 (routine) to level 3, are demanded, which may include being involved in the event and succeeding, thus showing that everything prescribed to prevent the action was complied with, and that back luck exists no longer.

If damages to third parties were incurred, remediation may be demanded, there may be answerability before a court, and eventual imprisonment, all within the aforementioned minimum requirements.

Operational enhancements, as seen, cover a wide variety and depth, but are always human factor related; for this reason, this chapter closes with the conclusions drawn in the year 2000 research work.

8.2 Conclusions

➢ A conclusion drawn from the surveys, powerful because evident, is the lack of specific training on safety issues related with crime in all its forms; this lack affects all civil parties, crew and on shore personnel within the maritime scope.

➢ This circumstance encourages the use of the maritime scope by the organised crime, which finds a favourable environment to its goals, with a low risk for detection or for undergoing strict control or inspection procedures that may limit their illicit activity.

➢ Groups lacking minimum knowledge on prevention, control and fight against illegal actions, as repeatedly identified beforehand along the study, are:

- Crew
- Shipping company personnel
- Concession holder personnel
- Port personnel
    Commercial port personnel
    Recreational port personnel
    Fishing port personnel

➢ This division, based on common overall objectives, should consider the specific aspects that differentiate them amongst themselves and make them peculiar; at the same time, it involves a last classification based on the pyramid of responsibilities and on each group's organisation; therefore, training levels should be established, the contents of which should be adequate and supportive of the highest effectiveness, based on contractual responsibilities.

➢ For nautical professionals, the required training approach is referenced in the International Convention on Standards of Training, Certification and Watchkeeping for Seafarers (STCW) and the specific IMO recommendations that may be issued on the matter. For the moment, the STCW does not contribute significant aspects; concepts are mentioned without discussing contents, which are left to the free choice of the responsible institutions in each State. As with all general scope conventions, content details are not addressed by this convention either; subsequent regulations should complete the originating legal instrument.

➢ Such situation results in there not being specific training programmes to develop courses beyond those standardised and approved, not even purposing to include them in the current academic curriculums for professional degrees. Organised crime risks are not and have never been included.

➢ The matter of specialised training on international crime is alien to the knowledge of professional and technical staff usually in charge of designing training programmes; therefore it becomes quite difficult to come across any personal initiative in this direction. Resolution A.872(20) itself does not provide regulations for the application of training actions; it only calls attention indirectly by exposing the non malicious shortcomings of seafarers on this issue.

8. Conclusions

➤ The circumstance above directs to the search for a shared responsibility solution, conducted in equal share between marine professionals and safety and public order professionals, given the well known existing unawareness of each other and their roles, which in turn is quite logical, but not to be concerned about once detected. A matter of great concern would be the negation of such fact, and not only that, but if there were an express will to maintain the tightness between the groups or of denying any active and positive joint participation.

➤ The need for a wide and in depth training on the acceptable knowledge required by maritime and on shore institutions is considered. The final result would cover deficiencies, inefficiencies and loss of opportunities that the sum of synergies from one part and the other have not managed to overcome to this moment.

➤ As a minimum, all aspects included in the ISPS Code should be covered, strongly developing those subjects that the State Security Forces may contribute based on their operating experience; as a whole, once delivered by the relevant organisations and received by their addressees, they should ensure a better understanding, a more intense approach and an enhanced collaboration and participation between the civil human block and the State Security institutional block.

➤ It may not be assumed by any means that this solution should be final in fighting against maritime crime, but awareness, involvement and participation of the industry, nowadays affected by this issue to a minor extent, should change attitudes by enhancing skills, closing ranks around general interest objectives and creating further difficulties to criminals through a specific culture that is consistent with the activity.

State Security Forces will in turn also be able to benefit from such actions, since the ship will ever be the great unknown in a hostile, complex environment, in which intensive drills should be performed in collaboration with the largest possible number of other participants, where practice work on vessel approach and boarding, internal ship police control, evacuation and retreat should be carried out with the appropriate means, both airborne and maritime, together with specific equipment to guarantee other operations. Evidently, drills should be performed with the assistance of merchant ships, their officers and the on shore maritime traffic civil control.

➤ Information actions are required to provide and update knowledge on public safety.

Variations will be focussing on:

- Information volume
- Responsibilities of recipients
- Organisational procedures.

Everything is designed so that information may flow smoothly through the dissemination means, either written or verbal, such as safety meetings or lectures.

➢ Again, here it is not simply a matter of delivering information to all, indistinctively, from specialised magazines, technical data sheet or official reports. The information should be screened and treated in order for it to reach the various recipient levels so that personal skills are not overwhelmed and it effectively serves to enhance the recipients' attitudes.

➢ Expertise, as with training actions, should be applied here also by establishing profiles and action lines, even coming to the detail of which magazines or articles should be deemed suitable for providing the expected effectiveness.

➢ Such actions should create an atmosphere of better understanding within each group, not creating mutual interferences and providing a better comprehension of the existing issue and of the enormous difficulties for solving it. With this situation, a better possibility is provided of receiving outside news and adopting a position fitting to the circumstances, with a directed, focussed opinion. In most cases, when the information comes from the outside it is better understood and accepted, in contrast to internal information, which is usually suspected of as being biased by misunderstood reasons that cause misgivings on its goals and purposes, and is often rejected.

➢ Materials inspection means should be used (for cars, lorries, containers, railway wagons) that allow inspecting large volumes and provide mobility.

➢ Trained dogs should be used on shore for various detection processes.

➢ Manned, CCTV assisted surveillance systems should be set up.

➢ A port security model should be applied, including:

- Sectorisation
- Physical external and sector perimeters
- Access controls
- Lighting
- CCTV surveillance system
- Intrusion detection system, covering container vulnerability
- Surveillance patrols
- Mobile materials control systems, covering large size goods
- Subsystem centralisation.

➢ An enhanced port-ship relationship should be created, i.e., between Port Authority-shipping company-concession holder and the ship.

➢ Restrictive regulations on circulation of persons within the ports should be issued.

➢ A single model for passenger terminals (ferries and cruise ships) should be created at European level, providing a sufficient level of safety and that may be demanded in non European ports at which ships may call along their routes.

➢ A single assistance, urgency and emergency call number should be provided for all ports and the maritime system, similar to 112, 061, 092, 062, 080.

➢ Commercial ports are not recreational areas for citizens, this being a rather extended trend, fostered by municipal authorities. When it may be necessary to maintain such policy, recreational areas should be clearly differentiated from commercial, sport or fishing areas.

➢ A procedure should be established for special control on ships flying a flag of convenience, particularly on cargo and crew. A crew database should be created for these cases.

➢ Ships coming from or having called at ports considered as a source of illegal immigration to Europe should be subject to special control procedures against stowaways and illegal immigration, as implemented in all European ports of all categories.

➢ Nodal control systems should be set up at ports and airports, allowing an optimisation of control operations on already warranted merchandise.

➢ Container transit is one of the main supports for organised crime.

➢ A technical radiofrequency and GPS local or international location system should be established mandatorily for:

- Identifying each container, its features, owner and cargo
- Knowing its location at all times, warehouse, port, ship, train, etc.
- Receiving locally or internationally an alarm upon safety and Customs seal violation
- Ensuring "empty container" condition (without safety seal)
- Establishing collaboration agreements with all container companies, or at least with the main ones.

➢ A specific Maritime Information and Intelligence Service should be established at European level, to be yet another section within Europol; it should be based on:

- Official sources of each EU Member States
- Establishing the legal basis for this information system
- Mutual assistance agreements between the EU and neighbouring countries
- The ratification of the Naples II Convention
- Private sources

➤ Private companies should be joined to this maritime integral information system: shipping companies, ship owners, container transport companies, marine container terminals, consignors, special private ports, manufacturers and suppliers of vessels, technology and maritime materials.

➤ A Maritime Transit Information System should be activated, including the following subsystems:

- Search subsystem, similar to NISAT (Navigation Information System in Advanced Technology)
- Ship information subsystems providing: position, route plan and destination of ships en route, similar to ARES (Automation Search and Rescue System)
- Dangerous goods information subsystem, reporting on movements of ships carrying dangerous goods or potential pollutants within the European maritime territory (similar to AIDS MAT).

➤ The database of MOU inspection reports located in Saint Malo (France) should be included in the Maritime Information and Intelligence System.

➤ A data collection and statistical treatment system should be established that takes into account the peculiar features of the maritime environment and may be operationally useful for the special Maritime Information and Intelligence System. It should allow to assess the contribution of the maritime scope to crime and at the same time provide a swift response with maritime and on shore research and security operating resources.

➤ Statistics should provide for data comparison between coastal and inland sectors in every country, seas and waterways, therefore identifying weakest points or areas in order to reinforce preventative and security actions and increase dedicated resources.

➤ Mandatory coordination and information exchange should be established between ships (Captains and crew) and Police services in each country, to assist in the identification of individual or small groups of the crew that may be on the fringe of the law.

➤ An operational maritime structure should be created in each country, with the following design bases:

- Maritime task force conception
- Single Command and Management
- Varied resources, respecting their command channels that act integrated by a common objective
- Action principles

➤ Coordination: resources should be coordinated under a single system.

8. Conclusions

➢ Collaboration: resources should collaborate with each other at all levels (information and operational) with no limitations.

➢ Specialisation: resources with competence or specialisation should act with preference.

➢ Replacement: competential or specialised resources may be replaced by other resources, under the Single Command's judgment.

➢ Subsidiarity: in case of lack of a specialised or competential resource, another available resource may act; action should be transferred to the competential resource as soon as it may be possible.

➢ Operational resources, probably from various sources, should:

- Act and move on shore
- Act and move at sea at normal speed (surveillance)
- Act and move at sea at higher speeds and be kitted with sufficiently dissuasive weapons (interception).

➢ Prolonged air surveillance should be in place:

- Long periods: aeroplanes (surveillance and verification)
- Short periods: helicopters (verification and interception)
- Permanent (surveillance and verification)

➢ Surveillance should be kept from on shore, at sea and from the air, by electronic means:

- Radars
- Conversation recording

➢ Capabilities for low intensity electronic warfare should be in place:

- Frequency interference
- Transmission point automatic location

➢ Action forces and services should be allocated resources in proportion to the significance of the issue and the coastal and territorial waters extension.

➢ Safety related subjects should be included in all training programmes at all levels.

➢ There is a need to make seafarers more aware and introduce a prevention culture.

➢ The crew have basic roles related to ship safety, similar to those of citizens regarding the public safety system:

- Right to be safe
- Right to participate and be informed
- Obligation to provide assistance and succour, limited by own physical integrity
- Obligation to collaboration
- Obligation to provide information about, and report, crime related activities or suspicions
- Obligation to self protection, individually and collectively.

➢ Crew members / citizens are the basic elements of a safety system. This concept is included as a general philosophy in the employment contract.

➢ International maritime transport companies should be obliged to verify every person's identity when boarding, together with the transport title, which should be personal.

➢ All ships should be obliged to establish an automated access control system, similar to those on shore.

➢ All ships with first berthing port in Europe should be obliged to contract private security companies at ports of origin for stowaway and immigration control purposes. Unified guarantees at European level should be established in order to prevent corruption within these companies and their personnel, based on:

- Quality based delayed payment of services.
- Depositing a guarantee with an internationally renowned bank.
- Establishing an insurance policy with an internationally renowned company, covering eventual damages incurred by the ship due to deficient service quality.
- Obliging all ships and vessels, based on certain navigational features, to be fitted with a permanent location system, in the same manner as other technical conditions are demanded.

Bibliography

Literature

MARÍ, R. *Situaciones de crisis en buques de pasaje [Crisis Situations in Passenger Ships]*. Barcelona. Ediciones UPC. I.S.B.N 847653 6852. 1998.

MARÍ, R., Librán A. *Seguridad pública en buques de pasaje [Public Safety in Passenger Ships]*. Barcelona. Ediciones UPC. I.S.B.N. 84-8301-692-3. 2003.

MARÍ, R. *IPEN Journal (Pan-American Institute of Naval Engineering)* "El PBIP y el reto para la construcción naval. [The ISPS Code and the Challenge for Naval Construction].", Issue no. 28, September, 2003. ISSN: 1011-5951. 2003.

MARÍ, R. *International Congress on Maritime Technological innovations and research.* "Influence of the Maritime Environment on the Casuistry of Organised Crime". 2nd. University of Cádiz. UCA Publishing Service, on CD. 2000.

Research Works

Identificación y análisis de la influencia de la vía marítima (puertos y buques) en la casuística de la delincuencia organizada [Identification and Analysis of the Influence of the Maritime Environment (Ports and Ships) on the Casuistry of Organised Crime]. European Commission. Task Force for Cooperation on Justice and Home Affairs. Police and Customs. October 1998/April 2000. Responsible and Main Researcher: Ricard Marí Sagarra. UPC.

Metodología y marco programático para el desarrollo de planes de protección de las instalaciones portuarias (PPIP) [Methodology and Pragmatic Framework for the Development of Port Facility Security Plans (PFSPs)]. Ports of the State Public Entity [Ente público Puertos del Estado]. November, 2003/March, 2004. Responsible and Main Researcher: Ricard Marí Sagarra. UPC.

Specialised Publications

ICHNIOWSKI, TOM. *ENR* "Domestic security defense covers multiple fronts: transit, seaports want bigger share of federal aid.", New York. 2004

HUGUES, DAVID. *Aviation Week & Space Technology*. "Still in deepwater: congress may boost funding further as USCG adjusts the program for counterterrorism." 2004

KERRY E. JULIAN. *Professional Safety* "Trucking Security.". 2003

CHO, AILEEN *ENR* "Containing container risks and connecting modes intermodal infrastructure planners take on security." 2003

WALL, ROBERT *Aviation Week & Space Technology*. "Coast guard nears decision on maritime patrol aircraft.". 2004

KIEFER, K. *Proceedings of the marine safety council*. "Establishing a port security committee." 2004

APPS, J. *Proceedings of the marine safety council*. "International port security program." 2004

MERRITT, M. *Proceedings of the marine safety*. "TSA administers grants for port security improvements." 2003

Links to Websites

Defence Security Service :	www.dss.mil
Federation of American Scientists:	www.fas.org
Global Defence:	www.global-defence.com
Global Security:	www.globalsecurity.org
Marine Corps Doctrine Division:	www.doctrine.usmc.mil
MI5:	www.mi5.gov.uk
Strategy Page: http:	www.strategypage.com
Navy Warfare Development Command:	www.nwdc.navy.mil
Revista Naval:	www.revistanaval.com
Special Operations:	www.specialoperations.com
Specwarnet:	www.specwarnet.net
US Coast Guard:	www.uscg.mil
The Free Dictionary:	http://encyclopedia.thefreedictionary.com
About.com:	http://usmilitary.about.com
Control Electronic Security:	www.controlelectronic.com
Insight Security:	http://www.insight-security.com
Security Worx:	www.securityworx.com
Autonomous Solutions:	www.autonomoussolutions.com
US Marine Corps Training and Education Command:	www.tecom.usmc.mil

www.ingramcontent.com/pod-product-compliance
Lightning Source LLC
Chambersburg PA
CBHW081215230426
43666CB00015B/2741